# IMELDA

Dec 17, 1988

Dearest mi + Daddy Jim,

w/ love,
B. + Joe

# IMELDA

## Steel Butterfly of the Philippines

## KATHERINE ELLISON

McGRAW-HILL BOOK COMPANY

New York  St. Louis  San Francisco  Auckland  Bogotá
Hamburg  London  Madrid  Mexico  Milan  Montreal  New Delhi
Panama  Paris  São Paulo  Singapore  Sydney  Tokyo  Toronto

1 2 3 4 5 6 7 8 9 DOC DOC 8 9 2 1 0 9 8

ISBN 0-07-019335-5

**Library of Congress Cataloging-in-Publication Data**

Ellison, Katherine
  Imelda, steel butterfly of the Philippines.

  Bibliography: p.
  Includes index.
  1. Marcos, Imelda Romualdez, 1929–    .  I. Title.
DS686.6.M36E45   1988          959.9′046/0924 [B]          88-9023
ISBN 0-07-019335-5

Book design by Eve Kirch

For Jack and for my parents

# Contents

# Preface

Imelda Marcos first caught my eye as she was crooning love songs one autumn evening to a few hundred sympathetic Filipinos wolfing down free chicken adobo and pizza inside San Francisco's St. Francis Hotel. The ballroom walls muffled the clamor from Union Square outside, where hundreds of other, unsympathetic Filipinos waved placards, shouting, "Marcos is a U.S. puppet!" But Imelda must have heard them at some point, maybe by the guarded back door on her way in, because she suddenly paused between songs, raised luminously smiling eyes, and whispered throatily into her microphone, "Marcos is not a puppet. He is a puppy dog."

It was then 1982, and I'd been a fulltime reporter for two years, covering courts and city hall for the *San Jose Mercury News*, a Knight-Ridder newspaper in California's Silicon Valley. What I saw then in Imelda most of all was a daily story that would write itself. Not until four years later, after I had traveled and reported throughout the Philippines, did I begin to understand how much more she represented—what an angry, fruitless struggle her life was, and how well, behind her silliness and charm, she embodied some of the saddest truths of her country and its long, strong ties with the United States.

In the spring of 1985, *Mercury News* reporters Pete Carey, Lew Simons, and I authored a series of stories describing how the

ix

Marcoses and their cronies had covertly funneled untold millions of dollars out of the Philippines. We also showed how the capital flight had demoralized the country and helped wreck its hope of economic success. In the months that followed, we and other newspaper reporters gathered more evidence suggesting that Ferdinand Marcos, through various complicated schemes, had for years been siphoning off public funds and sending the money abroad. Yet the only time we found the name of any Marcos on an incriminating document, it was the name Imelda. And almost always, in our interviews with Filipinos, the bulk of their outrage was aimed at their First Lady.

I grew more and more intrigued with Imelda as I worked on our series and traveled through the Philippines the following fall. In December, I conducted a three-hour interview with her at Malacanang Palace, and in the next few months returned three times to Manila, where I watched Imelda's desperate struggle and miserable failure to hold onto power. In the early morning hours after the Marcoses fled their palace, I returned to Malacanang and took notes on all the jewelry, clothes, and artifacts Imelda had left behind. But I found myself thinking more about her truer legacy, the cynicism that owed as much to how extraordinarily she had raised expectations as to how she failed to meet them. I ended up taking eight months off from the *Mercury News* to continue researching her story, traveling back to Manila and Imelda's hometown in Leyte to speak with her relatives, friends, employees, and antagonists, and to Washington to interview each of the U.S. ambassadors who had served during her era.

People often treat beautiful women like children, seeing in them not only innocence but vast romantic potential and hope. Imelda, whose beauty was notorious, invited hopes and continued to hold illusions for years after it was clear she had no right to them. With remarkable intuition, she gave Filipinos a mix of old and new that they found irresistible. By modeling herself after the former Spanish and American colonizers, she fed a profound nostalgia in a time she promoted as "Camelot." Yet she also drew support with her rage at the developed nations, and many secretly cheered her petty rebellions.

Swept up by the Marcoses' magic, both Filipinos and Americans handed the couple a chance to achieve more than any of their predecessors. It thus couldn't have been more devastating when they turned out to be just as self-seeking and dependent as previous regimes. By now, though, Imelda's sins are well known, and an indictment of them wouldn't serve much purpose. If I've written this book as I've hoped, it will instead shed light on what motivated her, who gave her the "bright and shining moment," and finally, why that moment turned to darkness.

—Mexico City, 1988

*In its beginnings, the national bourgeoisie of the colonial countries identifies itself with the decadence of the bourgeoisie of the West. We need not think that it is jumping ahead; it is in fact beginning at the end. It is already senile before it has come to know the petulance, the fearlessness, or the will to succeed of youth.*

—Frantz Fanon, *The Wretched of the Earth*, 1963

*In the different magazines and American papers, fashion magazines and all of that, you see beautiful homes, beautiful cars, beautiful dresses, beautiful jewelry, beautiful everything. . . . You see* Dynasty, *you see* Dallas, *and you see all of these beautiful women and beautiful people. And if it is for the white, it is correct, but if it is someone who comes from a third world country like me who is—has a skin colored brown—it does not seem right. And yet it is a basic human right to reach for excellence, for life, for love and beauty and God.*

—Imelda Marcos, interviewed on
*60 Minutes*, September 21, 1986

# PROLOGUE:
# THE LEGACY OF
# LAPU=LAPU

*The yo-yo was invented in the Philippines, but few outside the islands know the toy began as a weapon, a kind of retrievable missile used mostly to hunt the next meal. Like this island invention, Filipinos have often been misunderstood, making it worth a brief look back long before Imelda Marcos was born, to find the context that shaped her life.*

When Imelda Marcos restored Malacanang Palace in 1978, an imitation stained-glass portrait of a fierce native chief wound up on an interior door. The chief was Lapu-Lapu, a Philippine underground hero, for it was he who killed the first would-be colonizer, Captain Ferdinand Magellan.

By the year of Magellan's death, 1521, the Portuguese captain had laid claim to the Philippine archipelago on behalf of his sponsor, the Spanish king. A devout Catholic, Magellan was a zealous recruiter for the Church, yet never a man blind to commercial potential. He and his crew were intrigued with the lush new land, and especially by the fact that its inhabitants would trade gold for iron. In a practice that would become time-honored, Magellan sought power through a satrap, in this case the Rajah of Cebu, who held court on grass mats, wore a yellow silk turban and loincloth, and had purple and red geometric tattoos all over his body. Magellan had the Rajah baptized in the name of King Charles, and thereafter referred to him as the Christian king. He called

1

together all the other local chiefs and declared that any who didn't defer to the Christian king would be killed. He also said they must be Christian too, which meant they had to trash their shrines and burn their idols.

Only Lapu-Lapu, chief of the neighboring island of Mactan, didn't obey. He preferred local ways, which by then included not only idols but the use of bamboo manuscripts, a system of weights and measures and a variety of oral and written laws. He sent word to the Christian king that he'd never convert, and promised to fight any other leader who did. Outraged, Magellan sent off a detachment to burn his village. The soldiers sacked its homes and raped its women, yet Lapu-Lapu remained defiant. Magellan decided he'd handle the rebel himself. So confident was the captain of success that he took with him just sixty ill-trained volunteers. On landing, he met a native army of more than 1500 expert warriors, armed with bamboo spears and poisoned arrows.

The battle was brief, ending in a rout after Magellan, mortally wounded, vanished under the spears. The rest of the crew hurried back to Spain, temporarily abandoning their campaign to loot the islands of gold and pearls and women and carry on conversions to Catholicism.

Within forty-five years, however, Miguel Lopez de Legazpi had returned to take up where Magellan left off, beginning the era of Spanish and American dominance that Filipinos refer to as "400 years in a convent and 50 years in Hollywood." It was an era of passionate postures and no middle ground: in the 1890s, independence fighters would chip off the sharp noses of Spanish *santos*, or saint dolls, to de-Europeanize them. Yet hundreds of thousands of their grandchildren would later clamor to become part of the United States.

The boatloads of friars who followed de Legazpi held sway until the turn of the century, leaving, in their wake, grand estates and many mestizo offspring (a descendant of whom was Imelda, the granddaughter of a priest). Then came the Spanish-American war and the first ties between the United States and the Philippines—ties destined to be tighter than those binding any other two modern nations in the world.

Hungry for new territory, the United States declared war on the decaying Spanish empire on April 25, 1898. Eight months later, after Admiral George Dewey shouted, "You may fire when ready, Gridley," and sank the unarmored Spanish fleet in Manila Bay, Spain handed over Guam, Puerto Rico, and the Philippines in exchange for $20 million.

The deal infuriated Filipino nationalists, who had seen America as their ally in their two-year-old guerrilla war for independence. In a gentlemen's agreement with U.S. diplomat E. Spencer Pratt, the nationalists' commander, Emilio Aguinaldo, had rushed back from exile in Singapore to reorganize his army and support the Americans with 14,000 troops and precious intelligence. The reward, as he understood it, would be Filipino liberty, and soon.

Aguinaldo had been elated by Pratt's promise, though somewhat perturbed that he wouldn't put it in writing. He praised his benefactor, the United States, as "the cradle of genuine liberty...considering us sufficiently civilized and capable of governing for ourselves." And on proclaiming the Philippines a free nation on June 12, 1898, his fellow nationalists modeled their Declaration of Independence after America's.

By December, Aguinaldo's followers had set up a full republic on the main island of Luzon. They governed vast areas, issued a new currency, and set up schools and a new army and navy. On January 23, 1899, they inaugurated Aguinaldo as president.

They hadn't counted, however, on the American notion of benevolence. When the Spanish surrendered, there were close to 12,000 U.S. troops around Manila, and none seemed in a hurry to leave. Then, just two weeks before Aguinaldo's installation, President William McKinley came up with a reason for them to stay. After several nights in prayer, he announced, he'd concluded America's relationship with Filipinos must be what came to be called, "benevolent assimilation." They couldn't be left alone, he said. "They were unfit for self-government ...and there was nothing left for us to do but take them all and to educate the Filipinos and uplift and civilize and Christianize them, and by God's grace do the very best we could for them as our fellow men for whom Christ also died."

Pratt then denied having made any promise to the rebels, leading an embittered Aguinaldo to denounce his former friends as the "tormenters of mankind." The Philippine-American War began on February 4, 1899, and though it officially ended two years later, sporadic fighting lasted through the end of U.S. rule in 1946. Rudyard Kipling's famous poem spurred 126,000 American troops to battles 10,000 miles away, urging their families, with some irony, to:

*Take up the White Man's Burden*
*Send forth the best ye breed*
*Go bind your sons to exile*
*To serve your captives' need;*
*To wait in heavy harness*
*On fluttered folk and wild*
*Your new-caught sullen peoples,*
*Half devil and half child.*

In that short, obscure war, 4234 Americans and four times that many Filipino rebels lost their lives. By reliable accounts, more than 200,000 Filipino noncombatants also died, largely from war-related famine and disease. Aguinaldo renounced his cause in 1901, after his capture by General Frederick Funston of Kansas, who had entered his camp under the ruse of being held prisoner by a band of turncoat natives.

In the same year Aguinaldo was captured, the war's worst atrocities were committed by both Americans and Filipinos on the southern island of Samar. They began on the Sunday morning of September 26, when a contingent of Filipino bolo-knife warriors massacred fifty-nine members of a U.S. garrison in the town of Balangiga. The Filipinos had slipped into the camp disguised as women and laborers, and they rose to attack at breakfast, on the signal of pealing church bells. One U.S. sergeant was decapitated at the mess table; others were found dead with bloody forks clenched in their fists. The survivors roared, "Damn the infernal googoos!" and the U.S. troops retaliated, killing more than 250 Filipinos in an assault that sparked several more bloody weeks of mutual revenge.

By November, U.S. General Jacob Smith had taken charge of Samar and given orders "to kill and burn...it was no time to take prisoners, and...to make Samar a howling wilderness." Asked the age limit for the killing, Smith, who was later court-martialed, replied "Everything over ten." By one report in the *Philadelphia Ledger*, his troops' tactics involved killing "to exterminate men, women, children, prisoners and captives...."

"Soldiers have pumped salt water into men to 'make them talk,'" wrote the *Ledger* reporter, "and have taken prisoner people who held up their hands and peacefully surrendered, and an hour later, without an atom of evidence to show that they were even *insurrectos*, stood them on a bridge and shot them down one by one, to drop into the water below and float down, as examples to those who found their bullet-loaded corpses...."

From that time on, Samar represented the most savage memories of American involvement in the Philippines. But the region as a whole, the Visayan Islands, soon came to encompass more complex connotations. Between Samar's rocky shores and those of Mactan, where the first assuming westerner was slain, lies Leyte, a craggy, typhoon-blown island that the Philippine and U.S. governments have made into a theme park of statues and plaques memorializing Americans as World War II saviors. It was on Leyte that General Douglas MacArthur waded ashore on October 20, 1944, to declare, "People of the Philippines: I have returned." And it was on Leyte that Imelda Remedios Visitacion Romualdez spent her adolescence, saluting the U.S. flag and singing "The Star-Spangled Banner."

# I

# LEAVETAKING

*President Ferdinand Marcos and his armed forces chief, General Fabian Ver, meet in Hell. Ver is up to his neck in boiling tar; Marcos is up to his knees. Ver says: "Boss, I've been your right-hand man for twenty years, and I've done horrible things, but nothing compared to what you've done. How come you're only up to your knees?"*
    *Answers Marcos: "I'm standing on Imelda's shoulders."*
                                            —Manila joke, circa 1985

Ferdinand and Imelda Marcos were legendary rulers, but at no time more affecting than the night they ceased to rule. Only then, once American Marines had hustled them from angry mobs of their own people, did Marcos, 69 and ailing, finally lose the perennial poise of a late-night talk show host. Only then did Imelda, grown fat and fearful, face trouble she could no longer seduce or maneuver away. And only then did the world get a peek behind the shutters of Malacanang Palace, and a glimpse of answers to mysteries twenty years old.

On that humid evening of February 25, 1986, Manila went hysterical with revelations. All along Roxas Boulevard, en route to Malacanang, men danced in celebration around blazing tires. Within the palace courtyard, television quartz lights cast a white glare on thousands of destitute squatters, vendors, and garbage collectors, all streaming under palm and frangipani trees to gawk, loot, yell "Victory!" and spear frogs in the sculpted fountains.

Inside the fifty-four-room palace, the Marcoses' secrets were also brought to light as young soldiers, no longer loyal, strode through the chandeliered halls, breaking into rooms, tearing curtains aside with their gun barrels, rifling through desks, and peering into bathrooms.

They marveled at the President's sickroom, its oxygen tank, dialysis machine and well-stocked medical supply cabinets confirming his long-denied illness. In a closet were Marcos' specially built shoes (with padded insteps as well as stacked heels), and in his bathroom, packages of Adamson's disposable diapers, proof of the long-rumored presidential incontinence. There were also hundreds of pages of financial documents, which in the last hectic hours of the departure had been strewn through the ornate halls, stuffed in paper shredders, and clogged in the President's gold-plated toilet bowl. All would help build an intricate, shocking case of multibillion-dollar corruption in the months to come.

But the most outrageous emblems of the Marcoses' rule—those destined to live on in world memory—were found just down the hall, through a long, angled passageway and past a small kitchen and shrine, in the bedroom and downstairs dressing room of the First Lady. There were discovered the hundreds of black brassieres, the scores of jeweled and feathered gowns, and the infamous 1060 pairs of shoes.

Imelda's shoes captured immediate international attention. In the giddy first reports, they were counted at 3000 pairs, but even reduced by two-thirds in a later inventory, the collection was no slouch. There were Charles Jourdans, Ferragamos, Bruno Maglis, Guccis, and Oleg Cassinis; rhinestone-studded heels, spiked snakeskin sandals, sequined silk pumps, and dozens of boots of soft, shiny leather—all size 8½, in a rainbow of colors, with as many as five pairs of some favored styles. The *pièce de résistance* was a pair of plastic disco sandals with 3-inch-high, flashing, battery-operated heels.

In the months to come, government guides on tours of Malacanang Palace would linger in Imelda's bedroom, reciting its contents in voluptuous detail. With a care that smacked oddly of reverence, they kept in place her seance table of lapis and tiger's eye, her $275,000 Austrian grand piano, diamond-studded hairbrush, bullet-proof bras, foot-high bottles of French perfume, and vats of Christian Dior face creams. Likewise, they enshrined her bedside oxygen tank, meant for rejuvenation, and the old white purse Fidel Castro had autographed with a felt-tipped pen on August 26, 1975: "Para Imelda—carinosamente...." They whispered, privately, of items not left on display: the collection of x-rated movies from Copenhagen, the photo of an old mistress of Marcos with a large X drawn through her face. But they left her record albums of Sinatra, Verdi, and the disco group The Village People, and replaced her books in the shelves next to the canopied bed: *Verbal Self-Defense, Masterpieces from the House of Faberge, President Reagan's Quotations, How to Take Charge of Your Life, How to Look Ten Years Younger,* and *Lenin.* The door to her jewelry vault was left ajar, and the interior tidied from the night that she ransacked it before fleeing. The riches she had judged not worth taking—strands of pearls and semiprecious stones, glittering tiaras and gleaming ivory statuettes—were all displayed to their best advantage.

The discoveries might truly have been shocking if they'd had to do with almost any other woman. But Imelda's name had long ago become synonymous with greed and excess and ambition. After years of carefully preserving the image of a demure and loyal wife, she had finally nearly achieved her dream of taking over from her husband. Anticipation had helped push her over the edge, and in her last years in power the world knew her as a full-fledged Dragon Lady: scheming, red-clawed, dripping with diamonds. She had nurtured her dream from the early 1970s, after she'd wriggled into such an unprecedented sharing of power that people called the Marcos rule "the conjugal dictatorship." Before her excesses grew unfashionable, her opinions ridiculous and her image sinister, she had worked her spell with consummate skill, on Filipinos and on foreign leaders, diplomats, executives, and journalists. Lyndon Johnson called her the "Jewel of the Pacific"; Richard Nixon, the "Angel from Asia." As recently as 1977, right-wing commentator William F. Buckley referred to her as "that exquisite woman" whose "determination to help her people has an elemental force." Though her ultimate goal always remained out of reach, she acquired more power than any other first lady in history, or for that matter, many chiefs of state.

\*         \*         \*

*Palabas,* or dramatic spectacle, is basic to the Philippines, where the most faithful crucify themselves at Easter festivals, and politics is always personal. From her teenage debut as a provincial beauty queen on a papier-mâché throne, Imelda was an expert in the art, which she used with skill to enchant both Filipinos and Americans. Although each group would in the end grow anxious to forget the spell she cast, it ensured her popularity and power for many years after Marcos became president in 1965. When he needed some sparkle in his campaigns, Imelda was there to sing love songs. When important foreign guests had to be entertained, Imelda produced lavish fiestas. And when a payoff scandal threatened in 1972, some say Imelda went so far as to stage a miscarriage to win sympathy for her husband. Marcos never denied his wife's value: from the days of his first presidential campaign, he called her his "secret weapon."

What the Marcoses shared most was a sense of destiny so great that they often compared themselves to Malakas and Maganda—the Philippine equivalents of Adam and Eve. But Imelda never approached Marcos' famous political mastery. As the President's illness and isolation increased, his wife, through fate and through her flawed character, was to make the most of the public mistakes that undid them.

He oversaw the systematic looting of the treasury—a quiet, meticulous theft of up to several billion dollars, mostly funneled to Swiss bank accounts. She couldn't help but flaunt the wealth, bragging of their assets, spending millions on jewelry and making ostentatious tours of her properties in New York. He devised intricate and subtle schemes to paralyze enemies, while she recklessly provoked them in public. As Marcos slipped into the background, Imelda flamboyantly took on the couple's most dangerous critics, eventually alarming a series of American officials who at last told her husband it was time to go.

All the other sins of Marcos' long rule—the military run amok, the torture of prisoners, the accumulation of nearly $30 billion in national debt—hardly seemed to matter in the end. It was Imelda's strategic missteps and the specter of her taking over that finally cost the couple their rule.

Or at least that's how Marcos saw it, according to the news around Manila just a few hours after the family fled. It was said that in a moment sometime before the helicopters came, after the President's defiant speech to 3000 paid "loyalists" flocking under Malacanang's balcony—and after Imelda, tearful in a white gown with butterfly sleeves, had sung her staple love song, "Dahil Sa Iyo" ("Because of You")—Marcos turned and rasped in his wife's ear:

"It's all your fault."

# 2

# ORIGINS

*Les gens heureux n'ont pas d'histoire.*
*(Happy people don't make history.)*
—French proverb

Imelda was born the sixth child of a lawyer named Vicente Orestes Romualdez, himself a humble product of one of Manila's most illustrious families—"the 400," as they were known. The clan's spiritual founder was Vicente's mother, Trinidad Lopez Romualdez, a long-haired mestiza with deep-set eyes. Trinidad had come from Leyte province in search of absolution: she felt shameful for being the daughter of a priest, a philandering Spaniard named Don Francisco Lopez, and she hoped in Manila to blot out the past by becoming a nun.

She never did. The priest who took her confession insisted she couldn't be a nun in her state of disgrace, but offered a roundabout way to redemption. "The only way out is for you to get married first," he told her. "Marry a man who is dying, and help him die well." As a respectable widow, she might come back to him and try again, he suggested, and as it happened, he even had in mind a suitable fiancé: a stout Chinese teacher at the convent who suffered from tuberculosis and who had fallen in love at the sight of Trinidad. The young woman submitted, and her new husband had himself baptized for her sake and renamed Romualdez.

Doña Tidad, as the new wife was known, ruled over her sickly spouse and their many descendants for the rest of her 72 years. She convinced her husband to return with her to Leyte, hoping the sea

10

air and local palm wine, called *tuba*, would cure him. She also bore him three sons, while supporting them all as a music teacher. The family moved from town to town in Leyte, but at last settled in the seaside village of Tolosa. There Romualdez recuperated, thwarting his wife's dreams of the convent, and there Doña Tidad fought to cure her own chronic case of nerves. Though strong-willed, she was anxious. She suffered both insomnia—which her grandchild Imelda would inherit—and a host of strange fears. "She began to be afraid of the sun, the moon, the wind, everything. She was a nervous wreck already," recalls another grandchild, Loreto Romualdez Ramos, the most dedicated family historian.

Often Trinidad would try to calm herself by bathing in the Pacific Ocean under a large mosquito net. Her four brothers would stand guard around her and hold up the net's corners to protect her from the wind, another of her terrors. Yet fearful as she was of natural elements, she tyrannized her family, who came to call her "the empress." Her husband died relatively young, leaving her to manage the family finances and the education of her children alone. In her old age, she moved between the homes of her three sons, staying four months with each at a time. On these visits she struck awe especially in her female grandchildren, whom she warned never to marry, to be nuns if they possibly could, "because the world is evil and you'll suffer a lot." Meanwhile, she kept a worried eye on her favorite, the youngest son Vicente, known as Orestes, who had begun to show signs of a certain lack of drive.

All three of the boys had studied in Manila and stayed to make their fortunes as lawyers. With Orestes' elder brothers, Norberto and Miguel, Doña Tidad had no problems. Norberto grew up to be a justice on the supreme court, and in later years entrenched the family's political base back in Leyte. A Filipino Renaissance man, his other famous accomplishment was the scoring of the popular tune, "My Nipa Hut." Miguel fought alongside the Americans in the Philippine-American War, angering fellow Filipinos but leading to an American appointment as Tolosa mayor. Later he built a successful law practice and served as mayor of Manila.

Orestes did fairly well to start with as a lawyer; by 1926 he managed to buy a two-story home on General Solano street, in a prestigious section of the city with mansions and tamarind trees, not far from Malacanang Palace. But his drive paled beside his brothers'—

he refused, for instance, to learn English to attract more clients. And he couldn't seem to settle down at home.

Orestes' first wife, a farmer's daughter named Juanita Acereda, had died of leukemia the same year the couple moved into their new house. She left her 42-year-old husband with five children whose ages ranged from 9 to 17. A tall, portly man with a booming voice, Orestes started to play the field. "He was footloose and fancy-free; pretty ladies flitted in and out of his life," wrote Kerima Polotan, Imelda Marcos' official biographer in 1969. Orestes' mother at last grew alarmed when she discovered her son was involved with his household maid. Together with a cousin and a daughter-in-law, she trooped to a convent, the Asilo de San Vicente de Paul, more often known as the Looban Convent, to find a new wife for him. At the time, convents were useful for such things, serving as schools not only for nuns but for marriageable wards who were taught cooking and sewing.

Two pretty students passed inspection by the three women, who promptly concocted a ruse to summon them to a family *merienda*, or afternoon snack, at Norberto's home the next Sunday. The girls were asked to deliver Norberto a note—in fact, just a blank piece of paper in an envelope—and to wait for his reply. While they were waiting, they were invited to sit down and eat, and then to entertain. Orestes, who loved music, chose the less beautiful of the pair after hearing her singing voice, which had in it "the essence of sadness."

Imelda's mother was named Remedios Trinidad, a young woman whose humble birth was determinedly fashioned as illustrious in later years by palace propagandists. Polotan, the authorized biographer, described her as "well-bred...the daughter of a jewel dealer" and holder of a degree in music from the University of the Philippines. Carmen Navarro Pedrosa, whose unauthorized biography also appeared in 1969, likewise said Remedios' mother sold jewels, but portrayed her as an itinerant merchant who for convenience had to keep her daughter at the convent. A niece of Remedios, however, described her aunt's origins as even more déclassé: by her account, Imelda's grandparents earned their living by giving rides in a horse-drawn carriage in the northern Luzon province of Bulacan, while Remedios' mother also peddled carabao milk in the mornings.

It nonetheless was Remedios, instead of the well-bred Orestes, who balked at the marriage. She had already fallen in love with an engineer who had recently left for America, and at 27, she must also have been wary at the prospect of wedding a 43-year-old bachelor with five children. The Romualdezes rallied the convent directors behind them, however, and before long the nuptial plans were made. The two were married on September 8, 1928, at the San Marcelino Church, in the Parish of St. Vincent de Paul.

Imelda was born within a year, on July 2, 1929. With her large eyes, milky complexion, and delicate chin, she was easily the prettiest member of her family. "She got the most attention of all of us," said Dulce, one of her stepsisters. "We would dress her up like a doll and stand her on the table, saying, 'Now, you sing. Now, you dance!' She was always such a happy child." Still, in those early years, Imelda had little reason to be cheerful. She was the closest of any of the children to Remedios, and thus the most sustained witness of her mother's growing distress. Although she rarely showed it in those years, it was to influence her deeply.

Remedios was a hard worker and a skilled cook and seamstress— well prepared to be the kind of dutiful wife society then expected. But she was shocked by the coolness with which her new husband's teenagers received her. "Just imagine," recalled Dulce, years later, "We were free; we were happy; we didn't have anyone looking out for us. And then you get this other woman in the house. And she was so hot-tempered."

Hormones may well have played a part in Remedios' sour moods. In the ten years of her marriage, she was constantly pregnant, bearing six children and suffering three miscarriages. She tried also to mother her stepchildren, but they had already found a substitute in Lourdes, the stern eldest child from Orestes' first marriage. Seventeen at the time of Orestes' second marriage, Lourdes was so attached to her father that she would later leave her husband in Chicago to return to care for him in his old age. From the day Remedios moved in, she and Lourdes were rivals, constantly quarreling, while Orestes looked the other way. "He was out of the house all day, with his work or with his friends," recalled Dulce. "His attitude was just 'Let the women handle it.'"

As Orestes remained aloof, the stress increased on Remedios and her stepchildren. It was in these years that Victoria, the second eldest daughter and violinist, had a mild nervous breakdown. By Dulce's account, it lasted only a few days. But it was left for Remedios and the children to handle, since Orestes by then was completely absorbed with his increasing money problems. Never a huge success, his law practice dwindled two years after his marriage from repercussions of the infamous Bar Questions Leak affair of 1930.

Manila has always been a city of clans, and in that era especially, family fortunes rose and fell together. Fifteen years before the devastation of World War II, the capital was a genteel, idle place, its population less than half a million, where anyone with money knew everyone worth knowing. Horse-drawn carriages brought the American elite and Filipino *ilustrados*, the "enlightened" rich, to their respective exclusive country clubs. A consensus on *delicadeza*—in essence, what *looked* most correct—governed behavior.

"Anomalies" were then a much more potent danger than they gradually became, and thus the entire Romualdez clan faced disgrace when Orestes' niece, Stella Romualdez—Miguel's daughter and Norberto's secretary—was charged with helping applicants for the bar cheat on exams. Stella was later given a presidential pardon, but the charges nearly ruined the law practice shared by Miguel and Orestes. There was a court trial, a year of scandalous press coverage, and a steep decline in clients.

The notoriety hurt Orestes most, since the law office was his only source of income. Even before the trouble, he had suffered by comparison to his brothers. But now the gap had grown much wider and as servants left his household, Remedios had to work harder to keep up appearances, taking on more and more of the cooking, cleaning and laundry for the huge household. Eventually the work and the feuds with her stepchildren grew too much for her, and she began to give in to urges to escape. She supported her flights from home by selling her embroidery, and she almost always took Imelda along— partly since Lourdes doted on the baby and it was one of the few ways Remedios could strike back. Hugging the child on visits to neighbors, she would say, "I'll punish them. I'll take Imelda off forever."

Still, Remedios always returned, and in those next eight years bore her husband five more children. Her second child was Benjamin, or "Kokoy," who became Imelda's closest friend and one of the few men she ever seemed to trust. As a child, he was her confidant and errand boy; as an adult, he would become her palace spy and troubleshooter in Washington. Thereafter, in rapid succession, came Remedios' third through fifth children: Alita, Alfredo, and Armando.

Remedios grew more and more depressed, lost weight, and became lethargic. Almost every night, Imelda heard her sob herself to sleep. Toward the end of her ten-year marriage, she reached a sullen compromise with Lourdes by moving into a one-room garage in front of the family home. In that rickety, stifling room, with its bare cement floor, Remedios conceived her sixth and last child, Conchita, who was born in December 1937. The following May, after struggling with yet another huge family wash, Remedios caught a cold which turned into pneumonia. "We didn't know she was sick, and then one night there were doctors and priests all around," said Dulce. "It really wasn't until she lay on her deathbed that Lourdes took her hand and forgave her."

From that time on, Imelda rarely spoke of her mother. But throughout her life, she took a keen interest in the mothers of her friends, from those of her classmates as a girl to those of George Hamilton, Van Cliburn, and Muammar el-Qaddafi. It was just one of the ways in which Remedios' grief marked each of her daughters and stepdaughters. Another, as Dulce laughingly remarked many years later, was that "Most of us girls turned into spinsters."

Indeed, Dulce became a nun, taking the name of Sister Bellarmine, while Victoria never married and Lourdes left her husband in her middle age. As for Imelda, she became a famous flirt but a private cynic about sex. With a characteristic misuse of an Americanism, she'd tell friends it was "like washing your hands." But it went further than that. Intimacy unsettled her: some of her best friends felt they could only get so close before confronting a chilly reserve, and even Marcos once excused his later philandering by complaining of her "virginitis." Concluded her friend Cristina Ford: "For Imelda, sex was power."

By the time of Remedios' death, Vicente Orestes Romualdez was nearly bankrupt. In November 1938, he resolved to give his house up to his creditors and take his eleven children back to Leyte, where life was slower-paced and farther from the goad of his brothers' success. Orestes had already acquired a reputation for being soft, which his daughter Imelda would later fight to refute. While Marcos, she'd say years later, "taught me how to package and...present myself," she owed to her father "the basic essence and values." Orestes was misunderstood, she claimed, because "he always presented a picture of beauty and of goodness" which was "thought to be weakness and frivolity." And she insisted on recalling Orestes' flight to Leyte as a sacrifice he made so as to spend more time with his children.

Imelda had barely turned ten on the boat ride back to Leyte, but most of her half-siblings were by then adults. Orestes, like many Filipinos, prized education, and Imelda's stepsisters especially had gone far with his support. Lourdes became a physician, Dulce a doctorate-holder and director at her convent school, and Victoria a lawyer. Of the two older boys, Francisco became a lawyer and an army general, while Vicente, Jr., was an executive. In contrast, most of the later children rose to prominence on Imelda's coattails.

As the family sailed away from its financial shambles, it was also leaving the chaotic politics of the capital. Manuel Quezon, the "dilettante dictator," had been elected in 1935 as the first president of the new Philippine commonwealth—a transition stage from colony to republic. He had campaigned with the famous cry "Better a government run like Hell by Filipinos than one run like Heaven by Americans" and thereafter seemed determined to test the comparison. A gambler and tango-dancer who wore large topaz rings, he enjoyed his presidency in the scandalous style to which Imelda would one day grow accustomed: in his second year in office, he spent nearly seven consecutive months out of the country, on junkets with his family to Japan, Cuba, England, Mexico, Germany, France, and the United States. When he stopped in New York, he made news by paying $5000 to a single haberdashery.

Filipinos then were on their way to sovereignty but also clearly on their way to war. The islands lay directly between the tempting East Indies and a bristling Japan, whose invasion of Manchuria was already six years old. The retired General Douglas MacArthur had reorganized the Philippine army, but by 1941 that army's strength would still be no more than 4000. "Right now the Filipino is like a super in a gigantic Max Reinhardt spectacle," observed Florence Horn, an American visitor of the 1940s. "Churchill, Hitler, Roosevelt, and Hirohito occupy the limelight. But a baby spot has somehow cast its glaring light on the Filipino. All he wants is to get off that stage, somehow, anyhow, but which way and how? Whatever he does is certain to be either tragic or silly."

The pressures were mounting in Manila, but Leyte provided refuge. Its newspapers came late and the concerns of the capital seemed continents away. The Romualdezes settled in the provincial capital of Tacloban, a sleepy port town of about 25,000 residents. For the first few years, they stayed on Gran Capitan street, in a large, impressive wooden house that belonged to Orestes' brother Norberto. From there, Orestes oversaw the growing Romualdez properties on Leyte's coast and lived off revenue from the family's coconut, casaba, and copra crops. Imelda went barefoot and wore pigtails and over-sized hand-me-downs. She enrolled in a new convent school, learned to sing and play the piano, and carried vegetables home from the market in a basket on her head.

Before reaching her teens, Imelda had become caretaker for her five younger brothers and sisters. In a home where attention was in short supply, she grew to treasure so much the feeling of being needed that she later told friends she felt traumatized when electricity came to Tacloban in 1945, since it meant she would no longer be asked to grate coconuts to fuel the family lamps. Nor did Imelda ever lose her sense of duty to her siblings. In a culture in which families traditionally divide political spoils, she stood out for generosity. While Imelda was First Lady, Kokoy received ambassadorships to the United States, Peking, and Saudi Arabia, among other posts and financial favors, while her sister Alita won a top job at the government's Central Bank and Conchita found a post at the quasi-government Philippine National Bank.

The two halves of Orestes' family came closer together on Leyte, united by a gradual understanding that they were all poor relations as far as the Manila Romualdezes were concerned. Still, they were by no means poor by Filipino standards. The children all attended convent schools which charged substantial entry fees, and Orestes kept a maid, a driver, and a cook. Imelda used to carry a bracelet of tiny diamonds, which was once owned by her mother, hidden in her belt. When money was scarce, the family sold the gems, one by one, for food. But some bills remained unpaid and there were often days of hunger.

There's a saying in Leyte that no one ever needs to want for food, since so much fruit is at hand in the trees. As First Lady, Imelda used to recite the childhood homily in reference to all of the Philippines, and in the process she both denied a past she found shameful and insulted most of her people, who knew well how few fruit trees grew in Manila's vast slums. Still, Imelda did admit to remembering how it was to be poor. "It's like you're naked," she said to an interviewer in 1979. "Every little drop of rain you feel. A little of the wind that blows, you feel. When one is rich, you have clothes on, a shirt, a coat, a fur, an umbrella, come hell or high water, come typhoon, come heavy rain, come heavy snow, you won't feel it because you're rich. But when you are poor, it's just like adding insult to injury."

Imelda's father was equally sensitive, especially about his status in the family, and he often warned his children against being snobs.

"If you're drowning, don't tell people you'll wait for a senator to save you," he'd say. A serious Catholic, he was strict with his children, occasionally spanking them with a slipper and telling them all they were expected to study hard, be cheerful, and not complain. Imelda later said she "learned early to mask my annoyance, to be ashamed of anger."

In Tacloban, Imelda began school at the all-girls Holy Infant Academy. Her classmates called her Rapunzel because of her knee-length black hair. Throughout her youth, her teachers were mostly Americans and Germans. Classes were in English, and Filipinos in those years routinely learned American instead of Asian history. Their instructors were zealous, and it was common for students of that era to quote Lincoln or the founding fathers with precision rare among American natives. Imelda grew to love *Reader's Digest*, Ingrid Bergman movies, fried chicken, and ice cream. The idyll ended, however, after December of 1941, when the Japanese invaded the Philippines hours after bombing Pearl Harbor.

In Manila, it wasn't long before most of the *ilustrados* were collaborating, just as they had sided with Americans against the Filipino nationalist resistance forty years earlier. The Japanese set up a new government under a puppet president, Jose P. Laurel, but its rule hardly reached outside the capital. By 1944, every major Philippine island and many smaller ones had armed and organized anti-Japanese guerrilla forces. On Luzon, the most determined guerrillas came from among the tenants of Manila's pro-Japanese landowners; in 1942, they had formed the Hukbong Bayan Laban sa Hapon, or Huk movement, which translates from the Tagalog to the "People's Anti-Japanese Army." The well-organized Huks became prototypes for the modern-day New People's Army communist guerrillas. Just two years after they formed, there were some 182,000 guerrillas in all throughout the archipelago, commanding a clandestine network of more than 120 radio stations.

The early war years made up the warmest era of the American-Filipino relationship. MacArthur would broadcast announcements beginning, "To my commanders in the Philippines." His submarine officers smuggled in millions of "victory packages" of treasured, scarce items such as cigarettes, chewing gum, candy bars, and pencils. The packages were stamped with American and Philippine flags and with MacArthur's signature under the vow "I shall return."

Leyte was the last island to be occupied, in the beginning of 1942, and for several weeks Tacloban felt little of the war's effect. But soon the food shortages and rationing began, and there followed months of worry and violence. Conchita, Imelda's youngest sister, was barely five years old when she saw Japanese soldiers dragging captured Filipino guerrillas through Tacloban's streets. "They'd force them to drink gallons of water, and then they would push on their stomachs," she recalled decades later. Each morning, just after dawn, the occupiers woke Tacloban families to teach them Japanese songs and lead them in calisthenics.

The war intensified and grew closer, and soon the clashes between Japanese and American troops forced the Romualdezes to move about 25 miles inland to the town of Dagami. They returned to Tacloban a few months later to find their big house had been burned down, and ended up settling in a cramped Quonset hut. For the 13-year-old Imelda, it was a time of chaos and terror, punctuated by the scream of air raid sirens which would periodically send the family running to foxholes. The Japanese cautioned Leytenos to stay away from the beaches, but some families ignored or didn't hear the warnings, and were killed by falling flak from dogfights. Along with her friends, Imelda grew accustomed to the notion and the sight of violent death, which reinforced in her a kind of callousness, and a fierce determination to survive. The occupation was to drag on for two more years.

The Filipinos who saved "victory package" wrappers and longed for MacArthur's return seemed ages apart from the bolo warriors of Samar. Forty years of American colonization had left deep, pervasive, cultural changes—sweetened by investment and trade advantages that gave Philippine cities the highest standard of living in Asia. American governors had built bridges and roads and sent out vaccination teams that wiped out smallpox and cholera. They set up schools throughout the islands, created a judicial system and a constabulary, and reorganized a bloated civil service. The new bonds were so strong that they smoothed over memories of how American soldiers called the dark-skinned natives "googoos" or "niggers" and sang "The Monkeys Have No Tails in Zamboanga." A party of 200,000, the Federalistas, formed to advocate U.S. statehood for the Philippines.

What made the crucial difference was English; with language,

Americans forged stronger ties in forty years than their predecessors had in tenfold that time. The Spaniards had waited until 1863 to make public education mandatory, and even then forbade most Filipinos to speak Spanish. In contrast, Americans, beginning in 1901, sought to unify the country by persuading Filipinos to learn English instead of their more than eighty dialects. In a prototype of the Peace Corps, 1100 young Americans—called Thomasites for the first converted cattle boat, the U.S.S. *Thomas*, which brought them to Manila—scattered through the islands with English-language textbooks, teaching classes in private homes. So determined were they and so willing were their students that they gave the Philippines Asia's highest literacy rate and made them the third largest English-speaking nation. "Language never comes as an empty train," explained Doreen Fernandez, a professor of literature at Manila's Ateneo University. "It's always loaded. Our popular culture, the images in everyone's heads, the songs we fell in love to—they all were American."

But with English also came alienation. As Imelda later said, "I knew how to eat an apple before I knew the banana. I knew the American anthem instead of my own anthem." Americans wrote Philippine history and Filipinos studied their ancestors "as if they were strange and foreign peoples who settled in these shores, with whom we had the most tenuous of ties," wrote Filipino social critic Renato Constantino. "We read about them as if we were tourists in a foreign land."

By the end of the Spanish rule, the Philippines were already unique in Asia. The first colonizers had left the nation 85 percent Catholic, and, once English, apples and fried chicken were added, Filipinos felt so apart from their neighbors that at the arrival of the Japanese they showed little real enthusiasm for slogans like "Asia for the Asiatics," nor for General Wachi Tokaji's warning that "No matter how hard you try, you cannot become white people."

The split had formed, apparently for good, and there was special warmth in the Filipino welcome for MacArthur and his troops. After so much hunger and worry, they saw in the Americans a return to earlier, easier times, and that vision came loaded with sensory reinforcements: For the Romualdez family, Letty Locsin, and thousands of others in Tacloban, the Leyte landing was above all a food orgy.

"The Americans brought apples, cheese, corn beef rations, chocolate, and chewing gum," said Letty, who was then 9 years old. "There were fireworks—or at least we thought so at the time; we realized later it was flak—and lots of people dancing in the street. It was like a fiesta; ladies came out in their printed skirts and fluffy sleeves and brought baskets of fruit to the GIs." There were joyrides in American jeeps, K rations and Coca-Cola for everyone. "The impact," recalled Doreen Fernandez, who watched Liberation from her village in northern Luzon, "was like 'The Gods are back.'"

The Americans stayed in Leyte through Christmas, and it was in those months that Imelda learned to hustle. Though that term may have had a sexual meaning for many of her older contemporaries, whom awe and practicality pushed into liaisons with the new occupiers, for Imelda, at 16, it meant mere childish flirting—with chocolate, not cash, as its goal. Imelda craved chocolate all her life, and that year, she chased after the U.S. jeeps for it, in crowds of other youths, waving a "V" sign and yelling, "GI Joe!" Kokoy would push her to the front of the line. She and Letty and some sixty high school classmates sang Irving Berlin's "Heaven Watch the Philippines" over WVTK radio and on USO tours of the American camps outside Tacloban. Their repertoire grew also to include: "Don't Fence Me In," "Mares Eat Oats," and "You Don't Know How Much I Miss You."

The GI's, meanwhile, taught the local children their marching songs, which Imelda learned so well that she would sing them as an adult to entertain U.S. diplomats. Her sister Conchita also kept the songs close to her heart—so close, in fact, that as a portly 50-year-old in Manila, she burst into song during an interview one afternoon over cappuccino in an Italian restaurant, trilling:

> *There's none so fair*
> *As can compare*
> *With the U.S. Infantry!*

MacArthur set up headquarters at the Price house, a two-story stucco and concrete mansion a few minutes' walk from the Romualdezes' Quonset hut. He made a strong impression on Imelda, who later said she used to watch him pacing his veranda in his bathrobe, chewing at the stem of his long corncob pipe. As First Lady, she kept MacArthur's wife's picture on her piano, and, in one of her speeches on an anniversary of the Leyte landing, called the general "the original *balikbayan*"—a term usually reserved for Filipinos returning from abroad.

It was all part of such a thorough identification that, more than forty years later, Imelda would occasionally seem to slip and refer to "us Americans." She would also make elaborate—though mostly apocryphal—claims to special connections with the most powerful Americans who passed through the Philippines, telling some that MacArthur had once thrown her a candy bar, and telling others a detailed story of catching the general making love to her aunt behind a palm tree. In one of her most blatant revisions of history, she told *Playboy* magazine in 1987 that Irving Berlin had written "Heaven Watch the Philippines" for her. Berlin, at 99, flatly denied this. (Other, earlier versions of the story Imelda told to Filipino journalists have Berlin urging the young girl to get professional training after hearing her sing "You Are My Sunshine.")

As life settled back to normal in Tacloban, Orestes won appointment as dean of law at St. Paul's College, apparently an elegant sinecure. By then he looked "like Santa Claus," thought a neighbor, "big and fat and white-haired." He cultivated the image of a Spanish gentleman of leisure, strolling through the town's wide streets with his cane over one arm. He'd gone back to romancing women, but never chose to remarry.

In 1944, Imelda enrolled in the public Leyte High School. There she spent one year before transferring back to the private Holy Infant Academy, which served as both a middle school and high school. On graduation three years later, she wrote in her yearbook that she sought to be "a lawyer, at the same time a tourist." In a friend's autograph book, she noted her favorite motto: "To try is to succeed!" Her favorite dance was the rhumba, her favorite expressions were "Nuts!" and "Hubba! Hubba!" and her favorite subject, as she wrote, was "Lovemaking, Ha!" It was then still bravado, however: by the time she was 21, her father had not yet allowed her to go to a dance or a beauty parlor. He took a dour view of her high spirits: on her high school graduation, he told her he should feel happy but did not, "because my hardships are over, but yours have just begun."

In 1947, Imelda went to a commencement ceremony for her older high school classmates and came away impressed by the speaker, a glamorous young member of congress, bedecked with medals and touted as a guerrilla war hero. It was Ferdinand Marcos, just back from a trip to America. The girl, then 17, drew her friend Letty aside afterward and whispered, "That Marcos is really terrific!"

By that year Imelda herself was gaining fame, at least within

Tacloban's dusty limits, for her exceptional good looks. Tall and full-figured, with her hair long and shiny, she turned heads from a distance, but at close range her beauty was even more striking. Her eyes were wide-set and luminous, her expression invitingly vulnerable, her mouth and chin were delicately formed and her complexion light and flawless. In 1949, the town paid her its first homage when it christened her the Rose of Tacloban in a local beauty contest. It was a humble tribute: She sat on a throne of papier-mâché in a barn decked with paper flowers, and years later recalled that the sheep she had to hold in her arms relieved itself upon her in the middle of the ceremony. Yet the following months brought more formal honors. She stood in receiving lines when politicians visited, sang at Rotary or Lions club meetings and joined Independence Day parades dressed in a red, white, and blue gown.*

From 1948 to 1952, Imelda attended St. Paul's College, pursuing an undergraduate degree in education. Her family was still short of money, so Tacloban's town beauty owned only one party dress, of ruffled and tiered white organza. She wore it over and over, and sewed bands on the hem as she grew until her classmates teased her about it.

In college, Imelda earned mostly B's and C's. Her best grades were in teaching, American history, and physical education, her worst in logic, English, and ethics. She cared little for school and never took notes, relying instead on friends who would always let her copy theirs. Her memory was extraordinary, as she proved by reciting lines and lines of movie dialogue, but it often failed her when she tried to recall her lessons. "She was never serious about anything," said a friend, Lily Montejo. Orestes urged his daughter to study medicine or law, but she replied, "Oh, how *long* that would take." As she later recalled: "I was smart enough to know that being a lawyer or doctor would be useless for me as a woman because even if you were on

---

*Decades later, after most of her nation had turned against her, Imelda's province-mates in Leyte nearly unanimously remembered her affectionately. "Imelda-land," as the province became known, had thrived on her bounty: shortly after Marcos' inauguration, Imelda swore Leytenos would never again sing their traditional song, "Waray-Waray," which has been translated to mean, "nothing-nothing." She paved Leyte's streets, sent trucks of rice, meat, and canned goods to dole out at Christmas (when trucks with loudspeakers would announce the "gifts from the First Lady") and set up schools, libraries, and museums. She frequently also brought friends to Manila to tour her lavish quarters, advising them, "Don't envy me, because I'm one in a million."

the top of the heap, it would still be very difficult in a developing country for a woman to really survive. And I said, 'I'm just going to anchor my life to someone.'"

Imelda, Lily, and a half dozen other girls were members of an inner circle in high school and college, a noisy social club that called themselves the Pongers. The girls chose the name because they liked the sound of it, and Imelda later declared it an acronym for Popular Organization of Nice Good Energetic Romantic Socialites. Her role as the Pongers' ringleader was just an early example of her organizational skills: she loved crowds, hated to be alone, and was always giving away candy or planning spontaneous "blow outs," or parties, at the Romualdez beach property in Tolosa. She soon became so popular and politically adept that in 1951 she won election by a wide margin as St. Paul's first female student body president. In that office she started the first girls' basketball team, of which she was captain.

Many men paid tribute to Imelda in those days, or claimed afterward that they did. There was a lumberyard owner and an electric company head and a basketball player and a Protestant physician. Imelda liked the doctor best of all, but didn't seem especially bound to any of them. By town custom, young men then serenaded the girls they were courting, and many sang or played guitar outside Imelda's window. But the word around Tacloban was that Imelda never opened her shutters for anyone, which would have been the first sign of interest. Instead she stayed indoors, cutting out newspaper pictures of wealthy society women in evening gowns and putting them in a scrapbook after substituting photos of her own face for theirs. "She longed," noted biographer Polotan, "to beat her wings against challenges more exciting than chasing a runaway pig."

Into that void briefly dropped Teddy Lovina, a 25-year-old bachelor from Manila who stopped in Tacloban in 1950 to broker the sale of some scrap metal from the surplus army equipment then flooding the Visayan Islands. Teddy was bona fide elite: his father was the secretary of labor, he drove an avocado-painted convertible Oldsmobile, and his trousers were of white sharkskin, creased so sharp, he would say that "it would make you cry." He was born with four thumbs, which his family could have afforded to correct but instead left alone, since traditionally they were seen as a sign of good luck.

Lovina considered himself the first of Manila's society to recognize Imelda's potential and inspire her to leave the provinces. And for Imelda, the attention lavished on her by the slick city boy during his short visit was an important portent that her future lay outside Leyte. As Lovina recalled of the fateful first meeting, he was standing by the side of a dirt road on his first morning in Tacloban, wearing his sharkskin pants and a loud yellow Hawaiian shirt. While waiting for the town's only rental car to pick him up, he saw her walking toward him from afar. Tall and statuesque, she wore her hair in two Chinese buns. "My God, she's come down from the heavens," Lovina thought.

He asked his hosts in Tacloban who she was, and that night decided to serenade her. With a bottle of Dewar's scotch in his hand, he roamed the city's two or three bars, rounding up musicians with the promise, "I will pay you what you want." He finally collected a guitar player and a small brass section and brought them to Imelda's window, outside the wire fence which ran all around the small, one-story house. It was nearly 3 a.m., as he recalled, and his bottle was three-fourths empty.

The young bachelor had a terrible voice, so when he saw a Filipino soldier pass by on patrol, he pleaded with him to sing for him. The soldier sang three songs quite competently, but there was no response. Lovina at last decided to try, and sang the only song he knew: "Dahil Sa Iyo" ("Because of You"). A light switched on inside the house and the window opened. "She stood there, all in white, with her braids flowing. She looked like the Virgin Mary," Lovina recalled with emotion, thirty-seven years later.

"I like that song," said Imelda. "And I didn't want you to think we were snobs here. But won't you put down that bottle?"

Lovina complied, finished the song, and then excused himself in the current romantic patois, which he described as "Shakespearian Tagalog." He declared: "If I have caused you any repugnance, I am sorry," then bowed and walked slowly away, trailed by a crowd of about a hundred hooting neighbors. Both the neighbors and Lovina recognized the moment as special—the first time anyone knew of that Imelda had opened her window for a stranger. But Imelda's welcoming gesture even then seemed aimed much more toward Manila, opportunity, and freedom than at the skinny bachelor standing outside with his bottle of Scotch.

For the rest of the night, Lovina labored on a poem for his new love, calling her in one enraptured stanza, "the perfume of life to a grieving breast." When he went back to Manila, he sent her telegrams every few weeks, signing each one, "I shall return." It was two years, however, before Imelda and Lovina met again in Manila, where by that time Lovina had found another girlfriend. In the intervening period, Imelda began lobbying her father in earnest to let her travel to the capital, while her cousins from Manila also pleaded with Orestes to let his daughter stay with them. Loreto, Norberto's daughter, promised to find Imelda a scholarship to study singing with a friend who was a voice teacher in Manila. Daniel, the son of Miguel, said he would get the girl a job.

Orestes retained his old dislike of Manila, and wasn't eager to let any of his children go away, but he was beginning to worry about Imelda in Tacloban. During one of Loreto's visits, he caught his daughter sitting on the front stairs with the Protestant doctor. "I loathe that man," growled Orestes, who took pride in his family's unbroken line of Catholics. He began to brood: neighbors had also raised fears in the old man's heart that Imelda, who on graduation had begun teaching at the town's Chinese school, might even come to marry someone of that deprecated race. Clearly it was time to give his daughter a wider field from which to choose, and that very evening he told Loreto to begin preparing for Imelda's trip to Manila.

It was arranged that she would stay with Daniel, a member of congress and leader of the Nacionalista party. Daniel, who would soon become Speaker of the House, recognized the political potential of keeping so alluring a young woman at his home. Imelda was thrilled: she was by then 23, already late to be unmarried, but a wholehearted believer in the institution. "To find a husband is to find a sky above this earth," she would say later. Her father had often reminded her, meanwhile, that a rich husband, preferably a lawyer, would be her best security. She had taken the advice to heart, pointing out to her friends the elegant homes owned by lawyers in Tacloban. But she had already long been aware how many ambitious lawyers might be found in the Philippine capital.

Bored with the prospect of a teaching career and feeling stifled in Tacloban, Imelda, like millions of provincial Filipinos, looked to Manila for the things that made life worthwhile—not just romance, but Bob Hope, big bands, sodas, and ice cream. On the flight to Manila, she sat next to Daniel. Her suitcase was small, with just a few extra clothes, and her purse held exactly 5 pesos, the equivalent then of about $2.50.

# 3

# WAITING FOR DESTINY

*"Wedding is destiny, and hanging likewise."*
—John Heywood's *Proverbs*, 1546

The Manila Imelda returned to in 1952 was a hot sprawl of ruins and new construction. War had wrecked the graceful capital Imelda left fourteen years earlier, bringing more devastation to Manila than to any other city in the world except Warsaw. The Spanish columns once guarding public buildings had been knocked horizontal and Manila Bay had been filled with broken hulls of ships and patches of black oil. In the days before American bombing decided the battle, the Japanese had fought to hold on block by block, then house by house; finally they torched whole neighborhoods before they fled the islands. In all, nearly 1 million Filipinos out of a population of 20 million lost their lives. More than 100,000 of them were civilians in the capital.

Independence came with the war's end, but the nation's new owners found themselves with damaged goods. All over the country, industry was stymied; more than half of all the cows and chickens had been killed, while total losses in the sugar, rice, and mining industries approached $1 billion. There was little drive from the capital to solve these problems: Manila's political leaders were consumed with accusing each other of collaboration with the Japanese, even after the new president, Manuel Roxas, himself a former puppet minister, declared a blanket amnesty.

In the countryside, the Huks, armed and organized to fight the

27

foreigners, had refused to disband. Instead, they turned back against their original enemies, the rice and sugar barons who had kept their tenant farmers like slaves. Refugees from the rural poverty and violence streamed into the capital, where they joined hundreds of thousands more without homes or jobs: by one count, 2 million remained unemployed in the capital region as the 1950s began. Squatters pulled together sheets of tin in alleys, alongside public buildings and down the twisting banks of the Pasig River. Their children hawked cigarettes and candy in the perpetual dusty snarls of 1930s American cars, horse-drawn *calesas* and jeepneys, the U.S. Army surplus jeeps transformed into vividly painted public minivans.

Besides swelling the ranks of the poor, the war spawned a new class of legislative entrepreneurs who fed off the $620 million in U.S. war damages and the hundreds of new reconstruction contracts. Politics was the best of businesses then, and Senate President Jose Avelino coined the unofficial motto of the day when he demanded of President Elpidio Quirino, "What are we in power for? We are not hypocrites. Why should we pretend to be saints when in reality we are not?"

Manila's old and nouveau riche were still a tiny minority in a nation where most earned less than $140 a year, but they made up for their small numbers with their ostentation: they drank champagne for breakfast, threw parties for their pet cats, and whiled away the hot nights along the sparkling bayshore, between the Bayside and Riviera clubs. (The Bayside, it was said, was where you brought your wife; the Riviera, next door, was for the hours before dawn after the chauffeur took her home.) Each day there was some lavish *despedida* or *bienvenida* for someone newly leaving or arriving in the capital. Ladies attended in $1000 silk gowns as each host tried to outdo the rest.*

While few in power then or since fought against the outlandish excesses, President Quirino still raised eyebrows in the early 1950s when he bought himself a golden chamber pot and a bed that cost $5000.

Imelda found herself on the tantalizing edge of this thrilling new world of the wealthy. Her home was now her cousin Daniel's splendid

---

*At the time, the top 5 percent of Filipino families received almost one-third of the nation's income, leaving the lowest 60 percent with just a quarter of it. In contrast, according to 1986 U.S. census figures, the top 5 percent of U.S. households received 17 percent of the nation's income.

mansion on Dapitan Street in Quezon City on the outskirts of Manila, but on arriving, she was led to a room in the servants' wing. Daniel's wife, Paz Gueco, a petite but haughty woman, was the daughter of a sugar magnate in Pampanga, in central Luzon. She felt generous for having taken in Imelda at all, and let her know she had to earn her board by running errands and caring for the couple's three adopted young girls. As relatives remember, Imelda fetched Paz her slippers in the evening and her handkerchief when she sneezed. She summoned Paz's friends for mah-jongg games, fanned them when they complained of the heat, and ran out to buy the stinking black cigars they smoked with the lit ends stuck toward their tongues.

Finally Daniel produced the promised job, however, and Imelda went to work at the P.E. Domingo music store. The shop was on the Escolta, Manila's main commercial thoroughfare, where dandified shoppers mingled with raggedy vendors under awnings to guard against the beating sun, and teenage girls in pedal pushers and ponytails leaned on jukeboxes. Before long, it had also become fashionable for the young businessmen of the neighborhood to take detours past Domingo's to watch the new sales clerk sing as she demonstrated the pianos.

The Escolta was about a half hour's drive from Quezon City, and Imelda began by commuting on the jeepneys. But after a few days, Paz began to worry about her traveling alone in the evenings, and asked one of her nephews to escort Imelda home from work. Imelda's cousin-in-law was a fast-talking young *Manila Times* reporter and law student named Benigno Aquino, Jr.

Skinny and bespectacled, Aquino was three years younger and a few inches shorter than Imelda. But he cracked jokes, drove a white convertible Buick, and had a prestigious surname; his father had been Speaker of the House and secretary of agriculture under past administrations. More importantly, he was possibly the first eligible bachelor in Manila to whom she'd had a formal introduction. Lovina was in town, but their short romance was over, so instead of dating Imelda himself he said he escorted her and Aquino on walks along the bay.

The courtship with Aquino was little more than flirtation—an unassuming prologue to a rivalry that would last for thirty years. Both Imelda and Aquino would later tell friends that Aquino had broken it off—as he later said, because Imelda was "too tall and too old." But if Imelda was heartbroken in 1953, she didn't seem to dwell on

it. Her beauty was beginning to make her famous, bringing many
more admirers and opportunities.

*       *       *

One winter night, her sister Victoria, then a Spanish professor at
the Manuel L. Quezon University, brought Imelda along to a faculty
dance in the school's roof garden. The moment she appeared, "the
slim girl stood out like a clear silver chime," recalled one witness,
and "the male professorial mass advanced toward her like an ava-
lanche." The witness, who joined in the mass, was Angel Anden,
who besides teaching photography edited *This Week,* the Sunday magazine of the *Manila Chronicle.*

A few weeks later, Anden was trying to decide on a Valentine's
Day cover subject for his magazine. "I wanted something fresh and
dewy, like a newly washed cloud," he later wrote. "The kind of face
a man carries throughout his life behind a secret trapdoor in his memories." Behind his own trapdoor, of course, and already inspiring
his most abysmal metaphors, was the statuesque Imelda. He pictured
her "regal bearing and heart-shaped face," and placed a call to the
Romualdez home in Quezon City.

Imelda agreed to be photographed, and Anden suggested a pose;
she would sit at a desk and pretend to be writing a valentine. She
wore a scoop-necked, sleeveless dress and her full lips were painted
a deep red. The print that Anden chose showed her looking solemnly
down at her card over the caption "Girl Pens Valentine." "To the
maiden untried in the wiles of the heart, the pen falters, the struggle
becomes titanic," said the write-up, which also stated Imelda's age,
22, and height, 5 feet 6 inches. "A tall girl, she is slim (118 lbs.)," it
noted, and "rounded in the right places."

Imelda was delighted. "Imagine, taking a picture of me," she
wrote her sister Conchita, "as though I were some person." Manila
seemed to be opening up to her. She had been working just a few
months at P.E. Domingo's when her cousin decided to find her a
more prestigious job. Through his brother Eduardo, then a member
of the government's monetary board, Daniel found his cousin a position as a clerk at the Central Bank. There, she was known as the
Tacloban "beauty queen" who sang during lunch breaks, yet she was
hardly the center of attention. One of the officers, Benito Legarda,
Jr., said he forgot he had ever met her until nearly thirty years later,

when as First Lady on a trip to Moscow, she made a special point of dressing down his cousin, then the Filipino chargé. With seemingly fresh anger, she informed him that Legarda had once insulted her by sending her out with a peso to fetch him a Coca-Cola and then insisting she return the small change.

Each evening when she finished at the bank, Imelda would rush to the Philippine Women's University college of music and arts, where she was enrolled on a scholarship arranged by her cousin Loreto. The scholarship amounted to Imelda being tutored in singing after her working day by Adoracion Reyes, who offered the lessons as a favor to her friend Loreto. The favor came about through *compadrazgo*, or ritual kinship, in which *commadres* and *copadres* (godmothers and godfathers), are treated like blood relatives and tied with bonds of obligation. An important twin concept to *compadrazgo* is *utang na loob*, the debt of gratitude. Filipinos make the most of each by cultivating them with those of higher status and resources. Of those who succeed, it is enviably said, "X is a person whom Y cannot refuse."

Since Reyes' daughter was Loreto's godchild, Reyes couldn't refuse Loreto. But the voice teacher also liked Imelda, admired her fine mezzo-soprano and thought she had talent—so much so that when she heard applications were being taken for a Miss Manila contest, she felt Imelda couldn't lose. Fresh from her triumph on *This Week*'s cover, Imelda felt the same way. The former Rose of Tacloban believed her barrio debut had trained her for the big-city beauty contests, which were carried on much like political campaigns. With the Reyes' assistance, she set about collecting sponsors, while Lovina became her campaign manager. Reyes even managed to coax the Philippine Women's University president to let Imelda be the school's official candidate. When the votes were counted, however, Imelda's name wasn't even among the finalists chosen by the International Fair Board. The new Miss Manila was 20-year-old Norma Jimenez, whom the newspapers of March 1, 1953, announced would compete with three other regional winners for the title of Miss Philippines.

Imelda was distraught but not ready for surrender. There remained another angle to explore, one that would depend on all the charm she could muster, and one, she reasoned, worth a try. She would appeal her case in person to Manila's mayor, Arsenio Lacson, a dashing figure who already had a reputation for accessibility to pretty young women in need of favors.

Barrel-chested and gruff, Lacson, whose nickname was "Arsenic," was a former lead scout in the Battle of Manila. He drew on somewhat the same skills in his mayoral job, which was reasonable, considering the youth gangs, politicians' private armies and miscellaneous hoodlums who roamed the capital in the 1950s. With his .357 Smith and Wesson at his side, he would guide teams of police and reporters to raid gambling dens and brothels, seeking out such worthy foes as the Grease Gun Gang or the Canari Brothers. He became known as "Manila's Fighting Mayor."

Imelda cadged an appointment through Adoracion's brother-in-law, who worked in the mayor's office. On meeting Lacson, she wheedled and fretted, insisting the contest had been rigged. Blinking tears from her eyes, she then shyly asked if she might treat the mayor to coffee. "She was such a pest that he had to give in," recalled Luz Lacson, Arsenio's widow. On March 3, a second newspaper item appeared about the contest. It said that Lacson had disowned the fair board's choice and had selected Imelda Romualdez as Manila's official candidate for Miss Philippines. Lacson, it seemed, had discovered that "certain rules" of the contest had been violated, and on that basis claimed the right to choose the candidate himself.

The scheme faltered after the fair board overruled his objection, arguing that the mayor had no standing to intervene. But Imelda came away with a burst of publicity—her picture once again in the papers, this time in a chignon and strapless gown—and the consolation title of Muse of Manila.*

The contest was Imelda's debut at the center of scandal, a position she found essentially rewarding, and on which she would soon make a permanent claim. In visiting the mayor unescorted, she had flouted convention and invited the wide assumption that she'd won her title by seducing Lacson. It was an assumption even shared by the mayor's wife. "My husband was a very naughty man," Luz Lacson said in 1987. "He wanted to please her, naturally." As Luz recalled, she had harbored her suspicions for several days, until she could wait no longer and finally asked Arsenio directly, "Are you having an affair?" The response was purposely vague, as she recalled. "He just told me, 'Don't be silly.' But you know how men are."

---

*The distinction slipped away a dozen years later, and as First Lady, Imelda was almost invariably referred to by Philippine and American newspapers as "the former Miss Manila."

Manila was and is exceptional among world societies for its love of scandal and rumor (at last count, it had more than two dozen daily newspapers) and the Lacson-Imelda gossip was particularly juicy. It continued even after Imelda's marriage to Marcos, one year later, and especially after the birth of Imee, her first child, in November of 1955. It was taking a big leap to assume a new political wife in that chauvinistic time might have been free enough to conceive another man's child—and survive her husband's retribution. Nonetheless, Imelda's reputation was such that it grew into a minor society pastime to scrutinize Imee's features, particularly her jutting chin, which mirrored the mayor's. Even Lacson's daughter used to tell friends that Imee was her half-sister, while her mother Luz's friends teased Luz without restraint. Mrs. Lacson responded with her usual nonchalance. "Everyone was telling me: You never told us Imee was your daughter," she said. "I said I didn't know, but of course the wife is always the last to know."

Reigning as Muse of Manila, Imelda seemed unscathed by her new notoriety. She took a screen test at the Sampaguita film studio and told friends she passed it. Meanwhile, her attention turned to another man, a tall and elegant architect named Ariston Nakpil. The two would meet to stroll together on her lunch breaks from the bank down Dewey Boulevard, the wide, seaside throughfare that in more nationalistic times was renamed Roxas. Nakpil was 28, had fine, handsome features, and wore his fingernails long and polished. He came from one of Manila's most prestigious families, and Imelda seemed more serious about him than anyone she had met so far. The only problem was that he already had a wife.

Imelda's sister Dulce was the first of the Romualdezes to find out. By then a nun in Quezon City's Holy Spirit Convent, she heard from friends that her half-sister was dating a married man. "What's this? What's this?" the nun yelped. She called Imelda to the convent to interrogate her, but Imelda swore Ariston hadn't told her. Then Ariston appeared, his wedding certificate in hand, and earnestly attempted to explain.

While Dulce, tall and portly, stood inspecting him over her horn-rims, Ariston told her that his marriage was a sham. It had happened on New Year's Eve, he said; he'd been drunk and didn't remember any of it. He showed the nun his signature on the certificate: it was scrawled and nearly illegible. Dulce came to sympathize but couldn't think of any way out. Divorce wasn't an option under the Catholic Philippines' law. Until 1949 it could only be obtained after a criminal conviction for adultery, and thereafter it was banned altogether. And Ariston's wife refused to have the marriage annulled. The young man returned several times to the convent to plead that he just needed more time, but by then the rest of the family knew, and Imelda was caught in the middle of an even more serious scandal.

Life at the Romualdezes was hard enough before the Nakpil debacle: Paz seemed resentful of her charge's good looks, set a strict curfew, and scrutinized each man who called at the house. Maids were given orders to receive only those male callers arriving in well-kept private cars, while refusing anyone appearing in a taxi. Daniel, meanwhile, seemed to see Imelda as a political accessory, to be summoned for coffee and chats in the Leyteno dialect, which Paz couldn't speak, with his influential friends from the region. Imelda felt trapped and lonely, and would often weep when she told Lovina how she suffered—moving him so much on one occasion that he said he offered her cash to fly to Hong Kong and start over.

But now it was all unbearable. Daniel and Paz were mortified by the news about Nakpil and told Imelda's father, who shouted at her when she visited Tacloban that Christmas of 1953: "I'd rather see you marry a man sweeping the streets! You will always be a mistress." As 1954 began, Imelda returned to Manila in despair. She would soon be 25 years old, a dreaded age for unmarried Filipinas, since it is a well-known local male taunt that girls, like Christmas cakes, are "good 'til the twenty-fifth." But even as her confidence faltered, Imelda was on the verge of reencountering her future husband, who at the time was appropriately enough being touted as "The Man of Destiny."

# 4

# ROMANCE OF
# THE YEAR

*What political strategy!*
—Liberal Party Leader Diosdado Macapagal, regarding
Ferdinand Marcos' April 1954 courtship of Imelda,
in an interview, April 1987

The courtship of Ferdinand and Imelda Marcos is made of such sentimental stuff that in hindsight it seems likely it is simply another of the myths in which the couple clothed themselves. Considering the journalistic standards of the day, when reporters supplemented their salaries by fawning on or blackmailing the powerful, it is quite possible the romance was romanticized. But if so, the Marcoses have yet to concede it, nor has the most constant witness to the courtship, who happened to be a sympathetic newspaper reporter.

From the evening they met, April 6, 1954, the Marcos union was public property, with each development faithfully recorded in the notebook of Marcos' friend and steady sidekick, Jose Guevara of the *Manila Times*. Guevara accompanied the two for hours when no one else was present, roomed with Marcos as he pursued Imelda through the resort town of Baguio, and filed dispatches all the while. Left on the sidelines, the rest of Manila's society columnists embroidered on his accounts, filling in flowery details to what one magazine pronounced "the romance of the year."

By all published reports, it indeed had all the essentials of heroic courtship: love at first sight, gifts of rose buds and walks under pine trees, questions of intentions and vows of everlasting sincerity. Above all, however, it was a political match made in heaven. Marcos at 36

35

was a second-term member of Congress of rapidly expanding wealth, reputation, and ambition from the barren northwesternmost province of Ilocos Norte. Imelda had claim to the support and prestige of the Romualdezes, who by then controlled at least 550,000 votes on Leyte and Samar.

If the two had any initial emotional bond, it was that both were controversial outsiders to capital society. Marcos came from a particularly clannish northern tribe, the Ilocanos, often the butt of jokes in Manila. Nicknamed *saluyud* for a slippery green vegetable known as poor men's food, Ilocanos were looked down on as tight-fisted, humorless peasants. Only after the first Ilocano president, Quirino, gained power in 1948 did their provinces get decent roads or schools. For her part, Imelda never lost her feeling of having been spurned by the Manila Romualdezes, and seemingly, by the rest of the world as well. "I come from a third-rate province in a Third World country," she would often later say.

The courtship, appropriately enough, began in the halls of the Philippine Congress. Control of government was then held by the Nacionalista Party of Ramon Magsaysay, the nation's most popular president. Imelda's cousin Daniel was also a Nacionalista, the party's Speaker Pro Tempore. On that Tuesday evening, in April, the government was struggling to push through an omnibus budget bill. It was the last session before Congress retired for Holy Week, the middle of the brutal Philippine summer and a time when all signs of capital life traditionally disappear.

Marcos had seized the opportunity to launch a filibuster against the bill, and as midnight approached, the wiry congressman was strutting back and forth, declaiming the Nacionalistas' extravagance in the eloquent baritone that had won him the press nickname of "The Golden Voice of the North." At that moment, Imelda stepped into the spectators' gallery, accompanied by her cousin Paz, whose husband had invited them to drop by for some entertainment.

It is unclear whether Imelda recognized Marcos as the war hero who had made such an impression on her at the 1947 commencement ceremony. But it is a safe assumption that she knew of his reputation. It was known throughout the capital that Marcos was rich, aggressive, successful—and highly controversial. At 36 years old, he had already been accused, convicted, and exonerated for the murder of a political rival of his father. He had also maneuvered himself into a leading position in his party, while hinting he was headed for the presidency. Besides all that, he had had a string of well-known love affairs, ending in various degrees of disaster for his partners. Any woman then would have had to have been avid for attention and excitement to find the thought of loving him alluring. Imelda, at least it seemed, was not so sure.

Bored and slapping at mosquitoes in the hall, the women soon retreated to the cafeteria, and there, in a break in the session, legend has it that Marcos saw Imelda for the first time. ("I was brought to Ferdinand by the mosquitoes," Imelda later recalled.)

Legend also has it that the dimpled congressman stood motionless at the vision of Imelda looking less than her most romantic—in a housedress and slippers, with uncoiffed hair and munching on salted watermelon seeds. "Mr. Marcos 'knew' in the flash of the magic moment when his eyes first brushed her cheeks, that 'at long last he had found *her*,'" *Kislap Graphics* magazine gushed a month later.

Diosdado Macapagal, a fellow Liberal Party member who was soon to become president, watched the scene with a more jaundiced eye, and credited Daniel Romualdez, the speaker, for creating a distraction with his cousin. "What political strategy!" Macapagal murmured to himself.

The budget debate continued without Marcos as he sought someone to make an introduction. Several he approached were unwilling. "Don't you monkey with that girl," said one of the other members of congress. As *Kislap* coyly noted, Marcos "was no stranger to females who had an eye for matrimony." His friends had only recently read of his engagement to Carmen Ortega ("Miss Press Photography 1949"), with whom he had by then at least one child. Nonetheless, Marcos had for some time before that famous night been seeking to meet Imelda. He had seen pictures of her in the paper, admired her photogenic beauty, and had to have known also about her own measure of notoriety: the affair with Nakpil and the rumored liaison with Lacson. For a media-wise opportunist determined to capture the nation's attention, she was potentially an ideal match, and Marcos wanted to put that potential to the test.

At last he found someone to introduce him. By various reports, that person was either Congressman Jacobo Gonzales of Laguna ("who had a sense of humor and of destiny," said the papers who took his part), Daniel Romualdez himself, or Jose Guevara. By the mere fact of outliving his competitors, Guevara in 1987 made the strongest claim on the status. In the 1950s, he was also Marcos' chief hanger-on, having turned his congressional beat into a running story on the rising politician. At age 69, nearly four decades later, he described in detail the meeting that would give him his limited share of fame.

"He asked me, 'Hey Joe, who's that girl?'" he recalled. "I said, that's Miss Manila, and I brought him over to her at recess. I said, 'Miss Romualdez, this is Congressman Marcos—and, by the way, may I introduce myself? I am Joe Guevara.' I didn't know her either. I just bluffed."

Marcos got straight down to business. "Would you mind standing up?" he asked Imelda. When she complied, he silently turned his back to her and compared their heights with his hand. As it was widely, though probably inaccurately reported, the 5-foot 6-inch Imelda, in low heels and a flat hairstyle, came out half an inch shorter. "Fine," said the congressman. "Everything else is okay. I'm getting married."*

The next morning, two roses arrived at Imelda's desk at the Central Bank. One was open, and the other was a bud. The accompanying note read, "Everything is so roseate. I wonder why!" Imelda assumed her admirer was a miser until an Ilocano office mate at the bank explained that the roses were part of a tribal courting custom: the open flower symbolized his declared love, while the bud stood for Imelda's unknown feelings for him. In the next few days, more roses arrived, along with boxes of chocolates and cards. "I told her I felt bells, I smelled roses, I could quote poetry the whole night through," Marcos said later. "I had never felt like that about any other woman."

How Imelda felt in return was less clear. In later years, she would intimate that she was not at all interested in Marcos that first week,

---

*Imelda's height, like most other facts about her, has been in some dispute. I use the 5-foot 6-inch estimate here as it's the one she most often gave in her interviews. Yet her idea of her height may have varied with how she felt on a particular day, or more specifically, to whom she was talking. In a 1970 talk with the *Washington Post*, she said she was 5-foot 7½-inches, while a few other articles have described her as 5-foot 7-inches.

In any case, pages from Marcos' diaries, discovered more than two years after the couple fled Malacanang, set the matter of the couple's comparative heights to rest. Marcos concedes he later realized Imelda was the taller of the two, but that he had been confused because she was standing in flat slippers while he had his shoes on at the time he compared their heights.

and of course it was also to their mutual advantage to frame the courtship as a heroic pursuit. Nonetheless, two nights after their first meeting, Imelda accompanied Paz to Congress once more, and this time
wore a formal, décolleté evening dress. She had also braided her hair
a few hours earlier so that it would be wavy and full when it fell to
her knees. Marcos, it was reported, left the floor in the middle of a
sentence to get a closer look. Magsaysay's budget passed, and Congress recessed for the week.

The ensuing events were described in Guevara's breathless dispatches and *Kislap*'s day-to-day accounts, with newspaper column inches
squandered as if the romance were some grand war in a neighboring
nation. For weeks, capital readers gorged on details of how Marcos
cadged Imelda's unlisted phone number, how he realized, "Meldy is
all I have looked for in a woman," how he could not eat or sleep, how
he found her surprisingly intelligent—"She could talk with me about
Socrates and not bore me"—how his golf scores grew dismal, and how
he prayed to Santa Catalina, "Now that she's here, don't let me lose
her," and promised, "I will be faithful to her always."

The papers touted the backgrounds of each lover, reminding readers of Imelda's relation to Norberto Romualdez, the former supreme
court justice, and how Marcos had topped the 1939 bar exams and
had been valedictorian of his law class at the University of the Philippines. What they left out, but of which few Manilans had need of
reminders, were the scandals that made each of the pair so prominent.

Ferdinand Edralin Marcos had sparked controversy from his earliest years. There seemed little doubt of his brilliance or athletic prowess;
born September 11, 1917, to a lawyer-politician and a schoolteacher, he
was in college, says his biographer Hartzell Spence, "first in scholarship, first in athletics, first in military science, first in student activities.
The newspapers simply referred to him as 'Number One,' (or) 'The Top-
notcher.'" He studied by memorizing his textbooks, was fluent in
Spanish, English, and Ilocano, and at 32, was an accomplished lawyer
and the youngest member of the House of Representatives.

Still, some of Marcos' claims to fame were in dispute. In his official biography, *For Every Tear a Victory,* (later reissued as *Marcos of
the Philippines*) author Spence touted his subject as a national hero
for his daring World War II guerrilla exploits. But even in the 1940s,
there was evidence to challenge Marcos' assertion that he led a guer-

rilla force called Ang Mga Maharlika ("the Noblemen") against the Japanese. The dispute arose soon after the war ended, when Marcos, along with thousands of other Filipinos, applied for back pay. He certified that Maharlika was the preeminent guerrilla force on Luzon and that it frequently had clashed with the Japanese, but U.S. Army officers rejected the claims as "exaggerated, fraudulent, contradictory, and absurd." The records of their comments remained classified secret, however, until 1958, and were not publicly released until January 1986, when Marcos' rule was crumbling.

In the intervening years, Marcos flaunted what he and Spence described as his legendary wartime record, insisting he had won more medals for bravery than any Filipino or American in history. He commissioned a movie about his exploits called *Maharlika,* christened a government broadcasting network "Maharlika," dubbed the main north-south highway on the island of Luzon "Maharlika," and named a hall in the presidential palace, again, "Maharlika." In 1978, the Philippine National Assembly even considered renaming the entire nation "Maharlika." Yet all the while, many Filipinos remained leery of both Maharlika and Marcos' medals.

Also dogging Marcos when he met the young Imelda was his 14-year-old conviction for the murder of Julio Nalundasan, who had defeated Ferdinand's father, Mariano, in the 1935 national congressional elections. The campaign had been ugly, and Nalundasan's followers gloated over their victory by staging a mock funeral procession for their rival. They drove in an open car through the streets of Marcos' village of Batac, while in the rumble seat a man labeled "Marcos" lay in a painted casket. On arriving at Mariano Marcos' door, they catcalled, "Long live Nalundasan!"

Yet Nalundasan didn't live even another day. That night, September 20, while hard rains lashed the northern province, the re-elected member of Congress was shot once in the back as he stood near a lighted window in his home, having just finished brushing his teeth. The bullet that entered his heart was from a .22 rifle of the kind used in target competitions at the University of the Philippines, where the rifle team captain that year was Ferdinand Marcos.

Philippine electoral history is full of fatal shootouts in the countryside. Provincial politicians have traditionally ringed themselves with armed "goons" to defend against their rivals' armed goons, and, more recently, also to guard against the hit men of the guerrilla New People's Army. But back in 1935, Nalundasan's murder was a national sensation. The Philippines had just received status as an American commonwealth, and its leaders were anxious to show themselves worthy. A three-year investigation culminated in the arrests of Mariano Marcos, his brother, Pio, and his son, Ferdinand. The first two were charged with conspiracy and Ferdinand blamed for the shooting.

The trial drew crowds of reporters to the courthouse in Laoag, the provincial capital. Marcos, newly graduated from law school, joined in his own defense, greatly impressing his judge. He was nonetheless found guilty, on testimony from a handyman who said he had overheard Marcos volunteer to kill Nalundasan. His father and uncle were acquitted, but Marcos was sentenced to up to seventeen years in prison.

He spent about a year in Laoag's 200-year-old jailhouse awaiting his supreme court appeal. Before a courtroom crowded with diplomats and politicians, the defendant showed up in a costume meant to show him "pure of guilt as a nun": an all-white ensemble of double-breasted sharkskin suit and shoes, with garlands of flowers for good luck around his neck. For forty minutes, without notes, he cited what he called the errors of the trial judge and tore apart the reputation of the witness who blamed him for the murder.

The performance swayed Justice Jose P. Laurel, who, arguing how much the Philippines needed such bright young men, convinced his fellows to reverse the conviction. Laurel was unusually forgiving—a few years later, as president under the Japanese occupation, he declined to press charges against a man who shot at him point-blank. But his brethren followed his lead and set the 23-year-old Marcos free. Within hours of the reversal, the *Philippines Free Press* dubbed Marcos "Lawyer of the Year" and "a public hero." Still, Nalundasan's murder was to haunt him at each step of his climb to the presidency.

Sensitive, surely, to the well-known controversy and the twelve-year difference in their ages, Imelda naturally shied from Marcos' initial advances. Before agreeing to become his wife, she demurred for all of eleven days.

Guevara was in tow for the duration. On Wednesday of Holy Week, he accompanied Marcos on his first visit with Imelda at the Romualdezes. There, the two bachelors learned that while Daniel and Paz were heading for Hong Kong, Imelda was planning to take her three wards to the Speaker's summer mansion in the Luzon mountain town of Baguio. Marcos and Guevara quickly arranged to go too, and managed to convince Imelda to ride with them instead of in the convoy of other Romualdezes heading for the cabin.

With its pine trees and cool mountain air, Baguio was a perfect setting for a summertime political romance. One hundred and sixty miles north of the capital, and 5000 feet above the South China Sea, it remained the premier vacation spot for elite Manilans. But its tonic climate wasn't all that made Baguio chic. In a nation where all things American were still very much in vogue, it was the most American of towns. Back in 1898, U.S. colonial officials in Manila, backed by Secretary of War Elihu Root, had made expeditions to Baguio after reading enthusiastic records left by the Spaniards. Even the obese Governor William Howard Taft rode horseback for 25 miles on an exploration of his own, hoping to cure his amoebic dysentery. He sent back a cheerful endorsement: "Great province, this...air as bracing as Adirondacks or Murray Bay."

The Americans resolved to develop the land and build a center where government and army personnel could recuperate from tropical diseases. Over Filipino objections, they spent more than $3 million of the natives' taxes to hire U.S. engineers to build a road through the mountains. An American planner, Daniel Burnham, designed the new city with wide, American-style streets, and the American High Commissioner and most ranking Filipino leaders built imposing second homes with stunning valley views and deep manicured lawns, "like those of Westchester estates," said one visitor.

The height of Americana was the U.S. Army recreation base, Camp John Hay. Named after Teddy Roosevelt's secretary of state—famous for having called the Spanish-American conflict "a splendid little war"—it had a golf course, bowling alley, and cinema that played only American films. But the barnlike 100-room Pines Hotel, which one observer likened to a "large pink marble mausoleum," was the main arena for social reconnaissance.*

In its lobby stood 30-foot statues of the town's original founders, the 4-foot Igorot tribe members who still roamed the streets on market days, in g-strings and old woolen sweaters. In the evenings, Ma-

---

*The hotel was burned down by antigovernment arsonists in 1985 during a conference of U.S. World War II veterans. Eight U.S. citizens and fourteen other foreigners were either burnt to death or died after they jumped from windows during the fire.

nila ladies in gowns strolled under their frowning stares on the way
to the ballroom, while men in golfing costumes toddled past them in
the mornings en route to the country club.

The word *baguio* literally means "typhoon"; the town was named
for the Pacific storms that blast through the mountain ranges in the
rainy season. In 1954, "typhoon" was an appropriate metaphor for
Marcos' courtship of Imelda. The three romancers—Marcos, Imelda,
and Joe Guevara—sat together in the back seat of Marcos' white Plymouth as his driver navigated the five-hour trip through the steam-
ing central Luzon valley and around winding roads lined with pine
trees to the mountains. Guevara, plump and bespectacled, clowned
in the middle; when Marcos whispered to him that he wanted to hold
Imelda's hand, he chortled, "No, hold *my* hand, Ferdie."

Once in Baguio, they dropped Imelda off at the Speaker's govern-
ment-owned mansion on Cabinet Hill. The two then booked a room
together at the Pines, but mornings, noons, and nights were spent
commuting to see Imelda. Marcos quickly cultivated Imelda's young
charges and got them to call him "Uncle Ferdie." He made his best
impression in church on Good Friday, however, where he recited
passages of the prayerbooks by heart.

The papers recorded bits of the reputed courting dialogue that
would have made even *This Week*'s Anden blush. At one point, said
*Kislap*, "Meldy asked him about his reputation and he answered, 'It
looks like I have the name, but you can rest assured, not the game.
A worm becomes (sic) to look like a snake when mentioned in
stories.'" To the press, Marcos said that he liked Imelda because she
was so *mahinhin*, meaning demure and shy. He reportedly confessed
to her, "he was a spendthrift...that what little he has made has been
spent and he needed a girl who could help him save. To Meldy,"
the columnist averred, "it made no difference whether he was broke
or not."

Of course, Marcos was far from broke at the time. Though his
law practice was small, and his congressional salary less than $5000,
he joined with other politicians who routinely spent up to $200,000
apiece on election campaigns. The custom was to make back the deficit and more by squeezing "contributions" from wealthy Chinese
merchants and skimming off treasury funds allocated each year for
ambitious public works projects such as new roads and wells that
more often than not were never built. Author Joseph Burkholder

Smith, then a CIA agent working in Manila, said it was well known that Marcos had already grown wealthy by such means.

Each night in Baguio, Marcos' political allies lobbied Imelda on his behalf. Among the guests at the Speaker's mansion were two of Paz Romualdez's brothers-in-law, both Marcos supporters, who droned on endlessly about their favorite representative's intelligence and wealth. Even Mayor Lacson, who was staying at the Pines that week, urged her to make the match. Meanwhile, Marcos was intractable. It was "Operations [*sic*] 'Queen' Imelda," the papers declared. He followed Imelda around with his marriage license, demanding that she fill it in. "The refrain of the wild courtship," wrote Filipino essayist Nick Joaquin, was "not, 'Do you love me?' But, 'Will you sign?' The girl might have been a vital witness being wooed to sign a deposition, or a client pursued by Madison Avenue."

Years later, some of Imelda's friends and relatives came to believe Marcos' frantic courtship was inspired by his wish to marry her before she learned about Carmen Ortega. At the time, though, he must have seemed to offer what she wanted most in a man: a law practice, some prestige, and security. It was shortly after mass on Good Friday that Guevara delivered an ultimatum. "You better answer this guy," he told Imelda. "He is getting impatient."

"'How can I answer him? I hardly know him,'" he said she responded.

"Well, you've got to decide now if you want to become the First Lady of the land someday or not," said Guevara.

As the reporter later recalled, the words had an effect. "Of course I would," Imelda told him.

"Then marry the guy."

By Saturday it was decided. Marcos returned once more with his application to the Romualdez cottage and the two rode to Burnham Park, the town center named after Baguio's planner. There Imelda signed the papers, pausing only once, in apparent confusion, to ask Guevara if her new surname would be Marcos or Edralin, Marcos' mother's maiden name.

Getting back in the Plymouth, they drove to Trinidad Valley, about 12 miles away, where Marcos knew a judge named Francisco Chanco. A friend and former classmate, the judge nonetheless hesitated to marry them. Marcos' reputation as a womanizer had long ago reached that far north, and, at the time, there was also a scandal over a rash of fake marriages, for which some judges had already lost their jobs. Marcos was insistent, however, and the judge finally agreed, albeit nervously; by the time the three left his chambers, he was so flustered that he bade Guevara, the best man, good luck instead of Marcos.*

As soon as they got back into the car, Imelda began to worry. While Manilans later referred to the courtship as the "eleven-day whirlwind," it was really even shorter than that; the Marcoses married after just three days spent getting to know each other, making Imelda's acceptance probably the most impetuous thing she had done. Moreover, she hadn't received her father's approval, and she told Marcos she wouldn't consider the marriage official until they had a "proper" wedding in church, Guevara said. She grew even more alarmed later that night when the three stopped to celebrate the secret wedding at the Pines. An Igorot dance troupe was performing, and Guevara recalls that Imelda turned pale when he jokingly whispered to the new bride that her husband belonged to the same tribe.

Imelda repeated to Guevara that same evening that as a good Catholic, she would wait until her church wedding before consummating the marriage. As the reporter later recalled, however, he spent that night alone in the room he had shared with Marcos. The next day, Easter Sunday, the three returned to Manila, where Imelda went straight to her older sister Victoria. If she had expected congratulations, she was disappointed. "You're crazy!" Victoria shouted.

It was indeed shocking behavior, which seemed, once again, to enhance its attraction. Imelda had made a great, romantic splash, at once winning the attention she craved and freeing her from her worries of being a spinster. Marcos sent a telegram to Tacloban to ask his new father-in-law's forgiveness, but it didn't arrive before the Easter Sunday newspapers with their society page headline, "MARRIAGE CAPS 11-DAY ROMANCE OF BEAUTY AND CONGRESSMAN," and another seductive photograph of Imelda.

---

*In a nostalgic, hand-written paean to Imelda in a diary entry on June 21, 1971, Marcos listed other details of the romance, the memory of which he called "one of my most precious treasures." He recalled how he had sung to Imelda, in Baguio, "Torreador, don't spit on the floor, use the cuspidor...." He described "her decision secretly that I was the man she was going to marry and my observation that if I had known that early we could have saved a lot of money." Finally he recalled "her appetite, when she ate the two chickens we had ordered, one for each of us, while I quoted poetry, Whitman, Shakespeare and Tagore or Omar Khayyam...."

Conchita, then 17, burst into tears at the news. Imelda was the first of all the children to marry, and she felt she had lost her. Vicente didn't say anything. After reading the telegram and newspaper over a few times, the tall man walked slowly to his study and locked the door. When Conchita looked through the keyhole, she saw that he was kneeling in prayer.

After a day or two to get used to the idea, Vicente agreed to fly to Manila to give away his daughter in a formal morning wedding on May Day at the San Miguel Pro-Cathedral in Manila. With only two weeks to plan, the Marcoses managed to turn the ceremony into their first joint political extravaganza, a *palabas* no rising legislator could afford to miss. Nearly 1000 guests came to their reception, including most of the elected officials and cabinet. Among the sponsors were President Magsaysay (in a beige alpaca morning suit), Paz Romualdez (in a flesh-colored terno), Congressman Macapagal, and the minority floor leader, Eugenio Perez.

Imelda's wedding gown was designed by a leading Manila couturier; it was a "dream ensemble of satin and nylon," as the newspapers phrased it, that sported a cascade of mother-of-pearl flowers on each side of the billowing skirt. A long satin train trailed behind her and a veil of tulle bordered with white feathers framed her face. Calla lilies filled the church, and Imelda carried a bouquet of three cattleya orchids flown in from Baguio. Marcos wore gray striped trousers and an embroidered white native shirt, the barong tagalog.

The reception following the wedding was held at Malacanang Palace and featured a cake that was a 3-foot by 3-foot replica of the legislative building. Imelda's cousin Paz, noted the papers, gave the new bride a "rose-gold wristwatch, Paris-made and studded with three diamonds and three rubies." Imelda gave Ferdinand pearl cuff links, and he gave her a pair of 3-carat diamond earrings and a matching bracelet. Marcos also gave Imelda two rings: a 10-carat diamond engagement ring and a wedding band with eleven small diamonds for each day of their courtship. His own ring was a gold band fashioned like a rope, to symbolize, he told reporters, "his complete willingness to be tied for life" to his bride. After such a wedding, a single honeymoon might have seemed tame, so the Marcoses had two: a short return to Baguio and a four-month trip around the world.

Among other society events of the day, the papers also noted that an American business executive had commissioned more than 1000 candles to be lit in his driveway for a party for a visiting bank board chairman; Eugenio Lopez, one of Manila's most powerful men, threw a sumptuous *bienvenida* for his wife, returning from the United States; and a Colonel Edward G. Lansdale, a former U.S. military adviser in Manila, gave a speech at the Overseas Press Club on "Dien Bien Phu, Its Relation to a Free Asia."*

Another intriguing item from that week's society pages discussed a mysterious rash of pock-marking of automobile windshields in the United States. "In time," noted the writer, "it may become just as fashionable here to drive automobiles with pitted windshields as automobiles with American license plates." The comment was nonchalant, but most of its readers recognized the depth of the influence to which it referred in those Cold War years. In return for its postwar aid, the U.S. government had demanded and won "parity," giving American investors the same rights as Filipinos to exploit the archipelago's resources. Moreover, huge reminders of the lingering colonial presence came with the twenty-three U.S. military installations allowed to remain in the Philippines through a ninety-nine-year lease signed in 1947. The bases, of which the largest were Clark Air Base and the Subic Naval Station, remained under U.S. control until 1979; American flags flew above them; Americans collected taxes in their vicinities; and Americans tried any criminal offenders caught within their bounds.

All three Philippine presidents since independence had won office on the strength of a U.S. blessing. Most candidates openly coveted American support, and more than one would seek to raise their public standing by suggesting they worked for the CIA, whether or not they really did. Magsaysay had been elected just five months before the Marcoses' marriage, and his speeches sought to downplay a recent nationalist backlash. His cachet nearly carried it off: a former mechanic and son of a schoolteacher and farmer, he was the first "man of the people" to win the presidency. U.S. agents helped out

---

*Lansdale was doing more than talking about a free Asia in those days. By 1954, the colonel had already established his legendary reputation by helping Defense Minister Magsaysay wipe out the Philippine Huks in a covert war. Using a suitcase stuffed with $1 million in cash, he then secretly financed Magsaysay's presidential election. Shortly after his lecture in Manila, Lansdale went to Saigon as chief of a military mission working to sabotage the planned elections on unification. Using skills developed in the Philippines, his agents sullied the oil in Hanoi's public buses to cause breakdowns and broadcast phony alarms to frighten Catholic peasants to flee south from North Vietnam.

on the sidelines, deflating would-be critics. When Nationalist Senator Claro Recto attacked Magsaysay's closeness with America, for instance, the CIA went so far as to distribute condoms with tiny holes in strategic places, labeled, "Courtesy of Claro M. Recto—the People's Friend," according to Burkholder Smith, who found a packet of the condoms in an agency file.

The Marcoses were to learn both from Magsaysay's success and from the occasionally devious strategies of his U.S. backers. But in the wake of their marriage, they took a short break for domestic concerns. Before moving into Marcos' home in Quezon City, Imelda insisted that it be remodeled, and plans were underway to rename it "Trinidad" for her mother and for the site of their civil marriage. (Several years later, she convinced him to change the name of the street as well: to "Marcos," from "Ortega," with its unpleasant reminder of his previous mistress.)

If she didn't already know it, Imelda soon discovered that Marcos, in her words, "was no pauper." He opened a joint account at an American bank and handed Imelda a cash advance. "I saw three and a half million pesos," she said, and "I felt like a stupid little girl...that was plenty of money. I remember on our honeymoon...I spent buying some hi-fi's, two pianos, two rugs, I went crazy....He had a very good income."

While Imelda was learning to manage Marcos' money, Magsaysay was presiding over another marriage in which two more of the nation's most influential families were joined. After a ten-day engagement, Corazon Cojuangco and Benigno Aquino were wed in November at Our Lady of Sorrow Church in Pasay City, a suburb of Manila.

# 5

# EDUCATING IMELDA

*Mrs. Marcos must be a beautiful person.*
*—Ferdinand Marcos, circa 1955*

Her life's central drama ended, as she saw it, Imelda prepared to ease into the accepted role of upper-class Filipina wives of the 1950s. It was a role that required an especially high tolerance for ambiguity: While the overt wifely duty was sexless submission, the covert one was fierce managerial skill. Training came early, with males spoiled from infancy by *yayas*, or nurses, who left females more to their own devices, letting them grow up tough. Later, as a wife, the Filipina would be trusted each week with her husband's paycheck, doling out his allowance and often running his business behind the scenes.

The system made many men idle and foppish, while their women, though nurturing at home, grew aggressive and often hard-hearted in their dealings with the outside world. Women clung to their men both by tradition and necessity, since professional fields remained largely closed to them until the 1960s and 1970s. It was well understood, on the other hand, that a man's wife was critical to his success. Nonetheless, a woman's influence remained a touchy subject, men's sensitivity being acute to hints that they were, in the Tagalog phrase, "under the skirt." Aurora Quezon, the First Lady of the commonwealth, was an appropriate early model: a demure hostess in fluffy-sleeved dresses at charity teas, self-effacing with her reckless spouse, she made quiet and profitable investments in Philippine gold and chromite mines.

A 1952 magazine essay by journalist Carmen Guerrero Nakpil on

"The Filipina Woman" set forth a bit of the ideal, focusing on the soft, domestic veneer these hard-hearted women often feigned:

"Once married, she considers it wrong to continue to attract men, even her own husband. She begins to run to fat, to dress dowdily. At the same time, her whole manner towards her suitor-now-husband undergoes such a change that anticipation of it is what gives many men the endurance to go through a typical Filipino courtship. A Filipina will fan her husband all throughout a meal on a hot day, she will urge him to take a long siesta while she does the washing, she will change her hairdo and ignore her best friend at his prompting, and cry secretly into her pillow when he is faithful to her in his fashion and brings home his child by a mistress for her to educate. She lives only to please him, or so she tells him."

Imelda was ready to coddle and to manage—she had grown up far more independent than most Filipinas. Yet to her surprise, she found she was in store for an even more demanding sort of marriage. Marcos soon let her know that as well as a housewife, he needed a full-time political partner to aid in his plans to win the presidency—plans he cockily disclosed as early as 1949. A gifted public speaker and brilliant political strategist, Marcos was nonetheless a social dud. His impatience with chitchat was obvious, his taste in food ran to little more festive than boiled chicken and greens, and he couldn't bear the chores of political convention: the beauty contests, baby showers, and endless ceremonial meals. His choice of Imelda to lighten the burden made immediate sense, if only on regional lines: while the stereotypical Ilocano is grave, sluggish, and shy, Visayans are classed as the Philippines' merry hedonists, happy-go-lucky, generous lovers of music, wine, and company. Marcos was counting on Imelda's charm just as much as on the prestige of her surname. And Imelda did come through with both, though it was not until after a long, hard, breaking-in period.

In the months after her glamorous honeymoon, the new bride would hide out in the basement of the home on Ortega Street, dressed in her cotton duster and puffy-faced from weeping, leaving Marcos alone with his cigar-smoking crowds of hangers-on. She had a private telephone line whose number she shared with only her most trusted friends, and would spend hours in hoarse complaint to those few, who included her schoolmate Letty Locsin and Guevara, the newspaper reporter. "She was so nervous then, always crying," Guevara recalled. "She'd call up and say, 'I don't know how to cope. I wake up in my bathrobe and there's someone peeking already.'"

The official version of Imelda's problems at the time was that she was too "shy and retiring," as Marcos characterized it, to cope with the sudden lack of privacy. But "shy and retiring" doesn't square as a description of the young woman who went unescorted to the office of the Manila mayor to win virtual appointment as a beauty queen. More likely, Imelda was finally confronting her lonely, traumatic upbringing—inescapable now that her idealized marriage had failed to produce an ideal life.

The marriage, in fact, brought enormous new stresses of its own. After the honeymoon, Marcos had little attention to spare from his obsessive political climb. He delegated to his wife a variety of huge household chores including the supervision of a staff of thirty-five, who by one estimate catered 60 breakfasts, 250 lunches, and 30 dinners for visitors on an average day. Imelda made constant trips to the market to buy groceries, with a jeep following her to carry back the loads of produce and meats she selected. She took control of the household budget, helped answer constituents' mail, stood as sponsor at weddings and baptisms, and modeled clothes for charities. In the midst of it all, her father was stricken with lung cancer and came to Ortega Street to die in September of 1955. Two months later, Imelda gave birth to her first child, Maria Imelda, nicknamed "Imee."

Throughout this momentous first year, Imelda was also fighting in vain for acceptance from the other congressmen's wives, most of whom were at least ten years older and homelier than she, and who regarded her as a gaudy provincial upstart, overdressed and given to malaprops. Fearing their snubs, she rarely joined them in the legislative hall's wives' gallery, but began to court them privately with birthday cards and gifts of perfume. (When one of the wives complained that she couldn't find a good girdle, Imelda went so far as to send her two that she had bought in the United States.) Marcos' mother, Josefa Edralin Marcos, also held back her acceptance, reportedly having favored Carmen Ortega. Friends said Josefa and her daughter-in-law often quarreled.

Marcos kept up a steady pressure on his new wife behind the scenes, sometimes with criticism, sometimes with rewards of jewels and cash. He counseled Imelda on how to dress for effect—a knack he had displayed at his murder trial—and how to arrive at gatherings just late enough to be dramatic and not rude. "He'd plan her entrances," recalled Imelda's cousin Loreto, "saying something like, 'Ah, now you will see that woman who is not so attractive,' and then Imelda would appear, looking completely magnificent, and it would have such an effect on everyone in the room." After observing Imelda's uniformly beefy relatives, Marcos also began to weigh her food before each meal to restrict her diet, using a small scale he kept on the dining room table. "Mrs. Marcos," he informed her, "must be a beautiful person."

"He has a say, in fact *the* say, on just about everything that concerns his wife—from how much makeup she should wear (he frowns on heavy eye shadow) to how long her hemline should be," gushed a society columnist. "Far from hiding the fact that her husband is the boss, the family's undisputed ruler, Mrs. Marcos happily—and proudly—proclaims it, and like the Biblical Ruth, completely submits to it."

Ostensibly, she did try hard to please him, saying, "I live to see him look at me." When he looked at someone else, as he did increasingly often, she said she would study the woman and try to copy whatever she thought he found most appealing: her hairdo, for instance, or the color of her dress. But occasionally, in secret, she rebelled. Unlike her husband, Imelda loved to eat, and what she especially loved were pasta, candy, and ice cream. Like a child, she hid chocolates in her bedroom, and for the rest of her life maintained a running battle against weight gain. Her appetite was prodigious, and she alternated between stoicism and surrender to it, fasting grimly before each state occasion and gorging herself afterward.*

By nature cheerful, Imelda still found it a struggle in the early years of her marriage to maintain the required constant good humor: the memory haunted her of an early political event during which she was handed a poor woman's baby, and, raising its swaddling cloth, found to her horror that it had died. She also had trouble adjusting to her husband's frantic pace. Life with Marcos, a relative said, was "a crisis every five minutes," jarring to anyone brought up in southern languor. After only a few months, she began to suffer migraines,

---

*Imelda and Marcos weren't alone in seeing her weight as a central matter. Shortly after their exile, it became a political issue when the new Filipino consul in Hawaii sent gleeful dispatches to Manila that Imelda was tipping the scales at over 200 pounds. Her furious response was to send Philippine newspapers a Polaroid shot of herself clearly weighing less than that.

retreating to her room in a near faint, complaining of double vision and dizziness. To Guevara, she confessed that she wanted to go back to Leyte. To Letty, she confided that she wanted an annulment. Instead, she found a third way out: shortly after Marcos won his third congressional term in 1957, she had a nervous breakdown.

Like most other aspects of her private life, her collapse quickly became public domain, but with its aspects enlarged and tailored to fit her new, heroic persona. According to essayist Nick Joaquin, a prominent journalist given intimate access to the Marcoses, it began with intense, recurring headaches that "no pills could stop.... When her husband was around, she bore the pain grimly, betraying nothing; but when he had kissed her goodbye and left, she sought her room, locked it and struck her head repeatedly against a wall to kill the pain. Occasionally, she led days of sheer sloth: in bed the whole day, gorging on sweets, and nearby, a radio that ground out one soap opera after another."

This description, which couldn't have been released without the Marcoses' permission, amounted to a kind of apotheosis of Imelda's depression. Her husband finally realized he had trouble, according to Joaquin, after Kokoy found Imelda in bed one night, "cold, pale, motionless and hardly breathing," as if, he thought, "she would go any minute." Marcos took her to the Presbyterian Hospital in New York City, where she stayed for three months in 1958, and where a psychiatrist told her, "the cure was simple, and that it lay in herself ... she must embrace her husband's life, without reservation, not only accept, but love it and yes, enjoy it." The alternative was that Marcos quit politics, which he maintained he offered to do, "for the sake of the 'fulcrum of his life,'" but which Imelda naturally refused, since "it was like asking him to die." So instead, she performed "auto-suggestion" every morning, reminding herself how lucky she was to be asked for help instead of needing it. And one day, as Joaquin's record states, she awoke indeed feeling lucky for the "opportunities to help others," feeling, she said, "like a butterfly breaking out of its cocoon," her headaches gone forever, "and the double vision fused to become a single, concentrated look on the possible heights her husband's career might take."

Imelda's concentration nonetheless eroded over the years, while her behavior grew increasingly erratic. She also slept less and less as time went on. Yet for many years to come, she managed to function through the day, give her husband active support, and even gaily announce, "I really am a lucky girl. I really love crowning fiesta queens and cutting ceremonial ribbons....I wouldn't know what life would be without politics."

Joaquin believed Imelda's early hardships increased her allure, giving her, he wrote, in the high-blown style of the court journalists of the time, the look of "agonized vivacity [and] beauty in distress." In his *Philippines Free Press* essay, "Image of Imelda," he compared the Marcos couple's north-south "collision" of styles to historical regional confrontations such as the American Civil War and the Spanish conquest, in all of which, he said, "the languorous South too often suffer[s] ravishment.

"But from the ashes, like a phoenix, perpetually rises, in Southern womanhood, an image of beauty," he went on. And so with Imelda:

"When she speaks—" he wrote, "her voice becomes so full of feeling the very air seems to throb, and the great splendid eyes deepen, darken, and dazzle with tears....She is happy, but whatever the effort may have cost her shows in a deepened glowing of her charm. The loveliness has become poignant."

Following her recovery—which her official biographer, Polotan, said took two full years—Imelda began to refer to life with her husband as "an enchanted fairy tale." She took to advising reporters that young girls should always marry older men, "so that they, the girls, can be properly molded."

The next few years brought little besides more politics and more molding. By their end, even the newspapers were comparing Imelda's education to the story of Galatea and her sculptor, Pygmalion. Late in 1958, the year of Imelda's hospitalization, the couple had a son, Ferdinand, Jr., or "Bongbong." Imelda's brother Kokoy moved in with the young family and began to serve as one of Marcos' chief aides. Meanwhile, Imelda was taking advantage of her free reign over the household budget to dabble in finance. Without telling her husband, she used $500,000 of their savings to buy a warehouse full of garlic just after she heard the price would go up. Later, Imelda claimed to friends that she tripled the investment.

By 1959, Imelda had grown confident enough to help Marcos campaign for his Senate seat, his first try for a national constituency. She accompanied him as he stumped throughout the provinces, singing love songs to rural voters in three idioms (Tagalog, Visayan, and her husband's Ilocano) and making brief speeches, standing somewhat awkwardly with her hands clasped behind her. ("She was always afraid of appearing before a crowd—until I got her to sing," Marcos would recall. "She'd always been a good singer.")

Only Magsaysay before them had made such an effort to penetrate the countryside, where most of the votes lay. Imelda used her extraordinary memory that year as never before. She cultivated provincial leaders by learning each one's idiosyncrasies, always remembering who had gained or lost weight, how many children he had, and whether he needed a new roof or windows or equipment for his farm. "If I failed to send a greeting on a birthday, or failed to tell some politician's wife to get well soon when she was ill, well then, that would have serious repercussions," she said.

Marcos, meanwhile, pulled together what would soon become the Philippines' most efficient national machine. With sound trucks and crowds of loyalists, he appeared at hundreds of fiestas, visiting towns to which no candidate before had ever gone. He won his campaign by a wide margin, with 2.6 million votes.

The next year Imelda bore her third child, Irene. Though Imelda once said she wanted to have eleven children, like her own family, Irene was to be her last. The demands on her time were already too much. That same year, 1960, the Marcoses took a short vacation in Florida, where they stayed at the Fontainebleau Hotel and mulled over the future. Marcos had been the top vote-getter in the Senate election, making him the natural candidate for Senate president, if his peers voted him in, and boosting his stock to run for even higher office. The only question was when.

Following Magsaysay's death in a 1957 plane crash, his vice president, Carlos P. Garcia, had replaced him as president. Garcia's new vice president was Diosdado Macapagal of the Liberal Party, making theirs the first split-ticket term. Within two years, the Liberals had a good chance of capturing the presidency, and by October of 1960, there was open speculation that their candidates would be either Marcos or Macapagal.

The Liberals' convention was held that November, and the night before the Marcos camp had prepared thousands of buttons, leaflets and sandwiches to win over the delegates. A few hours before dawn that morning, however, Marcos woke Imelda to tell her that he had withdrawn in favor of Macapagal. He said he did it to avoid party strife, but later it was revealed that the two had made a deal. Marcos had agreed to withdraw on condition that Macapagal retire after one term and support him in 1965.

Macapagal and the Liberals were swept into power in 1961 by voters indignant at the spread of graft under Garcia's administration. Members of Congress were running smuggling syndicates, businessmen couldn't get government orders without paying kickbacks, and the bureaucracy was so venal that average people had to either bribe clerks or wait months to get the most routine sort of public service. The Liberals promised "moral regeneration" and Macapagal, whose propagandists called him "The Incorruptible," declared, "Shoot me if I steal!" Yet it was soon clear even Macapagal couldn't control his underlings, and corruption hit a new peak. The chief of Macapagal's antigraft commission quit in disgust, while his replacement, Bertolino De Joya, came to complain that the commission itself was graft-ridden. "My staff steals money and goods impounded as evidence in graft cases," he said. "Our only hope is to elect God president."

Increasingly, Marcos saw himself worthy of the call. In 1963, he was elected Senate president, after which he and his wife set out to court a crucial constituency: the American diplomatic community. In this endeavor, Imelda would stand and gracefully pass her first test as hostess and charmer.

Macapagal's relations with the United States had begun fairly well four years earlier, when the CIA donated $50,000 to his campaign.* He also won the esteem of William McCormick Blair, the U.S. Ambassador in Manila from 1964 to 1967 and a former campaign aide to Adlai Stevenson, who found him "honest and very easy to work with."

But even by 1963, Macapagal sensed he was losing the American mandate. One year earlier, he had ventured a display of nationalism by issuing an executive order changing the Philippine Independence Day from July 4 to July 12, the day in 1898 when Aguinaldo had declared the new republic. More meaningfully, he also began to pursue policies divergent from U.S. interests, warming relations, for instance, with the nationalist leader of Indonesia, Achmad Sukarno,

---

*Macapagal, in an interview in 1987, said he turned down this money when it was offered him "by an American businessman who wore a straw hat." But Burkholder Smith, who supervised the payment, says not only did the agent who delivered the cash tell Smith that Macapagal accepted it, but that Macapagal, "that two-faced son of a bitch . . . thanked me for it."

and slowly beginning to close previous open-door incentives to foreign investors.

Meanwhile, American embassy analysts had also begun to view Macapagal as a "hesitant introvert," too wrapped up in his political maneuvering and increasingly ineffective in daily government. Like others before him, he had come to office with promises of land reform, and had even managed to pass a new law to curtail tenant farmer arrangements. But by the end of his term, only a tiny share of rice and corn lands had been touched, leaving nearly half of existing farmland in large estates owned by one-tenth of 1 percent of the population. Rural voters—as well as Americans who understood the urgency of reform—were impatient and frustrated. Sensing their opportunity, the Marcoses stepped in.

Heading the long line of Americans they set out to cultivate was Lewis Gleeck, Jr., who arrived in late 1962 as the new U.S. consul general. A short, brusque right-winger, Gleeck and his wife, Fira, were immediately "adopted" by Kokoy Romualdez, who was fast becoming the political point man in Marcos' evolving shadow administration. By 1964, Fira became godmother to Kokoy's youngest son, Ferdinand Martin, drawing the Gleecks into an ever more binding tie with the Romualdezes and naturally the Marcoses as well. Gleeck understood the intent: *compadrazgo* required him to be friends with his new friends' friends and cool towards their rivals. Meanwhile, he spoke highly of the Marcoses in conversations with his embassy colleagues. "They used us, and we were quite willing," he recalled. "We were their first foreign friends, which flattered me and did a lot for my reporting. And they made their first steps in international society through us." The Gleecks' tie with the Marcoses stayed tight through the 1965 presidential elections, after which, Gleeck said, the Filipinos abandoned it.

The Marcos-Romualdez international debut came in 1963 at the mansion of the Gomez family, Kokoy's in-laws. Gleeck invited a dozen other embassy officers to look over the new Senate president, whom he championed as a bright new hope. "It was rather peculiar, in that there was no one there but us U.S. Embassy people," he said. "They were no longer local politicians. The Marcoses were following their star." The embassy staff appeared impressed, and the party was followed by another for the American business community, for which Gleeck also helped with the guest list.

As a hostess, Imelda "was off and running very fast," Gleeck said.

"She had a wonderful capacity for being briefed, and literally within a year was wowing visiting congressmen, cultivating the delegations who came through Manila." In those years, however, some rough edges remained. "She was still awkward about some things. She didn't really know how to set up a dinner party correctly, and certainly didn't do much holding forth on her own. Back then, she was simply the demure, elegant wife, beautiful and charming, a kind of emerging butterfly."

Imelda's winsome struggles and her obviously rising stature inspired others besides Marcos to play Pygmalion. "She was like raw clay," said a friend. She gradually improved her English and Tagalog and even learned some Spanish, but she remained most comfortable with her native Waray and often blithely embarrassed herself in other languages, inspiring either scorn or earnest tutelage.

"She would sing this one love song in Tagalog that she hadn't learned well," recalled Loreto, her cousin. "And by accenting the wrong syllable, she would say, instead of *Ako ay mama'matay*—I'll die without you, *Ako ay mamama'tay*—I am a criminal. And I couldn't stand it. I called her aside, and said, look, that's wrong. No author will write such a crazy thing—a lover will say, I am a criminal? No lover, even if he were a criminal, he would not admit it. He would say, I'm going to die for you, but not I'm going to kill you or something like that! She'd shrug her shoulders, saying, 'Ah, it's all the same.' I'd have to tell her, 'Look here, I'm a nobody, but if you mispronounce a word, what a terrible example.'"

Marcos, meanwhile, was building up his own public image. He had hired propaganda men to nurture comparisons between him and President John F. Kennedy, whose image in the Philippines was, if anything, more glamorous than in the United States. When Kennedy was killed, the senator's young image-maker, Blas Ople, rushed over an expansive eulogy for Marcos to read on television. In this endeavor, too, Imelda was an obvious asset: she served as both the southerner, to match Lyndon Johnson's appeal and a glamorous Jackie figure as well.

Macapagal's wife, Evangelina, could never have elicited such comparisons: a physician, she was older—close to 50 by the time of the election—and much more drab than Imelda. She had already drawn rebukes for what some saw as too obvious a political role, appearing, as she had, with her husband at several state affairs. Even this was such a departure from earlier habits of first ladies that some in government began to call her "Mrs. Rule," leading her husband, as he recalled, to warn her to keep her distance. "This is how it is," he finally told her. "I've been elected to be president. I'm responsible to the people. I want all the public decisions to be my own."

Macapagal seemed already to have decided he wasn't about to honor his promise to Marcos. In April of 1964, Marcos resigned from the Liberal Party to join the Nacionalistas, who, it was clear by then in any case, had a better chance of capturing the presidency. His switch was controversial, but not seriously so. The Liberals were reputedly more pro-American than their rivals, having been responsible for "parity" as well as the first bases treaty. But few doubted the Nacionalistas would have done the same, had they been in power at the time. Leaders of both parties exchanged affiliations, sometimes several times in a political career, at the mere whisper of opportunity. "There is only one party," U.S. Ambassador William McCormick Blair would later say, "and that is the party of the politicians."

Among his own reasons for leaving, Marcos cited "the pleasure and privilege of defeating Diosdado Macapagal," whom he charged had tried to dislodge him as Senate president. Imelda's cousin Daniel Romualdez, known as the Nacionalistas' kingmaker, gave him a hearty welcome: Marcos was a rising star and the Nacionalistas were eager to get back in power. Those who later came to see Marcos as the consummate chess player said he'd planned the move long before his "impulsive" marriage. But Imelda greeted the change with pure enthusiasm, saying it felt "like coming home."

In June of that year, Marcos suffered an infected gallbladder. Although his doctors advised surgery, he asked instead for antibiotics to get him through the November convention. At a Lions club meeting later that month, with Imelda at his side, he announced his decision to run for president.

Nearly 1400 delegates were chosen for the Nacionalistas' convention, and the Marcoses set forth to court each one. They split up to travel to the provinces on a house-to-house campaign, the kind of politicking in which Imelda was becoming expert. In Cebu, she was said to have traveled more than 500 miles for one vote, chasing a delegate back and forth until she finally won him over. She took boats through shark-filled waters and small planes in bad weather, bearing with her gifts and up to eight changes of clothing for each day.

Though she'd earlier favored dresses of soft pink or beige, she now wore chartreuse, shocking pink, and canary yellow, as well as strong perfumes, explaining later, "I wanted people to spot me in a room. After all, I couldn't stand up and holler, 'Here I am!'"

By the time of the Nacionalista convention in late November, the number of candidates for the nomination had boiled down to five: Marcos, former vice presidents Pelaez and Fernando Lopez and senators Arturo Tolentino and Gil Puyat. Each descended with his entourage on suites in the stately Manila Hotel, the capital's main stage for political events. On the edge of Rizal Park, facing Manila Bay, the hotel's white stucco, Spanish-style facade, marble floors, and huge chandeliers heightened the drama of the posturing going on inside.

On Friday, November 20, the eve of the convention, banners and posters covered the high-ceilinged lobby, while the kimono-wearing society girls and starlets who formed shock troops for each aspiring nominee sidled among the delegates. Imelda arrived late, as usual, to find all the seats in the wives' section of the stage had been taken. Since no one offered to share a chair, she stood for nearly two hours. By her return early the next morning, it was clear that the aggressive Marcoses were being seen as common enemies of the other four delegates. The four, it was said, had even signed a pact to stop the young senator, out of sudden concern for his shady past and fear that he might threaten the party, if not the country.

Imelda squared her shoulders in her red, white, and blue sailor dress and set out on a renewed lobbying campaign for each delegate. She remembered every name, asking each about his wife and children, and recalling their last meeting in intimate detail. She once described her phenomenal recall as "a capacity for remembering with my skin and my heart." Combined with her beauty and verve, it made her an unrivaled campaigner. "She was the focus of attention throughout the convention," said Celia Laurel, a former theater actress who had married aspiring Nacionalista politico Salvador Laurel. "She wore these bright, vivid costumes and would play up to all the delegates, most of whom were old men, and who loved it."

Beneath her coquetry, Imelda was taking careful notes. "I watch the eyes," she said. "I watch how he smiles, mark his expression, and study how he acts when he's left alone."

Of at least equal importance to the Marcoses' charisma was the Marcos money flooding the Manila Hotel that weekend. After formally agreeing with the other Nacionalistas not to bribe or promise favors to the delegates, "Marcos virtually bought the convention," *Life* magazine reported. "His supporters flung 100-peso bills about like confetti." Imelda, as Celia recalled, handed out envelopes containing the equivalent of about $125 each, with notes saying proof of a "yes" vote would earn another $125. In private, Imelda demonstrated to Celia how to slip the money across in an unobtrusive handshake. Nor were the delegates the only ones to profit from the windfall. As Imelda later described it, "We had the bellhops; we had the waiters; we had the elevator boys; we had the desk clerks; we had everybody talking up Marcos, 'It's going to be Marcos.'" "But most importantly," she said, "we had all the telephone operators, so the other side never got their calls."

The Marcoses assigned commandos to each committed delegate to guard against defections. They spent $2500 for sandwiches alone. When the vote came, Saturday night, it went easily their way. Yet Imelda's most brilliant moment was still to come, when it was left to her single-handedly to corner her husband a running mate.

After the vote, Marcos' party rivals retreated in anger. He realized just how grim the situation was when he tried to convince Fernando Lopez, an ideal candidate for vice president, to run with him. The tall, affable Senator had already served a term as vice president, and had clout both in Manila and in the south. His family, a sugar dynasty, virtually controlled the province of Iloilo, and also owned the Manila Electric Company, the Philippines' largest public utility, and a vast media network including twenty-one radio and television stations and the influential *Manila Chronicle.* Popular and not at all controversial, Lopez offered by far the best hope of unifying the Nacionalistas and helping Marcos defeat Macapagal. Nor was it any small matter that his family could provide millions of dollars in campaign funds. But Lopez, out of loyalty to his defeated friends, refused one Marcos emissary after another, including former President Carlos Garcia. He said that he was too old—he was already 61—that his family disapproved, that he'd decided he was through with politics. At last, Imelda cornered him in a hotel hallway, and literally stood in his way until he agreed to see her for five minutes in his suite.

Once past his door, Imelda theatrically dropped to one knee and began to cry. She pleaded with him to accept, telling him how hard she had worked already, and promising that he wouldn't have to tire himself campaigning; she would do it for him. She reminded him that he and Marcos were "brothers" in the Senate, and how, though they had long been of different parties, they had worked together for the good of the country. The sight of a woman in Imelda's high position so openly begging was rare, and it soon became stressful for the courtly Lopez. He found himself buckling; his chest hurt and he groped for his medicine. "My heart!" he muttered. Sensing her advantage, Imelda later said, she told him he had no heart, "for a heart could feel compassion, and he had none for my need."

"I was flattered, of course, her coming to see me like that—but that she was beautiful had nothing to do with it," Lopez recalled in 1987. "Finally, I'd say it was just too much persuasion on her part." After a few minutes of silence, he told Imelda to talk to his brother, Eugenio, the powerful publisher of the *Chronicle*. She grinned through her tears.

At 9 p.m., the Marcoses and Lopez strode back onto the convention hall stage. Imelda wore a gorgeous formal terno, low-necked and weighed down with seed pearls, her hair in a Burmese bun. Under the glare of the television lights, Lopez reached for her hand, caught and kissed it, and asked, "Are you happy now, Imelda?"

\*      \*      \*

Macapagal won his Liberal Party's nomination with ease, kicking off a year of campaigning that *Life* magazine later reported was "the longest, roughest, dirtiest, most scandal-ridden and most expensive in the 19-year history of this republic." ("Politics is the national disease of the Philippines," the writer added, "and another attack like this one could be fatal.") In addition to the presidential contest, nearly 500 candidates were running for congressional seats. Hundreds of millions of posters appeared around the islands, with leaflets dropped from planes and even hung on the horns of water buffalos. The U.S. Embassy called the campaign a "year-long propaganda orgy," and, for once, apparently did not intervene to support either of the presidential contenders.

That disappointed Macapagal. During Johnson's campaign, he had visited the American President and driven with him through San Francisco in his motorcade, an appearance that Macapagal believed helped Johnson attract votes among the many Filipino Americans on the west coast. Subsequently, he said, Johnson promised him in Washington, D.C., that the United States would help in his campaign. "He said, 'I'll send you 100,000 tons of rice,'" the former Philippine president recounted. "And I said, 'Oh, you know our customs!'"

As Macapagal remembered, Johnson indeed sent the free American rice, but it never landed in Manila. Instead it went on to Saigon, convincing Macapagal that Johnson had finally abandoned him, and leading, he believed, to his defeat.

In Manila, however, it was clear other factors played parts in Macapagal's loss. Issues, to no one's surprise, took a back seat to images in the election, and although Marcos was still scorned by much of Manila's society, he was gaining popular appeal among the neglected majority of Filipinos, the rural farmers and fishermen. He appealed to them with his war-hero image, his can-do speeches, his dedicated supporters, and far from least, his effervescent, energetic wife.

In 1965, the Philippines' population was almost 32 million, close to 70 percent of whom lived in stark poverty in the countryside. A typical voter of that time in central Luzon's rice basin, for instance, was 30 to 35 years old, married, with a family of six or seven, and farming about five acres of land for a landlord to whom the family was in constant debt. While successive governments, including Macapagal's, had made stabs at setting up better marketing arrangements, graft, neglect, and inefficiency brought each program to a quick defeat.

Other conditions were deteriorating. The country was so overpopulated that it no longer could provide enough food and education; the number of children lacking elementary education in 1960 was seven times as great as in 1948. At least one third of the country's work force lacked full-time jobs, and violent crime was sharply on the rise. During the war tens of thousands of guns had been smuggled in to fight the Japanese and there remained about five guns in circulation for every male adult.

The 1960s did bring one improvement, though its blessings were mixed. Radios, newspapers, and even television sets were appearing in formerly isolated areas, sharpening visions of the world outside the provinces. Reports brought unsettling news of the phenomenal growth and new riches of Japan, Taiwan, and Hong Kong. Filipinos began to understand and resent how poor they were.

People wanted change, but they would settle for hope, and Marcos, younger, livelier, and, best of all, less familiar than Macapagal, seemed to embody a brighter future. Imelda visually reinforced the dream of wealth and glamour that all the squatters, soda vendors, and tenant farmers longed to share, appearing like a celluloid fantasy in sparkling, sequined ternos in their dusty barrios where few national candidates—and no Manila ladies—had ever come. Macapagal, for his part, stumped through 1300 Philippine towns, claimed to shake "3 million" hands, and drained the treasury by handing out tens of millions of dollars worth of subsized food to voters. But Imelda drew crowds seemingly without effort. "Since the masses have always known that we are far from impoverished, it would have been a terrible mistake for me to have appeared before them in old or shabby clothes just because they themselves dress shabbily," she reasoned. "They would have thought I was belittling them. On the other hand, it flattered them to no end to see that I always took the trouble of wearing my best ternos—I would even wear dangling earrings to make them feel important."

It wasn't just that Imelda was beautiful—she was beautiful in a *certain way*. Both Filipino and American writers describing her would often point out her unusual height—about 6 inches over the average Filipina—and the lightness of her skin.

At the same time, she oozed empathy, her large, tearful eyes fixing on the crowds to whom she sang love songs and assured, "I believe in Ferdinand. He is a good man." In Leyte and Samar, she declared, "I am from the south myself. If Ferdinand wins and turns out to be what his enemies say he is, I would not be able to return, I would be so ashamed. And I do want to come back here, for this is where I belong."

For months, she traveled almost constantly, with her small staff and large wardrobe, jostling for hours in jeeps over rocky dirt roads and sleeping in roach-infested provincial hotels. Once, after three days spent visiting fifteen of eighteen towns in a province, she heard that people in the other, more remote towns had felt slighted, and she returned to see them too. "She became Marcos' best asset, with her lovely singing voice and sweet manner," said one of her campaign aides. "There was still a hint of sadness about her in those years, and it made her all the more bewitching."

The people she met "admired her frankly, loved her secretly, and sometimes felt a little sorry for her—for her prodigious efforts to make her husband win," one Manila paper reported. When the couple campaigned together, Marcos began most of his speeches with the vow, "I will give you everything you want—except my wife!" But for the most part, they exploited their advantage by splitting up the country between them. "When Marcos was east, I was west; when Marcos was south, I was north," Imelda said later. "Only 30 percent of this country's votes can be bought, if you wish to buy them. The rest you must win."

The 1965 campaign was Imelda's watershed, and it brought plenty of immediate payoffs. She proved herself invaluable to her husband, won wide acclaim for her beauty and charm, was constantly challenged, and kept blissfully busy for the full year. The cost, however, was a rift with her children which later years did little to mend.

Never an especially motherly sort—after all, she had little time to learn from example—she was always more awkward and physically restrained than her husband with their children. Still, until the presidential campaign, Imelda had taken great pride in doting over her brood. Not once, at the house in San Juan, did a Marcos child come home from school to find that his or her *merienda*, or snack, was not ready. And as soon as the snack was consumed, Imelda would supervise homework. Josefina Verzosa Ocampo, a politician's wife from Ilocos Norte and Imelda's close friend during Marcos' Senate years, said Imelda employed a maid for each child. Yet several times, on the ten-hour car rides the two women often shared to campaign in the north, Josefina recalled that Imelda insisted on placing her children around her: one on each side and one on her lap. She would never let anyone else share the duty, saying, "In case of an accident, you know, I want to be sure that I will be holding my children."

By the 1965 campaign, however, it was already clear that Imelda had begun to crave politics in her own right. Through that hectic year, Manila newspapers made much of Imelda's "sacrifice" in leaving her children with relatives for weeks on end. More likely, she enjoyed herself far more than she let on, yet she did recognize the consequences. In later years she often referred guiltily to the time she had to choose between tending to Imee, who was then 10 years old and in a hospital with a high fever, and keeping a political engagement on the southern island of Negros. She chose Negros, but would later complain to friends that her eldest daughter had suffered the most from her absences, and had never really forgiven her.

When Imelda wasn't traveling, she helped oversee operations at the Ortega Street home, which had taken on the air of a military camp: squadrons of college student volunteers were fed with rice from army vats on cooking fires in the backyard and meat delivered by trucks every few hours. Fabian Ver, a distant cousin of Marcos who had become his chauffeur and bodyguard, was put in charge of security, while Juan Ponce Enrile, a friend and Harvard-educated attorney, helped with legal research. Marcos put together an intelligence group that monitored Macapagal's campaign and brought back daily reports of his itinerary.

Imelda oversaw the campaign budget, but made a public point of staying clear of her husband's decisions on policy. "Ferdinand will never be under the *saya* [skirt]," she swore. "I am afraid of my own decisions. I'm a woman who knows her limitations....If he needs an opinion, he can get it better elsewhere." Her approach was an intentional contrast with that of Mrs. Macapagal, who, despite her husband's best efforts, was known as a political meddler. Imelda, instead, played hostess, beginning in August, to large tea parties in the garden for diverse occupational groups, such as medical workers, academicians, clerks, factory hands, and even market venders. For the first of these teas—a lavish lunch of roast pig and paella—she invited some thirty female reporters, sending chauffeurs to pick each one up and return her to her office with a Marcos badge, brochure, and box of Go-Marcos candy. "I was a little tense about this lunch," she confessed afterward, "because...if there's anything I'm afraid to do, it's to invite any member of the press. I don't know, perhaps I have a complex or something, but I have always been scared of them."

Imelda's most ingenious contribution was in mobilizing the enormous power pent up in Filipinas. Already advanced among their Asian peers, Philippine women had won the vote in 1937, just seventeen years after American women, and by the time of the 1948 census were trickling into the professions, with 1194 registered nurses, 1268 pharmacists, 304 lawyers, 161 dentists, and 20 opticians. But politics remained a mostly male preserve, as if in this single field of leadership the Spanish ethos still held, classing women as custodial material, along with idiots and infants.

Imelda sensed the results of this repression and took full advantage of it. She began to exploit what she recognized as vast untapped potential at the Nacionalista convention, when she recruited seventeen society beauties to help her hand out brochures and sandwiches. Most of the women were ripe for the job, bored by their idle lives and thrilled by the energy and zeal radiated by the Marcos camp. Those who still seemed hesitant were won over by Imelda's tenacious personal lobbying. The recruits wore white kimonos with blue sashes, emblazoned MARCOS across their chests. Following that weekend, their ranks increased exponentially, their uniform changed to an aquamarine shirtwaist dress, and they became known as Imelda's "Blue Ladies." High-spirited, ambitious and loyal, they were natural successors to Imelda's high school club, the Popular Organization of Nice Good Energetic Romantic Socialites.

In the first stages of the general campaign, Imelda organized about 100 of these women, all young and attractive and of the most prominent families, to speak at rallies in Manila and tour the provinces with her. (She later called them "my childhood friends," although that was patent wishful thinking.) They went to bus depots, markets, and schools with gifts of pens, combs, and hats. Imelda, in her fervor, made them into a kind of high-heeled Peace Corps.

"I realized that these girls were spoiled, pampered young women ...preoccupied only with themselves," she said after the campaign. "I am very glad to have taken them along on my provincial trips for, seeing misery and poverty at first hand, they began to develop a social conscience. Now, on their own, they give of their time and money to help the poor."

She admitted, however, to some initial problems in breaking in the girls. At some of her teas, at which the Blue Ladies acted as hostesses, she had to monitor them closely so they didn't offend the lower-income guests—the jeepney drivers or market vendors. "They are used to saying 'Call for my car,'" she explained. "Because it is so easy for them, they have a dozen cars perhaps. But suppose it's a market vendor and they say: 'Are you leaving, shall I call for your car?' That might lose votes for Marcos!"

She inspired the women to tap their family funds for her teas and work for hours on end tying sacks of rice or sugar to send to victims of floods and typhoons. She took obvious enjoyment in commanding the "blue bloods," whom she perceived as having snubbed her in earlier years. "She used to gather all these ladies around her and make fun of us, saying, look what I made you do, how I made you work; your hands are bleeding!" said Presentacion Lopez, a Blue Lady who was the niece of vice presidential candidate Fernando.

Imelda was a merciless example, single-minded, praised for her "paratrooper's stamina," and by then needing only a few hours of sleep a night. "She'd be fresh while we'd be dying," Presentacion said. Yet Imelda was working harder than anyone. She felt intimidated by the new demands on her to understand the political issues of the day and began to surround herself with experts, as if she might improve her own intelligence by osmosis.

The Liberals countered the Blue Ladies tactic with a group of 100 matrons called the Lakambini 1965, led by Eva Macapagal. Capital reporters played up the rivalries; the Blue Ladies sneered that their counterparts should be renamed Lakambini 1865—since many, they said, were old enough to have been born around that year. The Liberal Party women urged their rivals to hand out toothbrushes along with their gift combs, a cutting reference to the murder of Nalundasan, who, as everyone remembered, was assassinated while brushing his teeth.

Indeed, any Filipino who hadn't known of Nalundasan before the 1965 campaign surely knew of him by its end. Macapagal's supporters made Marcos' old murder conviction a central issue in the campaign, going so far, at one point, to call for a nationwide commemoration of Nalundasan's death on September 20, with rallies all over the country. There was also a television special, the "Inside Story on the Day of Infamy," featuring commentary by the dead congressman's sister.

As the year wore on, Macapagal grew ever more willing to sling mud, but the tactic soon backfired, showing just how desperate he'd become. His supporters began to sound shrill when they attacked Marcos as a "murderer" and charged him with stealing land from northern peasants. And Macapagal seemed shrillest of all: at a rally in Cebu late in October, he said Marcos had "his hands dripping with the blood of murder." At another point, he claimed Marcos would turn the Philippines "into another Cuba," and four days before the election charged him with "a black litany of deceit, dishonesty, greed for money and power, and pride in the use of violence and death."

Imelda made the smear campaign sound silly just by smiling at the crowds who came to see her. "Do you think I would like this fellow and stay with him if he was like that?" she'd demand of rally after rally. So touching was her appeal that it prompted one western reporter to conclude, "If Marcos has the human touch, it is because he has Imelda."

But having made herself a figure in the campaign, Imelda became another target of the flak. In what she branded "black propaganda," the Liberal Party campaigners spread word of her déclassé origins. They called her the daughter of a "laundrywoman," and further charged that the stylish Senator's wife had been raised in a garage.

Finally, in September, crude photographs began to circulate of nude female torsos with Imelda's face pasted above them. On learning of them, Imelda locked herself in her room in the dark, shaking with outrage. "I was so furious," she said years later. "They were very naked, very ugly bodies.... If they had used Marilyn Monroe's body, then I would have had no problem. I might," she added, laughing, "even have ordered some." Her public response at the time, however, was simply to say, "The more they smear us, the harder I work."

By one estimate, Marcos spent well over $100,000 for his own propaganda. His biography by Spence was out and circulating, and he'd commissioned a movie and comic strip along the same lines. Macapagal supporters retaliated with their own biography, *Macapagal: The Incorruptible*, by Quentin Reynolds and Geoffrey Bocca, and a similar biographical film. But the President made one of the worst missteps of his campaign when government censors on September 1, 1965, banned the romantic Marcos movie, *Iginuhit Ng Tadhana*, (*Destined by Fate*). The film had already been out long enough to win mass appeal, particularly in the provinces, and largely due to its depiction of the whirlwind courtship of Imelda.

The Marcos camp, under Enrile's legal guidance, made an immediate appeal which brought a quick victory: the supreme court lifted the ban, reversing an appellate court affirmation, on September 17. The damage of the government's overreaction had been done, however, and the Nacionalistas capitalized on the thwarted attempt at censorship. Many thereafter regarded the affair as the turning point in the campaign.

The Marcos forces also hit Macapagal for the government's record on rice; from once being self-sufficient in the grain, the Philippines had begun to import hundreds of thousands of tons each year. In the meantime, the President, who had repeatedly aimed his appeals to the "common man," was facing the traditional campaign charges of personal extravagance. The newspapers featured his purchase of a $3500 Cadillac and expenses of nearly $30,000 for travels to the United States and Africa.

Stung, Macapagal resorted to full-page ads calling for bids for final phases of construction of a magnificient pan-Philippine highway connecting northern Luzon to the southern tip of Mindanao, to be completed in 1966. But the ads seemed incredible even then, and only called voters' attention to the abysmal state of most existing roads. In the last stages of the campaign, Macapagal suddenly charged he had been narrowly missed in an assassination attempt, declaring, "Never underestimate my opponent's capacity for evil." The Nacionalistas' response was to beam radio programs at the south, characterizing the President as henpecked by his wife, Eva.

Voters went to the polls on November 9, among them Marcos, in Laoag, in his "lucky" striped shirt, and Imelda, in Manila, in a dress with a v-shaped border. By the time ballots were counted, some three days later, they showed Marcos the winner by more than 705,000 of the 8 million votes cast. Marcos credited his wife with winning him 1 million votes out of his total. In her base, the Visayas, where many had predicted he couldn't win, he exceeded Macapagal by 65,000 votes.

In a confidential assessment of the election, William Owen, first secretary of the U.S. Embassy, credited Marcos for "superior generalship" in the campaign, adding that he appeared "more colorful, expert, and determined," with the extra appeal of his "dramatic wartime exploits." Owen then devoted several paragraphs in praise of Marcos' young wife: "Combining regal looks and bearing with the simplicity and directness of a successful young career woman in a more technically advanced society," he wrote, "the highly photogenic and intelligent Imelda, who appears not to have made a misstep during the entire campaign, must have represented to many Filipinos of both sexes the embodiment of the most desirable qualities in a prospective first lady..."

The transformation was complete, and it was reasonable to assume then that Imelda—at 36, the youngest Filipina First Lady in history—would continue to be the asset Marcos had fashioned into an ideal running mate. Her own devotion to that end was obvious from the night of Marcos' victory, when Blue Lady Presentacion Lopez said she came upon Imelda making stiff motions with her arm in front of her mirror. "How does she do it?" the new First Lady was muttering. "How does the Queen of England wave?"

# 6
## CAMELOT

*Whenever he makes a decision, I barely mumble. Whenever he speaks, I hardly utter a single word. Whenever he gives advice, I scarcely dare make a suggestion.*
—Eva Peron, speaking to crowds about her husband, General Juan Peron, in 1948; from *Evita, First Lady* by John Barnes

*I am afraid of my own decisions. I'm a woman who knows her limitations.... If he needs an opinion, he can get it better elsewhere.*
—Imelda Marcos, speaking to reporters about her husband, Ferdinand Marcos, in 1965

The grandstand of Luneta Park, alongside Manila Bay, was stifling long before the inaugural music began at close to noon on December 30, 1965. But the new President and his wife looked fresh and cool as they flanked their guest of honor, Vice President Hubert Humphrey, who was sweating in his dark morning coat. Lopez, the new Philippine vice president, stood idly by, just out of hearing.

Marcos wore striped trousers and a lacy white barong tagalog, while Imelda's dress was ivory with a cinched waist, low neck, and sharp puffs of shoulders. Her hairdo was dramatic: a tall, teased bubble dubbed "the Round Look" and created just for that day. Her expression was demure, though; she kept her eyes down, clutched her white fan, but stuck by Humphrey's side.

Such was her image in the first years of the presidency—the unblemished, utterly loyal political wife—and Filipinos, male and female, loved her for it. "You should have known her back then," old friends said in the 1980s, asked why she held their allegiance so long. In 1968, when a group of female college students in Manila were asked their opinion of the Marcoses, they gave their president mixed reviews, with at least one-third calling him "average." But the students were united in their high regard for Imelda, with one considering her an "unqualified, resounding success," another, "so gorgeously presentable," and still another declaring she "can do no wrong."

Throughout Marcos' first term, Imelda left to her husband the controversial tasks of governing. During the campaign, she said, "I was so full of politics people even said Mrs. Marcos must be wanting to run for the Senate! Immediately after the elections the President told me that image would have to be changed. In my administration, he said, I'll take care of the framework, you see to the trimmings." She said she was happy to agree. She made few speeches, rarely traveled by herself, and kept her attention on such feminine pursuits as cultivating the arts, redecorating the palace, and improving the menus at presidential parties. She revived the terno, the butterfly-sleeved traditional dress that she said suited her figure, and she threw out the plastic flowers that once decorated Malacanang, ordering fresh blooms in their place. She proudly told reporters that the Marcoses were the first couple ever to share the same presidential bedroom. "The President and I see as much of each other as ever," she said. "We have our meals together. We try to work together; we inspire each other."

To all appearances, Marcos indeed depended on his wife. He never started a speech until she made her entrance, and was notoriously dull at parties without her. Yet despite the warmth Imelda shared with her husband, she was growing more and more awkward with her children. Acquaintances who saw the family together would remark how much Marcos seemed to enjoy the kids, who flocked around him, chattering of horses or astronauts. Yet Imelda stood to the side, increasingly preoccupied with palace photographers' camera angles and spots on the children's charming coordinated outfits.

As early as she could, she enrolled each child in strict Catholic private schools in England. She believed all three to be in grave need of discipline, and there she had a point. Ever since the campaign, Imelda had been giving in to guilty urges to indulge her children, and now that they all were installed in the palace, the temptations had become unavoidable. To begin with, there was twenty-four-hour attention for each child—a corps of maids and guards followed them everywhere. Meanwhile, Imelda was buying them all sorts of gifts for any excuse of an occasion. Giving things or doing favors had always been a quick and easy way to make herself feel better. And besides criticizing common enemies—a ploy for which the children were too young—it was one of the few avenues she used to get close to people. Still, the closeness never lasted very long with either technique. And with her children, there was the added danger of spoiling them.

Her real and simpler passion had already become her work outside the palace, and she was moving quickly to realize a host of plans that would leave her mark all over the Philippines. At her first press conference in January, she promised a year-long capital beautification drive and plans for a new cultural center, which she announced as her husband's idea to "revive national pride." She also set off a burst of other construction, commissioning five major centers for orphans and the elderly and, according to palace records, 2000 new day-care centers. She started dropping by building sites for impromptu inspections, and on occasion made workers toil through the night to meet her deadlines. She commissioned two restorations of historical sites, ordering the rebuilding of the gates of Intramuros, Manila's old Spanish section, nearly leveled in World War II, and turning the route of the Bataan Death March into a tree-lined memorial. At the same time, she established popular programs such as Share for Progress (a seed dispersal effort for backyard gardens with the motto, "Viva the vegetables!") and Save-a-Life-in-Every-Barrio, through which her secretaries arranged free medical care for the poor on a case-by-case basis.

Her work then was mostly personalistic—showy handouts instead of lasting reform—but few before her had done things much differently, and she quickly distinguished herself by the zest she brought to the job. "She beats miracle drugs in Instant Relief," wrote Filipino journalist Luis Beltran, who many years later was to turn critical. In her emphasis on culture, her photogenic young children, her high fashion, and her self-effacing style, she often seemed a conscious copy of Jackie Kennedy, who only two years earlier had won unprecedented popularity as America's First Lady. The likeness was often noted in Manila's newspapers and fit naturally into the Kennedyesque "Camelot" motif offered from Marcos' first speech in the Luneta.

"We are in a crisis," the new President had intoned at his inauguration. "Our government is gripped in the iron hand of venality, its treasury is barren, its resources are wasted, its civil service is slothful and indifferent, its armed forces demoralized, and its councils sterile.... Public officials combine with unscrupulous businessmen to defraud the government and the public—with absolute impunity."

Rather than mourning his news, however, the audience of 80,000 warmed to his confident tone and the proud smile of his lovely wife. They found it a good omen that the ceremonies had not begun late, as was the custom, but in fact eight minutes before noon, the scheduled hour. They also noted with awe that Marcos barely glanced at his notes throughout his thirty-one minute speech. When he promised to "make this nation great again," punsters replied, "This nation can regret again." But once again, if somewhat wistfully, Filipinos allowed themselves to be inspired. "Not religion but the polls have been the opium of the people," wrote a Filipino journalist in later years.

Like the Kennedys, the Marcoses offered glamour, youth, and a palpable sense of destiny. "They hit the mother lode of the Philippines," said David Briscoe, then a Peace Corps volunteer who later became Manila bureau chief for the Associated Press. "They played on people's weaknesses—their love of fun, their need for faith...." After the divisive, violent elections, Filipinos were eager for faith, and so were the Americans. Less than a week earlier, Lyndon Johnson had ordered a pause in air attacks in North Vietnam as part of efforts to negotiate a settlement. His emissaries, including Humphrey, were visiting capitals all over Asia to seek support for his approach, and Marcos seemed like someone with whom they could deal.

American approval was just one of the advantages Marcos enjoyed in his first few years in office. Of equal importance was his union, through his Vice President, with the powerful Lopez clan, whose total assets were gauged at close to $400 million. The Lopezes were "old wealth," grounded in their southern Iloilo province sugar plantations, while the Marcoses, as far as Manila society was concerned, were hopelessly nouveau. Nor did the Lopezes try to downplay their clout: *Chronicle* publisher Eugenio Lopez used to boast of wielding more power than any Philippine president. And in 1968, Vice President Fernando Lopez celebrated his golden wedding anniversary by importing an American dance band, flying in a group of European nobles, and stocking his three garden fountains with Dom Perignon champagne. The clan's victory party for the Marcoses had been no less sumptuous. Thousands of red lights were strung in the trees around Eugenio Lopez's mansion in the capital subdivision of Paranaque. Guests stubbed out their cigars in gold-plated ashtrays, and Imelda danced in a stark, black gown through the vast, glowing garden.

For several months afterward, the Lopezes' enthusiasm for the new president continued to resound in the *Chronicle*, with optimistic echoes throughout the Philippine and American press. Of the two Marcoses, Imelda often won more column inches, especially when space for photographs was counted. Her spirited charity drives, endearing confidences about family life, and choice of dress for each interview made much more intriguing reading than Marcos' Sisyphean struggles with rice shortages, graft, and bad roads.

*The New York Times* described Imelda as "a statuesque beauty who wears her skirts above the knee 'to make me look shorter'" and commiserated with her new problems. No longer, for instance, could she push her own shopping cart, since everyone wanted to do it for her, and the "between 500 and 700 people" a day dropping in meant "Ferdie can't get any work done." *Parade* magazine touted her "magnificent honey-colored skin, eyes of fiery topaz...figure of a beauty queen [with] brains and energy to boot." *Life* called her THE PHILIPPINES' FABULOUS FIRST LADY and put her photo on its August cover, which showed her seated on a thronelike chair with her hands clasped childishly. *Life*'s writers likened the "busy beauty in the barrios" to Jackie Kennedy in looks and Eleanor Roosevelt in energy, saying she had the "constitution of a water buffalo, the political savvy of a Boston Irishman, and the unflagging zeal of a Carrie Nation." As one Filipino reporter conceded, creating a word for the occasion, "It's difficult not to queenify her."

With the aid of palace handouts, U.S. and Philippine papers generally reduced Imelda's age in their reports by three years, while adding to the glamour of her upbringing—*Time* called her "the sugar-rich Imelda Romualdez." She told reporters that her wardrobe was nearly exclusively Philippine-made, including off-the-rack dresses for $25, as well as "the occasional Paris dress or Italian knit." And she declared: "From now on, I'll probably be traveling even less. People don't like their officials to go off on junkets, and I can get a wonderful wardrobe right here."

Shopping at home also made her self-conscious, however. "I went to buy two pairs of shoes the other day at a downtown store, and suddenly, I felt like Elizabeth Taylor buying up the whole place," she confessed. "Yet, in the past, whenever I went shopping here or abroad, I would think nothing of getting myself two dozen pairs of shoes at a time or a dozen dresses off the rack—just like that. Now it's frightfully different. I'm always thinking of what people might say."

There's no reason to think her comment then wasn't sincere, and that she wasn't conscious of where the line lay, in society's eyes, between elegance and excess. That awareness made her outrageous later indulgences all the more pitiful, apparent emblems of self-destructive anger more than the means to any kind of joy.

In her early years as First Lady, Imelda indeed was frankly obsessed with how others saw her, and most of all with her image in the eyes of her husband. Sol Vanzi, a television reporter who became one of her first press aides, recalls taking an overnight boat trip with the Marcoses to Fuga Island, off northern Luzon, and encountering the First Lady in a cabin bathroom shortly before dawn. (Vanzi, like Imelda, rarely slept more than three or four hours a night.) The younger woman watched in wonder as Imelda washed her face, carefully brushed her hair, and completely reapplied her makeup before returning to bed with her spouse. "You must always be pretty, Sol," Imelda advised her later. "Your Sir has never seen me without makeup."

The Blue Ladies who formed Imelda's retinue shared in her obsession with looks, and in her willingness to take drastic measures to enhance them. The fashion among the Blue Ladies then was to take diet pills that combined amphetamines and an extremely strong laxative. An ambassador's wife later recalled that she spent a night in agony after the Blue Ladies persuaded her to try one of the pills. "They would give those drugs to their kids," she said, "which I really think was going too far." The rumor then was that the pills were causing Imelda's insomnia, but no one had any proof that the capsules she took with her meals were anything other than the vitamins she said they were.

Another tactic in the palace women's battle for beauty was to travel to the resort town of Baguio once or twice a year and have the skin on their faces peeled off by a chemical process that left it whiter and smoother—after a painful week or two of looking horribly red and raw. The same ambassador's wife said Imelda once urged her to come with her to get the treatment but that this time she had thought twice and declined.

Imelda tended her political image with the same devotion she gave to her looks. In the wave of publicity that engulfed her, in the Phil-

ippines and the United States, she rarely strayed from the humble
role of making Marcos' "house" a "home." She described herself repeatedly as simply a wife, a mother, and occasionally, a student. "We
have grown together because he has allowed me to learn from him,"
she told one interviewer. "He has shared his thoughts and learning
with me. He has tutored me so generously." Marcos did treat his
wife as his disciple, though a rather slow one. He'd tell his bodyguards and cronies, "Don't mind her, she's *tangá*," a Tagalog word
meaning "stupid," which he pronounced "*tan* G-A," as if hiding the
meaning from a child.

Imelda nonetheless learned swiftly, adapting her husband's lessons to her own warm, impulsive style: At one large party, she sought
out Manila Mayor Antonio Villegas, one of Marcos' most vocal enemies, first for a dance and then to insist that he pose with her for a
picture. At another time, when one of the capital newspapers criticized her, she visited its publisher and his wife in their living room,
where she sang to them in honor of their wedding anniversary.

In those years, especially, Imelda was like Gloria Steinem's vision
of Marilyn Monroe: a kind of "female impersonator," so intent on living up to what she thought society wanted that she often seemed silly.
In a speech at the Philippine Women's University, which gave her an
honorary doctorate in humanities, she quoted Lord Byron's dictum that
"Man's love is of man's life a thing apart. 'Tis woman's whole existence." She spoke of woman's origin as Adam's "help like to himself"
and went on: "In that tiny word, that slender syllable, help, is mirrored
the ideal of womanhood." Her grave conclusion was to warn career-
minded Filipinas not to sacrifice husbands and children "on the altar
of...personal ambition or pride." It was beginning to be clear that she
was leaning over backwards to hide her own burgeoning enthusiasm
for power in her own right. Yet though her antifeminism was to become an increasingly obvious facade, it suited her purpose that year to
make the most of it.

There were still many times, even in that early phase, when
Imelda cast aside her humility and took open delight in wielding
power. She still held sway over her Blue Ladies, dispatching them
like servants to raise funds for her projects, help her entertain, and
above all, keep tabs on their families, the oligarchs who dominated
Philippine life. She also used the glamorous women as a kind of moving backdrop. When she brought a sampling of them with her to Osaka for the Expo in 1970, her "boys" put out the word before the

opening night's dinner that she had chosen a red gown. The message was clear: no one else was to wear the same color and prevent her from standing out. "I'd brought with me just one formal, and of course it was red," said one of the women. "I was really in a fix; I had to borrow someone else's dress."

Still, to most of the public, Imelda seemed so guileless throughout her husband's first term that she inspired defenders at the slightest sign of affront. When the Beatles rock group seemed to tarnish her honor on their July 1966 Manila tour, it led to a minor international incident.

Imelda's self-appointed knight in that episode was Willie Jurado, a wavy-haired Ilocano aide to Marcos who was serving that year as director of the Manila International Airport, and who had been put in charge of seeing to the Beatles' every need during their stay. The day before their departure, he was chatting with reporters at a coffee shop near the Manila Hotel when the chief of police and chief of detectives arrived with shocking news. Imelda, they said, had just ordered them to pick up the rock stars for a "command performance" at the palace, but the Beatles had refused to come along.

"They said if the First Lady wanted to see them, why didn't she come to their bedroom for a special exhibition!" Jurado fumed in recollection, two decades later. "I got white-hot angry. My ears were stung. They were insulting the whole of Filipina womanhood. Oh my goodness. What do you *think* they meant by it? What do you do in the bedroom in the first place?"

That morning, however, his only response was to leap to his feet and announce, "Tomorrow, when they leave, I'll beat them up!" He then bet columnist Teodoro Valencia 1000 pesos that he wouldn't back out.

The next day, Jurado picked up the British group as scheduled. On the surface, he said, he showed no sign that anything was wrong, but he had already ordered the porters not to carry the Beatles' bags and had stopped the escalator so they had to walk up it, lugging their instruments. Jurado also brought along four of his "boys."

At the top of the stairs, he said, he confronted the group's manager, Brian Epstein, saying, "So you are the guys who are more popular than Jesus Christ?" Without waiting for an answer, he shoved him, and his "boys" followed suit. "It was one-to-one," Jurado said. "No one got seriously hurt." The quartet went running to their plane, while a crowd of airport workers, passengers, and news reporters shouted, "Go to hell, Beatles!" Drummer Ringo Starr was quoted as saying he had been "scared stiff." John Lennon later said, "If we ever go back, it will be with an H-bomb." The British Embassy made a formal apology, and Jurado felt he had performed his chauvinistic duty toward "the woman that everybody loved," but he received an official reprimand from Marcos, who called the incident a breach of Filipino hospitality.

If the national reputation indeed was harmed by this incident, it was soon restored on the Marcoses' first state visit to the United States in late September 1966. First in Washington, then in New York, the couple feted U.S. politicians, society leaders, and journalists, and in return were lionized like few foreign leaders before them. IMELDA TAKES WHITE HOUSE BY STORM, declared a proud *Manila Times* headline back home, and it wasn't far from the truth. The U.S. Congress gave her a three-minute standing ovation when she appeared in the gallery. A White House dinner for the couple featured a dessert called Glacé Imelda.

The Marcoses owed much of their visit's success to Imelda's brother Kokoy, who was making his own debut as their overseas fixer. Kokoy by then had been given the rank of ambassador-at-large, and he had come to Washington three months before the couple's arrival to plan their parties and set up their schedule for maximum impact.

Imelda's brother was a figure of great intrigue in those days. Tall, stout, and silent, he hovered about her so constantly and with so surreptitious an air that her friend Cristina Ford later took to calling him "James Bond." He wore safari suits and loafers without socks, occasionally stuttered and swore in Tagalog, and often gave an initial impression of a bumbler. (A Manila columnist once dedicated a column to his brain and left the space blank.) Throughout the Marcoses' rule, however, many diplomats would become convinced that Kokoy, as one said, "was Imelda's Rasputin, a very cunning, ruthless man who clearly, deeply influenced her."

Kokoy was after power, and he infected his sister with his hunger to dominate events while tutoring her in the art of manipulating friends and scheming against enemies. In the meantime, he made the most of her connections, growing rich and influential in his own right. Within the next few years, he would be governor of Leyte province, ambassador to the United States, Peking, and Saudi Arabia, the owner of the *Manila Chronicle* newspaper, and the controller of the nation's largest electric utility. In 1966, however, he was just starting out: overseeing press releases, cadging invitations, and lobbying determinedly for the limelight.

In his toast at the White House dinner, Lyndon Johnson said he had long awaited meeting Marcos, particularly after Humphrey and other emissaries to Manila had returned with identical three-part reports: "The Philippines are on the march. President Marcos is a great man. He sure has a beautiful wife." The sad-faced Texan continued to flirt with the willowy Filipina throughout the visit, dancing with Imelda to the Marine orchestra's "Hello Dolly" and telling the other guests she was with only one exception the prettiest woman in the White House. (The exception wasn't Lady Bird but the blond wife of a writer.) During one pause in the music, Johnson eyed Imelda's pale yellow gown and said, "You people must have a pretty good CIA...that yellow is my favorite color." Imelda quickly rejoined, "It is my favorite color, too!" She later confided that her favorite color really was pink, "but he *is* the President!"

Weeks earlier, Marcos had pressed his wife to cram for the trip, and she had memorized Johnson's favorite color, scents, and hobbies, as well as the names of all the former U.S. Presidents, and histories of each of the fifty states. Her cousin Loreta said Marcos tested her at each meal.

The Marcoses also brought their hosts gifts, including a set of mahogany furniture and large portraits of the Johnsons that had been painted on black velvet. The Johnsons gave the Marcoses a silver engraved box with a presidential seal. And the next evening, the Marcoses reciprocated for the state dinner by toasting the President and Lady Bird at the Shoreham Hotel. Backed up by Peter Duchin's Orchestra, Imelda sang "Because of You," shooting longing glances at Johnson as she warbled the Tagalog injunctions, "You redeem me from pain. You alone, my love, are my only hope...Because of you I want to live...."

Both Americans and Filipinos saw the trip as a thorough success. Marcos hailed Johnson as the "liberator of Asia." Johnson, who apparently thought he was returning the compliment, called Marcos his "right arm in Asia." Marcos left Washington with the prize of the United States' agreement to shorten the lease on its Philippine bases so that they would expire in 1991 instead of 2050, as had earlier been negotiated. In turn, the American President found Marcos a willing new champion for his policy in Vietnam.

The glow lasted several more days in Manhattan, where the Marcoses had breakfast with Cardinal Spellman and were hosted for cocktails by *Time* and *Reader's Digest*—and on a quick side trip to Chicago, where Marcos, in a speech to business leaders, praised the United States as the "greatest democracy ever known in the history of the world." In Manhattan, Mayor John Lindsay gave a dinner at Sardi's restaurant in Times Square, where the guests included Johnny Carson and Angela Lansbury, and where Imelda sang "Strangers in the Night." Of all her whirlwind impressions, Imelda remembered most vividly her trip to the Rockefellers' mansion. "Imagine, an estate right in the heart of New York," she gushed on her return. "With its own golf course, an orchard of rare fruits, flower gardens of the best blooms, and stables—what stables! Beautiful horses and they did not even stink!"

She told Filipino reporters she had met "a minimum of 1500 people" at every stop, and that her shoulder had been scarred by the dozens of corsages that admirers had pinned to her. Though she declared she was merely "supporting cast—only a secondary actress," she added, "I put in my two cents' worth with the American politicians, warning them: 'Help us in Asia, otherwise we might be forced to play footsie with Peking.'"

*The New York Times* printed the Philippine First Lady's full-length portrait on its front and inside pages, while the *New York Post* captioned another front-page picture of her with the advice that readers turn the page for a look at her husband. President Johnson and Lady Bird escorted the Marcoses to the grand opening of the new $45 million Metropolitan Opera House in Lincoln Center, where Leontyne Price in *Antony and Cleopatra* was eclipsed by the parade of celebrities creating what press reports called a "crescendo of splendor."

"My God, the Rockefellers, the Duponts, the Fords, the Magnins, the Lindsays, the painter Marc Chagall!" Imelda recalled back in Manila. "And the jewels the women were wearing... wow! Strands and strands of them around their necks. My, in America, when they're rich they're really rich!"

Imelda felt, correctly, that her fascination was reciprocated. "We were called the Kennedys of the Far East," she said, "because we were fighting for the same thing America stands for." And indeed, that image was to endure for several years—despite the prescient warnings in a secret cable that had preceded the Marcoses from Manila two months earlier. Noting the obvious appeal of "a genuine war hero who speaks eloquently and a beautiful, charming, and talented first lady," U.S. Ambassador William McCormick Blair had advised his State Department colleagues to guard against "extravagant expectations" that would ignore the serious continuing problems in the Philippines.

After two years in Manila, Blair, a rich but idealistic lawyer who'd helped manage Adlai Stevenson's presidential campaign, was well versed in those problems. They included a nearly 4 percent rate of population growth—one of the world's highest—political chaos, and rampant crime. The homicide rate alone was eight times that of the United States, and fear of thefts and assaults had grown so great that there were nearly 18,000 gun-toting private guards in Manila. Guards with machine guns were particularly well represented behind the high-walled fences of Forbes Park, the "millionaires' barrio," where wealthy Filipinos and Americans lived in enormous mansions shaded by tamarind and flame trees.

Other problems were more subtle but also more pernicious. Corruption, as one journalist wrote that year, "approached the miraculous." Politicians continued to regard their offices principally as means of enriching their families and compadres. Foreign executives built allowances for bribes into their budgets. "The Philippines," said one veteran corporate officer in 1985, "is, always has been, and always will be a whorehouse on wheels."

The rampant graft showed just how desperate most Filipinos were to make it big, and just how easily society condoned their desperation. The gulf between the tiny upper crust and the rest of the country remained one of the widest in the world, with no sign of narrowing. A short drive from the lavish Forbes Park compounds led to sprawling, fetid slums where children died each month for lack of adequate food and sanitation. As a senator, Marcos had favored decentralization of government, which Blair thought might have discouraged graft and brought more equity. But Marcos reneged on decentralization as soon as he became President, and the ambassador soon lost faith in the top-heavy government.*

One of Blair's greatest concerns was the Philippine press, which

---

*In 1967, Blair's dark vision of the Philippines frustrated listeners at a secret congressional hearing at which he was a witness. "I am horrified," exclaimed Congresswoman Frances Payne Bolton, an Ohio Republican. "I always thought the Philippines was such a very nice place."

Declared Representative William Murphy, the Illinois Democrat chairing the hearings, "I would like to know how we are going to change their thinking and their traditional pattern. . . . What about a dictatorship? Somebody just takes hold. . . ."

he found "the most abusive, irresponsible press you will find in the free world." He spoke with insight, having been one of the main targets of that abuse since his arrival, in the midst of one of the periodic waves of Philippine nationalism. Nearly $1.5 billion in U.S. grants and military aid since 1946 hadn't swayed many Filipinos from bitterness over their former colonial status, and the bitterness only increased in the Vietnam war years, when as many as 16,000 American sailors at once would take shore leave around Manila, creating a boom of bars and brothels. When news of the U.S. atrocities in My Lai reached the islands, some journalists compared them to earlier American brutalities on Samar. Still, the loudest critics of the American role were neither pacifists nor moralists, but Manila's wealthy executives seeking chiefly to end "parity"—the equal rights for U.S. investors—and cut back foreign competition. Their most vigorous mouthpiece in the 1960s was the *Manila Chronicle*, owned by the Lopezes, the family of Marcos' vice president.

The *Chronicle*'s snipes at Blair began the day he arrived in the capital, after he had stooped to pick up his crying young son in welcoming ceremonies at the airport. The next day, a *Chronicle* editorial derided him for doing "women's work." Blair also received taunts after his wife, Catherine Gerlach Blair, made an international best-dressed list; newspapers took to calling him the "Ferdie Marcos of the U.S."

Blair's troubles extended past the newspaper pages. As student antiwar protests increased in U.S. cities, they also arose on the streets of Manila, where demonstrators regularly burned Blair in effigy. (A graffiti of the day, paying homage to the local fondness for elegant women, read, "Blast off, Blair! Mrs. Blair, stay!") The conflict echoed in the Philippines' rowdy parliament, where some members tried to declare Blair *persona non grata* and the Speaker of the House challenged him to a duel. But despite his travails, Blair stressed in his cables the "enormous assets" of the Philippines—particularly the military bases, "worth at least hundreds of millions," and the islands' store of "more genuinely pro-American sentiment than perhaps any place in the world." Those qualities, he said, warranted renewed U.S. commitment to "nudge this nation along the road to real progress."

Blair's experience typified America's confusion in the Philippines then and for decades to come. To be sure, there was some element of noblesse oblige, but also the grittier economic motive—besides the bases, U.S. private investment in the Philippines then totaled nearly $3 billion in oil, mining, communications, manufacturing, and trading industries. There was also a rather optimistic view of the local regard for Americans. Filipinos themselves were (and are) torn over their own feelings toward their erstwhile colonial masters. Antiwar demonstrators would shout, "Yankee, go home!" but whisper, "and take me with you!" And polls continually showed Filipinos had an exceptionally high opinion of the United States. But there was always some doubt about the polls' accuracy, partly since Filipinos by nature would tend to avoid giving answers they thought would displease interviewers. One critic of the prevailing belief in mutual affection was *New Republic* writer Alex Campbell, who in 1969 called the Philippines, "a smiling cesspool of hate as far as Americans are concerned." The Filipinos smile because they want to be loved by the Americans, he wrote, and hate since they strongly suspect they are not.

Blair found signs of the resentment all around him—except in his relations with the Marcoses, who mastered, among other skills, the culturally prized capacity for "smooth interpersonal relations."*

Accessibility was their hallmark, and it won them continuous goodwill from diplomats and journalists. In the 1960s, Blair saw the President every day; after games of pelota, Marcos sometimes would show him his "war wounds," and Blair believed him to be idealistic and truly concerned about improving the country. He found Imelda then to be "pretty, attractive, always charming, lovely looking, always gracious and warm."†

Marcos distinguished himself early on as more determined than his predecessors; he wore a constant grin, walked with a jaunty spring, and claimed to work twenty hours a day. He made it an immediate priority to break the islands' shameful 80-year-old habit of rice importation, and by election year 1969 had done so in a Green Revolution, which relied on new seed strains and guidance from the U. S. Agency for International Development (AID). He also managed

---

*Smooth interpersonal relations is defined by sociologist Frank Lynch as "being agreeable, even under difficult circumstances...and a willingness and ability to change tack (if not direction) to catch the lightest favoring breeze."

†Asked during his 1967 testimony if he thought Marcos was rich, Blair said, "Nobody knows." In fact, Marcos reported his total income in 1966 as $65,000, about $15,000 of which constituted his presidential salary and the remainder receivables from previous years' law practice. But even that year there was evidence that Marcos was depositing large sums in Chase Manhattan Bank. And by 1968, the Marcoses were stashing more money in Swiss banks under the code names "Jane Ryan" for Imelda and "William Saunders" for Ferdinand, according to court documents later filed by the Philippine Commission on Good Government.

to curb smuggling, which was costing the Philippines nearly $350 million a year, and improve tax collections, raising revenue that he poured into new roads, schools, and dams in the countryside.

Many were inspired by his approach. "Before Marcos, we'd grown up with pork barrels and never seeing anything being built," said Imelda's former aide Sol Vanzi. "With him, we saw the roads really being laid and we thanked God for low expectations. Put all the presidents together and Marcos did more than all of them. Maybe he was richer than all of them, but he did more."

Imelda, building away, was definitely part of the package. She soon established herself as an expert fund-raiser, garnering nearly $35 million from private donors in her first two years and pouring it back into her projects, such as "Operation Snakepit"—a high-profile emergency outlay for a crowded and filthy insane asylum—and a new showcase village of Filipiniana, aimed at tourists and built near the airport.

Another share of the funds went to the Marcoses' mutual project of cultivating loyalty among their employees, from cabinet staff members to the household maids. At Christmas, palace workers would line up to receive cash in envelopes, which Imelda would personally hand out. "If someone became sick, they would hear about it, somehow, and take care of it," said Colonel Saturnino Domingo, then a member of the presidential security command. "Or you'd go along on the campaign trail, and not be home for fifteen or twenty days, and Imelda would be sure to give you a bonus, a few hundred dollars, maybe, saying, 'Take this home to your family.'"

Marcos consolidated his political base with the same cash-intensive means. In 1967, he doubled the previous military-budget and began to lard provincial officials and friendly executives with gifts from the public treasury. Reinforcing the incentive of gratitude and debts was a large and efficient spy network established in those years, known as NISA, the National Intelligence and Security Administration, and controlled by Marcos' most trusted ally, Fabian Ver.

Though rapid in cementing his power, however, the President remained nearly as slow as his predecessors to speed along land reform, which he, too, recognized would have antagonized the politically powerful for the sake of the politically weak. His Green Revolution thus ended up raising profits for landlords while tenant farmers sank further into debt. The Philippines remained effectively colonized, the old Spanish and American rulers replaced by some fifty Manila families who flaunted their wealth and exploited their workers more than any foreigner might have dared to do.

Imelda steered clear of the land reform debate, but had an interest of her own in the wealthy Manila-based landowners. On the day after Marcos' 1965 victory, Guevara, the *Manila Times* reporter, said he accompanied her to a party where she began whispering to him of all the families she looked forward to "snubbing," including the Lopezes, the richest of them all. "She thought she'd been snubbed herself, but she'd been an insignificant person before then; she just couldn't see that," Guevara said.

In carrying out her early revenges, the new First Lady often fought dirty. If she heard of a party planned by a society woman she didn't like, she'd call a party of her own at the palace on the same date, thus drawing all the guests of her rival away. Within two years, Imelda also struck back at the wealthy branch of her own family, who she felt had patronized her during her first years in Manila. Seeking out a meeting with Norberto Romualdez, Jr., then Liberal Party governor of Leyte, she discouraged him from running for reelection, saying his job would instead go to her brother Kokoy. Norberto initially refused to back out, but he understood the power of the presidency in local elections and soon surrendered.

Nor was Imelda shy to use her office against another rival—her fierce, widowed mother-in-law, Josefa Marcos, who had long ago been a provincial beauty queen like Imelda. Josefa, who went on to teach school, had strongly influenced her son Ferdinand; even as an adult he called her "Mommy." For years, she had worked devotedly to support his political career, stumping for him in 1965 with an energy that belied her 72 years. G. Mennen Williams, the U.S. ambassador from 1968 to 1969, said Imelda was "very jealous" of and competitive with the elderly woman, who had lived with her son before his marriage but moved out once Imelda moved in. When Josefa and Williams' wife, Nancy, planned an antique fair at the ambassador's residence, Imelda tried to interfere, sending an aide to the embassy to object that official approval was required before anyone could sell antiques. Yet Josefa was not a woman to be deterred by such schemes, and Nancy Williams supported her in simply ignoring the objection. The fair went on as planned, and Imelda was left to brood about her growing list of antagonists.

# 7

# A SHARE OF
# THE BRICKBATS

*Ferdie is hiding behind the skirts of a woman.*
— Senator Benigno Aquino in a Senate speech, 1968

As the 1967 parliamentary elections approached, it grew clear that Imelda was keeping yet another grudge dating back to her early days in Manila. This one, the most bitter and fateful of all, was aimed at Benigno Aquino, the former suitor who was becoming her husband's most dangerous opponent.

Had Aquino and Marcos not been such fierce rivals, they should certainly have been friends. They belonged to the same fraternity (Upsilon Sigma Phi), had each jumped parties for convenience (Aquino publicly worrying he was "staining my moral shield forever"), and had fathers who collaborated with the Japanese during the World War II occupation. Each was Machiavellian, and each a notorious philanderer. By one account they even shared a dentist. But in 1965, as the Liberal Party's governor of Tarlac, Aquino had delivered his province to Diosdado Macapagal. "This was to be my undoing," he said later. "Marcos would never forgive me for his losing in Tarlac, which is 63 percent Ilocano. So I knew my days were numbered."

At the time, however, Aquino was undeterred. The very next year, he decided to run for the Senate, and, as he might have cockily predicted, the Marcoses' hostility paled next to the lustre of his résumé. As a teenager, Aquino had been a war correspondent in South Korea; at 22 he was mayor of his home town, and at 28 he was the governor of his province. Moreover, by the time he reached his thirties, he was wealthy in his own right. According to income tax statements each candidate submitted, Aquino was earning about $75,000 a year in 1966, making him the second richest entry of the field of eight. He was easily also the most flamboyant: he campaigned tirelessly in his butch haircut and a neon red jacket with a skull and crossbones grinning over his left pocket.

Imelda took Aquino's campaign personally. Shortly before the voting, Nacionalista Party member Celia Laurel visited her at the palace and received advice Laurel remembered for more than twenty years. Imelda, arms crossed over her chest, delivered her campaign instructions in a low, authoritative voice. "You must dress in bright colors," she began, "and wear a very strong perfume so people know you're there. You must know who to give money to. And last but not least"—here, she made a sudden mortar-and-pestle motion with her hands—"it's *pulverize* Ninoy Aquino."

Taken aback, Laurel murmured that she couldn't possibly oppose Aquino, who was so close a family friend that he had slept at the hospital the night she gave birth to her first child. "He's like a son to me," she protested. But Imelda was unmoved. "You must understand, in politics there are no sons, not even mothers," she said.

When Laurel continued to resist, Imelda, frowning slightly, muttered, "It's up to you." But a few moments later, her tone turned confidential, as she said, "You know why I don't like him? He used to court me, but when he met this rich girl he dropped me like a hot potato."

Imelda's best efforts couldn't stop Aquino, who won his Senate seat on his thirty-fifth birthday. But her instincts proved correct, as very soon thereafter he made his mark in the legislature with a direct attack—of a type never heard before—against Imelda's most cherished project.

Aquino's target was the Cultural Center, which Imelda had envisioned as "something like Carnegie Hall," and launched with elaborate ceremony on April 17, 1966. Artists, society members, and all high government officials had been invited to hear of her ambitious scheme to reclaim about ten acres of underwater land beside the Philippine Navy headquarters and build on it a complex including a performing arts theater, museum, art gallery, library, and a huge amphitheater. Her plans were based on exhaustive studies she commissioned, just weeks after

Marcos' inauguration, of modern theaters in Los Angeles, Sydney, Australia, and Tokyo. Imelda meant to have the center built quickly, to be ready for use before 1969—and the next presidential election.

Initially, the plan met with great enthusiasm from Manila's social leaders, who felt a new cultural center was long overdue. Previously concerts had been given at the Philamlife Auditorium of the Far East University, which had good acoustics but seats for only about 650 people. Under Macapagal, a joint Philippine-American endeavor had been studied whereby the United States would provide some funds and the Philippine government the land. Architect Leandro Locsin had come up with a design, and a Philippine commission collected $15,000. Despite a burst of publicity, however, not a stone had been laid—until Imelda made the project her own.

"Everybody was knocked out when she announced it," said Bing Roxas, a society matron who took over the Cultural Center under the Corazon Aquino administration. "They said, what's this? We don't see her at concerts. But there was definitely enthusiasm."

"She had wide support from the artistic community," said Locsin. "She was at the height of her popularity; she was received like a movie star everywhere. And her idea caused a lot of excitement."

Not all of the excitement was positive, of course. The Cultural Center was Imelda's most ambitious fund-raising venture to date, and she went just a bit overboard in her enthusiasm. Her first ventures were more or less benign: she collected some $50,000 from ticket sales for a sponsored performance of "The Flower Drum Song," and in a major coup, persuaded President Johnson during the Marcoses' state visit to commit $3.5 million from a $28 million Special Education Fund marked as part of a settlement for war-damage claims. But as months wore on, she increasingly put the squeeze on what she called "the gift-minded rich"—the wealthy executives seeking favor with the palace. Before any of her parties, for an anniversary, birthday, or holiday, she warned guests to bring their checkbooks, expecting each to make donations—not only to the Cultural Center, but to a host of other rarely precisely defined charity projects. "What I am asking them to do for the poor will be good for their conscience," she insisted, adding, "It's the rich you can terrorize. Not the poor. The poor have nothing to lose."

To those who questioned her values in a nation where indeed the vast majority had nothing to lose, Imelda replied that her mandate was to provide for poor and rich alike. "In some cases, water is the priority," she said. "In some cases, it's food. In some cases, it's medicine. But in some cases it's music. It's just as much of a priority for the rich to want a symphony."

Liberal Party critics came to brand her style "sophisticated extortion," with some, even then, raising suspicions that not all her collections were reaching their announced destinations. But the newspapers were full of ground-breaking ceremonies; Imelda was flitting charmingly back and forth between ribbon-cuttings, and no one could possibly trace every peso anyway. Still, by the time the date finally approached for the center's completion, the project had mysteriously sunk into debt—and in the process had become a glaring liability for the Marcoses.

Back in 1966, the center's price had been announced at just below $4 million, but by Christmas of 1968 it was learned that it had already cost more than twice that amount, with only three-fourths of the work completed. The board of trustees, which Imelda chaired, decided to negotiate for a foreign loan. It was at that point that the Liberals seized on the issue, calling for a Senate investigation. The oppositionists had already been building heat on the issue for months, with a series of speeches on the Senate floor by the Marcoses' increasingly noisy nemesis, Senator Aquino. By December his speeches had grown into unstinting attacks on Imelda.

"At a time when the impoverished masses groan in want, she resorts to a display of ostentation and high living," he declared. Aquino claimed, despite Imelda's denials, that she had ordered two bronze statues of herself and Marcos to be placed in the center—"a monument to a nation's elite bereft of social conscience." He then charged that rather than being financed by private donors, the center had received a $5 million loan from the government's National Investment Development Corporation, which by law was meant to fund only agriculture, commerce, and industry. (Imelda was forced to acknowledge the loan, but contended it was a mere "guarantee.")

Aquino's charges drew quick rebukes from some who called him unchivalrous. But they also unleashed the newspapers, whose editors until then had been painfully uncertain of how to treat the suddenly powerful post of First Lady. To be sure, they'd sanctioned one or two snipes of their own before Aquino's attacks: a columnist denounced one of Imelda's parties as a "bacchanalian orgy," while a magazine had published a photograph of her wearing a huge, sparkling necklace. Yet the general tone remained florid tribute, such as that contained in journalist Nick Joaquin's description of Imelda's trip to Rome that May for the investiture of new cardinals. "Whenever she appeared in public, the Romans wondered if she was some empress from the orient," he wrote, "and in her wake swelled a cry in crescendo, Bella! bella! bellisima!"

Now, however, it was open season; Imelda had finally been recognized as a politician in her own right. The papers were full of her confrontation with Aquino, who, privy to her déclassé past, went so far as to compare her to Argentina's Eva Peron.*

Still, even Aquino in those days felt the need to pay some tribute to the Philippine First Lady. "No amount of effort could deglamorize Imelda," he declared. "She is a thing of beauty, a joy forever... the prettiest Filipina of our generation. In fact, I will go further and say I consider her a national treasure. But a president should not use his wife for politics. We're handicapped. When she's criticized, they go saying, she's a woman. Woman? Baloney... Ferdie is hiding behind the skirts of a woman; Ferdie uses Imelda as a shield. She is a lovely woman, but I think that if a woman indulges in politics, then she should share in the brickbats."

Imelda burst into tears after Aquino's first speech: a photograph of her weeping appeared in the *Far Eastern Economic Review*. "Imagine comparing me to Eva Peron," she wailed. "It's part of the game. God knows I have never stolen a cent and what I am doing I do for the Filipino people.... People say I should dress up as Robin Hood."

Unconvinced, some of Manila's artists joined in Aquino's complaints. They charged that the Cultural Center wasn't truly intended for their work, but for more prestigious international performers Imelda sought to draw to the capital. And they protested that the enormous complex, with its fountains, grand lobbies, contoured chairs, and seating for nearly 2600, would intimidate the poor. (They were right on both counts, as time proved. Imelda used her center to lure the likes of Van Cliburn and Margot Fontayn, and while she made public promises of discounts

---

*Aquino's comparisons were valid even aside from the obvious parallel between the two women's ascents from squalor to vast power and wealth. Both had developed constant themes concerning how much she loved and worked for the masses, how she hated her country's privileged "oligarchy," and how well she complemented her husband, of whom Eva once said, in phrases redolent of Imelda, "In different ways we had both wanted to do the same thing: he with intelligence, I with the heart... he master and I pupil." Nor was Imelda blind to the likeness; under the Marcos rule, the rock opera *Evita* was banned from the Philippines just as it had been banned in Argentina.

for the poor, her \$1 and \$2 tickets still exceeded most Manilans' daily wage.)

The challenges built up momentum, and with the approach of September 10, 1969, the target date for the center's opening—and just two months before the Philippine presidential elections—the project was in clear danger. The U.S. Embassy in Manila wired Washington that the Marcoses needed help, specifically some kind of high-level administration figure who might briefly drape the center with the American mantle. The cable reached the hands of Henry Byroade, the appointee to succeed former Ambassador William Blair, and Byroade figured he might be of use.

Then 56 and a former army engineer from a farming family in Maumee Township, Indiana, Byroade came to Manila wearing red, white, and blue suspenders, after a swashbuckling career that included ambassadorships in South Africa, Egypt, Afghanistan, and Burma. In the late 1940s, he had been adjutant to General George C. Marshall, under whom he had personally concluded a cease-fire between Nationalist and Communist generals in Central China. But his favorite post of all was the Philippines. "I love that country," he said during a three-hour interview at his Potomac, Maryland, home in March of 1987. "The Filipinas, the girls, are terrific. They really are. They make the best nurses in the world."

A tall man with dark eyebrows, dimpled chin, and burning gaze, Byroade loved the company of women, and his enthusiasm often was returned. "I've had a lot of affairs with a hell of a lot of people," he said, chuckling. He conceded, however, that it deeply annoyed him during his term when his boss, Secretary of State William Rogers, took to calling Imelda "your girlfriend." The ambassador acknowledged that he found Imelda "very attractive," and furthermore worthy of respect—"if she had had a good adviser, she could have run the country all right." Yet he maintained that an affair with her never occurred to him. "Which is funny," he added, "because most women I'd like to go to bed with. But I never even liked to dance with Imelda. I don't think she really liked sex."

Still, Byroade liked the Marcoses, and from the start he also liked their Cultural Center. "When you look at the state of [most people's] livelihood then, you say 'Jesus Christ,'" he conceded. "But I'm not so sure. That center makes our Kennedy Center look cheap. The Filipino architects did a good job."

On his way to the Philippines from Washington, Byroade stopped in San Clemente, where he visited President Richard Nixon and his National Security Adviser Henry Kissinger. With the elections coming up so soon, he told the President, the Marcoses were "absolutely desperate" to get some high-ranking U.S. official—from Nixon himself to a cabinet member—to show their support. At first Nixon objected to the appearance of interfering in the domestic elections, but Byroade countered that it was "desperately impossible" in any case for Americans to stay out of Philippine politics. And as he spoke, a new idea occurred to him. "We just can't ignore it," he pleaded. "Why don't we send a governor? They don't have anything to do with foreign affairs. You know, we've got a guy like Reagan here sitting on the Pacific."

Nixon, he recalled, turned to Kissinger and said, "That's absolutely brilliant." Within the hour, Ronald Reagan was reached by phone in Sacramento and presented with the idea. "It turned out to be a good trip," Byroade recalled. "He didn't goof it up."

Reagan brought along his wife Nancy and his teenaged children, Patti and Ronald, Jr. At the time, the Marcoses clearly would have been happier with someone of higher rank. But Reagan's journey, his first trip overseas, was to lead to one of the warmest relationships between a Filipino and an American president. The Reagans stayed with the Marcoses at Malacanang and were toasted with champagne at a reception of 500 people. Afterward, Imelda danced with the former screen star, her sequined white silk gown wafting before her under chandeliers draped with palm fronds.

Earlier that day, in a speech at the opening of the Cultural Center, the First Lady sought to answer critics who called the mammoth complex inappropriate for a nation whose average per capita income was below $200 a year. "This center shall serve as a shrine of the Filipino spirit," she said. "It shall be our Parthenon, built in a time of hardship, a spring-source of our people's living conviction of the oneness of our heritage. . . . Reason and circumstance demand that this sanctuary should be built now, when the spirit of our young nation is first being tested and tried. . . . it is not during times of luxurious ease and plenty that great art is achieved or its inspiration most needed."

The words made an impact, but Reagan stole the show. "His gracing the inauguration was the ultimate imprimateur of approval," said Amelita Reysio Cruz, a *Manila Bulletin* columnist who admired the Cultural Center despite her disapproval of the Marcoses. "It showed the Center was not in bad taste."

Imelda also won a favorable write-up in *The New York Times,* then and now well-heeded in Manila, which called the center "lovely" and praised Imelda for the determination she'd expressed to use it to support the Filipino arts.

\*          \*          \*

Though Aquino would return to plague the Marcoses, the Cultural Center opened as a salvaged success. And indeed, the first presidential term in general was successful for Imelda, who enjoyed a series of pure triumphs, the most visible being the 1966 October summit, a conference of Southeast Asian nations held in Manila to discuss the fate of Vietnam.

At the time, President Johnson was depending on the Marcoses to build regional support for the unpopular American war. He had agreed to attend the Manila summit at the state dinner in Washington one month earlier—a decision which both confirmed Marcos as his most trusted Asian ally and turned full American attention on the Philippines.

Imelda was ready for the attention. Like the Marcoses' splashy state visit, the two-day summit was half policy and half party, with Imelda starring as the most glamorous and attentive of hostesses. Guests remember her dancing the fox trot with Johnson on the lantern-lit patio of Malacanang, alongside the river, and looking, said one, "as if it were the greatest moment of her life."

By day at the palace, Johnson and Marcos conferred with the chiefs of state of Australia, New Zealand, Thailand, and South Korea, and with South Vietnamese leaders Nguyen Cao Ky and Nguyen Van Thieu. Meanwhile, Imelda took their wives on a tour of Manila. They strolled through the walled city of Intramuros, flanked by Filipino presidential guards carrying carbines. Later Imelda, who through earlier research had discovered Lady Bird's interest in archaeology, led the tour to a seaside excavation site where fifteenth century artifacts lay partially exposed, laid out in advance so that the women could conveniently "discover them." Imelda, decked out in purple stretch pants and a purple Emilio Pucci top, was photographed leaping into one trench to pluck out a half-unearthed burial vase.

"So many of these Oriental ladies are like butterflies," later recalled Lady Bird in her memoirs. She was particularly charmed by the vibrant Imelda and Madame Cao Ky in her white silk turban and dress. And she was equally impressed by Imelda's beautification efforts in the capital (including banana trees planted the night before for a rustic effect), but she was curious to see several areas where coconut matting shielded views into the capital's tumble-down shanties, homes of a type shared by the great majority of the two million residents in Manila at that time. In other pre-summit cosmetics, Marcos had released $190,000 to patch the city's potholes, while Imelda had performed a rushed face-lift of the palace.

To celebrate the end of the conference, the Marcoses hosted 3000 guests at a Barrio Fiesta, a pageant combining Malay spirit, Spanish colonial traditions, and flamboyant material excess. Preparations for the party produced what *Life* magazine called "the most frenetic Filipino activity in a hundred years." Nearly 8000 colored lanterns hung in the great banyan trees on the palace lawn, while the white stucco halls of the palace were festooned with 400 dozen African daisies. Guests arrived in little buggies drawn by prancing white horses, their harnesses garlanded with flowers. There were dozens of booths of food, arranged in groups of seven—the Marcoses' favorite number—as well as exotic native dance troops and a cockfight sans steel spurs to spare the guests the sight of blood.

Orchestrating everything was Imelda, whose drive so bedazzled one American guest that he called her "the Lyndon Johnson of Asia." She ordered her Blue Ladies to study the histories of each country represented at the summit and to find the measurements of each chief of state and first lady, so that each could be presented with a barong tagalog and lavishly embroidered terno. She also had the police round up the city's pickpockets and homosexuals and keep them on board a ship just offshore for the summit's duration. To guard against rain on the critical night, she followed an old Filipino tradition and donated baskets of eggs to the church every day for a week. No rain fell.

The lovely Blue Ladies worked the crowd, handing out crowns of sampaguita blossoms to the chiefs of state and their wives. (Johnson drew the line at wearing his, which he placed near his plate while grinning at Imelda.) The fifty-dish dinner was piled on plates of woven palm leaves, and included roast pig and *balut*, an unhatched duckling roasted in its shell, regarded as a Philippine delicacy. Imelda joined a choral group singing, "Deep in the Heart of Texas" for the Johnsons. There was also "Waltzing Mathilda" for Australian Prime Minister Harold Holt, and "Arilang" for South Korean President Park Chung Hee. The festivities began late, the summit pact having been finished just that afternoon, and while still at the lush banquet table, several chiefs of state were seen signing the agreement to resist aggression and improve the economic life of the Vietnamese.

By the time the guests left Manila the next morning, however, it was clear that the results of the conference were mixed: the pact offered little of substance and ultimately had scant effect on the war. But the symbolism was powerful: Johnson's trip made it at least seem he was doing something, while the Marcoses' spectacular hosting of the conference boosted their standing in Asia.

As with quite a few other world leaders, the Marcoses soon came to find international issues more appealing in their simplicity than their own grinding domestic problems. With the approach of the 1969 elections, it had become clear that provincial handouts had drained the national treasury, while the usual midterm disillusionment was sinking in as Filipinos realized that Marcos had no miracle cures for the economy. In January 1968, the couple sought relief in a second dramatic state visit, using Imelda to full advantage, through Malaysia, Jakarta, and Thailand. There they were treated with a burst of favorable coverage in the regional press, which was still sympathetic. "I came," Marcos told the airport crowds on their return, "but Imelda conquered."

While Marcos vaguely touted the value of greater Southeast Asian cooperation, Imelda wowed the newspapers and skillfully hosted return banquets for officials in each nation they visited. In Kuala Lumpur, she posed under golden ceremonial umbrellas; in Jakarta, she had a deep purple orchid named after her. In Bangkok, she made friends with Queen Sirikit, the other "most beautiful woman in Asia," describing her social welfare programs to her and sharing techniques for applying false eyelashes. "You are like a Greek goddess," Sirikit was reported to have told Imelda.

But on arriving back home, the couple reencountered the same mundane problems. The budget was no less anemic, and Congress was refusing to pass Marcos' bills to increase taxes. Dependence on imports had swollen, as had the trade deficit, and inflation was rising fast. A congressional leader gave a press conference to warn that the Huk guerrillas in the countryside were recovering from their Magsaysay-era defeat and convincing peasants they could offer quicker reforms than the government.

The Marcoses were not at their best that year. The President had

had his gallbladder removed in 1967, after which Imelda began suffering from what she later would only say was a "congenital...kink in the tube" from her kidney to her bladder. (Manila buzzed with rumors that her problem was more serious—leukemia by one account, or a gynecological illness by another—but all that was revealed was that she underwent surgery at Walter Reed Hospital in Washington, D.C., early in 1968.) It thus came as an especially welcome boost when President Nixon chose to stop in Manila in July of that year.

For the occasion, Imelda completely refurbished the palace and even gave up her own bed, with its large purple headboard, for Nixon's use. (First Lady Pat was put up in her own suite in what was then the guest wing.) Imelda also produced another sensational Barrio Fiesta and arranged performances of costumed dancers who reenacted scenes from Philippine history along the motorcade's route. The government ordered public employees and students to participate in exchange for having the next day off.

At the formal state dinner in Malacanang, talk centered on the successful Apollo II moon voyage announced that day, prompting Nixon to recall that Marcos' son, Bongbong, had once said he would like to be the first Filipino to go to the moon. In his toast to the Marcoses, the American President promised, "On the first vehicle that carries passengers...to the moon, Bongbong will be on that space vehicle."

As was their wont, the Marcoses naturally squeezed every drop of political potential from the Nixon visit, which preceded yet another frenzied year of presidential campaigning. The watchword for the 1969 elections was "overkill," since Marcos' one challenger never really had a chance. Sergio Osmena, Jr., 52, was a prominent Liberal politician and the son of a commonwealth president. But he began with serious disadvantages: he was unglamorous, gaunt and wizened, a stiff speaker, and bereft of Marcos' colossal financial resources. All told, in 1969, the Marcoses handed out some 20,000 checks for $500 each to local officials for "local development." Often, the couple delivered the money in person, after which several photographs were taken of the beneficiaries smiling gratefully at the President and First Lady.

To be sure, Marcos also ran well on his achievements, which even critics conceded were more tangible and numerous than those of any of his predecessors. He claimed to have built more than 1000 miles of concrete roads, 1200 miles of asphalt roads, 500 bridges, 105 municipal sea-

ports, and 80,000 new classrooms; he would zip around the country by
helicopter pointing out the new buildings and highways. Despite all that,
the 1969 campaign was yet another in which droves of foreign journalists produced variations on the phrase "typical Philippine politics." Mud,
once again, flew freely. The Marcos camp repeatedly reminded voters
of Osmena's reputed collaboration with the Japanese, while Osmena's
backers revived Marcos' murder rap and charged he was taking kickbacks from Japanese executives. Osmena said Marcos was stashing the
funds in Swiss banks and he called the government "the most corrupt
the country has ever had."

Indeed, most remnants of faith in the Marcos government's honesty were destroyed in the wake of the campaigning. "I have covered several Asian elections where dirty tactics were used," reported
*Newsweek*'s Hong Kong bureau chief, Everett G. Martin. "But never
have I seen so much personally." In several instances, armed "goons"
working for Marcos intimidated voters and in some cases blatantly
seized control of polling places and forced election workers to fill out
ballots for Nacionalista candidates. Resisters paid a steep price. In
the six months before the polls closed, 107 people died and 117 were
wounded in political confrontations.

Again, there was little debate on the issues, and little disagreement
between candidates. Marcos now posed as the nationalist, having lately
"talked tough" with Washington, begun trade with Eastern European
nations, and suggested he might warm relations with China. But in fact,
he differed little from his ostensibly more pro-American rival in matters
that counted. Both candidates favored retaining the U.S. bases, though
Marcos sometimes hinted to the contrary; both agreed on trade policy
highly favorable to the west, and both meant to seek more foreign investment. "What Rochester is to Jack Benny," a *Manila Chronicle* columnist lamented at the time, "the Philippines is to the United States."

Former Senator Raul Manglapus spoke of a "vacuum of ideology"
in which people went through the motions of democracy, "as weight-
less astronauts in airless space, getting nowhere for lack of ideolog-
ical weights that will enable them to move forward." A coalition of
peasants, workers, and students called for a boycott, since they said
neither party had raised any meaningful issues. But cynicism remained mostly in the cities. The bulk of the votes were still to be
found in the countryside—as was, once again, Imelda, singing and
stumping her heart out.

Besides his other deficits, Osmena had nothing approaching Imelda. The First Lady had resumed her provincial journeys early that year, handing out money to key local leaders and telling her rapt audiences that Marcos would leave her if she didn't get him reelected. It was a measure of her persuasive powers, as well as the rural innocence and goodwill, that many country women voted for Marcos on that basis alone. The provinces kept their affection for Imelda. In town after town, crowds waited for hours in heavy rains to catch a glimpse of her, something they never did for her spouse. Women would dart up to touch her hand, exclaiming afterward that they wouldn't wash their own hands for days. It was Imelda's headiest moment to date, and it raised her expectations more than ever of her own political potential. Among other tributes, an article in *The New York Times* called her "the most effective campaigner in the islands."

She continually showcased that campaigning skill. She won admiring headlines for her bravery, for instance, after her helicopter made a crash landing on a campaign stop to a Visayan island. "She looked dazed for just a moment when she hit the ground," recalled her escort, Colonel Domingo. "Then she jumped out smiling, and immediately started looking around for the reporters."

It was no coincidence that set for publication that election year were two biographies destined to enlarge the First Lady's growing legend. Only one had been prepared with her consent, however, a queenly portrait by the writer Kerima Polotan, whose husband, Juan Tuvera, joined the Marcos cabinet soon afterward. Not surprisingly, Polotan doggedly air-brushed the unglamorous aspects of her subject's life in pursuit of her conclusion that "Compassion is the essence of Madam." But a second, unauthorized book appearing in draft in March of 1969 zeroed in on what Manilan society might have regarded as Imelda's warts. Prepared by a younger journalist named Carmen Navarro Pedrosa, *The Untold Story of Imelda Marcos* revealed for the first time Imelda's early years in the Manila garage, her half-sister Victoria's nervous breakdown, and the squalid tragedy of her mother's marriage. It also hinted at Imelda's father's affairs, and detailed Imelda's own infatuation with the married Ariston Nakpil.

Imelda's defenders saw the book as a political plot waged by the wealthy Lopezes, who in four years had shifted from allies of the Marcoses to increasingly vocal adversaries. Indeed, Pedrosa had worked for the Lopez paper, the oppositionist *Manila Chronicle*, while her husband was a rising executive with the Lopez utility firm, Meralco. There were also at least some indications that the Lopezes sought advantage in what they knew would be the Marcoses' discomfort at the spotlight on Imelda's sordid background. In an interview, Fernando Lopez, then Vice President, said copies of the book had been stored at the *Chronicle* warehouse, adding "I think there was some kind of deal," but refusing to elaborate.

The Marcoses struck back with visible alarm. As Pedrosa wrote in a later edition, palace officials sought to suppress the first draft, first with an attempted bribe of $125,000 and then with telephone threats.*

Still, their concern seemed excessive. The book's slights to Imelda were slights only to the capital's pretentious elite: in the vote-rich provinces, the Cinderella story had obvious potential to increase the First Lady's appeal. Moreover, *The Untold Story* was fundamentally a flattering one. In her preface, Pedrosa wrote that her husband had urged her to undertake the project, saying Imelda was a "woman to emulate." She called Imelda's life "a Cinderella story" and praised her so freely that the *Philippine Free Press* declined to print excerpts on the grounds that it might affect the election.

The rift between the Marcoses and Lopezes was more significant. It had first come to light in the spring of that election year, when Fernando Lopez started hearing rumors that Marcos wanted him off the ticket. By that time, both Marcos and Imelda had also been making rather pointed comments about the need to restrain Manila's "oligarchs," among whom the wealthy Lopezes were obviously counted. Lopez finally confronted Marcos, who assured him that he wanted him to stay. But that March, Fernando's brother Eugenio broke ranks on his own by printing a front-page editorial in his paper, the *Manila Chronicle*, charging Marcos with full blame for the nation's economic distress.

Following his sense of duty, Fernando stuck with the Marcoses through the 1969 elections and the first year of the second term. But on January 14, 1971, he finally resigned his cabinet post as agriculture secretary (by law, he couldn't quit as vice president) and joined the opposition Liberals.

---

*I found validation of Pedrosa's claims in one of the documents strewn through Malacanang the night the Marcoses fled. An unsigned contract, it set out a complicated deal: the author of *The Untold Story*, it stated, would agree to waive rights to the book, in exchange for which the government would finally validate a long-delayed contract that would have benefited Pedrosa's father, the owner of a Philippine shipping company.

By that time, however, the formal post of vice president was nearly meaningless. To the surprise of few, the 1969 elections had ended in a Nacionalista landslide. Winning nearly two million votes more than his rival, Marcos became history's first reelected Philippine president. His fellow party members triumphed in all but one of the Senate races and ninety of 110 House districts, effectively silencing the Liberals for at least two years and virtually eliminating checks on the presidential power. But with the end of the campaign came bad news. The election had sapped the treasury, forcing Marcos to call for public spending cuts and layoffs. Moreover, the cheating had left people demoralized, while the resulting one-party control was new and frightening.

"Neither wealth nor power shall purchase privilege," Marcos declared in his second inaugural address, which he used to attack the Philippines' "profligate rich" and call for a "new morality." U.S. Vice President Spiro Agnew joined in the applause from the stands. But this time, Marcos' oratory failed to have the same inspirational effect that it had four years earlier. At the ceremony's end, a crowd gathered to protest American influence in the country, and a small bomb exploded near Agnew's car. No one was hurt, and Agnew dismissed the participants as a "few...rambunctious" students. But less than a month later, Marcos and Imelda were pelted with stones, bottles, and tomatoes by a mob of angry students waiting for them outside Congress after Marcos' state-of-the-nation address.

Imelda had never been so close to violence. She froze for a moment as Colonel Ver grabbed for her husband, pushing him into the limousine so quickly that his head bumped on the door. In his panic, Ver briefly seemed to forget her existence altogether. She lingered, dazed, outside the car until Marcos sprang back out and yanked her roughly in beside him. "Nobody dared lay a hand on her to pull her to the car, so I had to go back and pull her myself," Marcos later recalled. "I'm afraid I pushed her too hard. It's good she didn't suffer any contusions on her lovely face." But Imelda's face was pale against the window of the black limousine as it sped from the shouting students and back toward the heavily guarded walls of the palace.

That night, January 26, 1970, ushered in what came to be called the First Quarter Storm—the worst peacetime rioting in Manilans' memory, bringing the Philippines as close as it had been in six decades to civil war. At the most grisly moment, a rally of 2000 Filipinos turned into a riot when some of the students rammed the gates of Malacanang Palace with a commandeered fire truck. The students fought police with slingshots, rocks, and gasoline bombs, and the police turned fire hoses on them. But as the demonstrators retreated down the broad Mendiola Avenue, either army troops or police opened fire, killing three students and one high school boy. More than 150 others were injured.

The rallies went on until the start of summer vacation in April. Marcos denounced the violence as a communist-inspired attempt to overthrow him and twice suggested he might declare martial law. American analysts, however, saw the rioters' motives as less influenced by foreign than domestic concerns: the students were outraged at the unrestrained election cheating and the increasing gap between the country's rich and poor. Their placards and chants called for an end to "opportunism in Congress."

In the midst of the disturbances, Imelda granted an interview with *Manila Chronicle* journalist Paulynn Sicam, who, like Imelda, had been brought up on Leyte and schooled by Benedictine nuns. "She had researched my background in advance," Sicam said, "and I guess she decided that she could relate to me." For the next two hours, in the palace music room—the antique-packed study where Imelda received her visitors—the First Lady made a long, rambling case against the increasingly popular notion that she'd fallen in love with luxury. At times tearful, at times smiling sweetly, she professed her love for "my little people" and waxed nostalgic about the simple life she had sacrificed to serve them.

"You don't know what it's like," she said sadly, at the end of the interview. "I'd rather be back in the provinces, any day. I'd rather be back in the Quonset hut." Then, suddenly pointing to the ceiling, Imelda demanded, "Do you realize that in an earthquake, that chandelier could fall on my head?"

Sicam listened and shook her head gravely. Years later, she realized that she had been one of the first journalists to witness Imelda's peculiar perspective of her life and political mission. At the time, however, Sicam merely felt stunned. As she walked from the music room, down the deep maroon carpets past the gilded Louis XIV sala sets, she pondered the effects of vast power on eccentricity, and of that combination on her country.

# 8

# DISENCHANTMENT

*Even the angels in heaven were beginning to hold their noses....*
—a member of Imelda's bodyguard in an interview, 1987

In the pageant of Philippine history, there's no avoiding the clown act of Ferdinand Marcos' philandering. In few other countries or times has politics been so bizarrely shaped by a political leader's personal life. But in the Philippines of the late 1960s and 1970s, scandals continually lurked behind policy, making it crucial for outsiders to keep up to date. Along with the rest of Manila, diplomats and CIA agents found themselves gossiping about Marcos' string of conquests and whether they left time to cope with constant national crises. Tracking his affairs also gave clues to the rise and fall of public careers—a notable case being the advance of Colonel Fabian Ver, a loyal "facilitator" who in 1981 became chief of the armed forces.

Most importantly, Marcos' infidelity soon drove Imelda to build her own power base, according to friends and aides. Within a year of the time she was forced to confront Marcos' infidelities, an Imelda-for-president movement was underway, and the couple's "enchanted fairytale" was often looking like a cynical limited partnership. "It was the girls that did it," said a retired CIA man who knew Imelda well in the late 1970s. "That gave Imelda her power, her hold over Marcos. It was profound. It put her out of his control."

Imelda's transformation began with her discovery in 1970 of Marcos' most sensational affair with a blond, B-movie Hollywood actress

103

named Dovie Beams. The *palabas* of the ideal marriage ended forever after Beams stuck a tape recorder under her bed while making love to the Philippine president. When she played the tapes for foreign correspondents, it caused Marcos his most intense public and private turmoil to date. Even almost two years after she finally left Manila, her story was still "being peddled chapter by chapter," said Hermie Rivera, a close Marcos aide, who compared the scandal to Watergate. (The martial law decrees of September 22, 1972, immediately silenced Manila's rowdy media, which had had a field day with the Beams affair, and replaced its score of newspapers with the lone, sycophantic *Daily Express*. But the President's revenge became even more explicit with the arrests of all the editors of *Graphic* magazine, which had produced the most sensational reporting.)

A former church organist from Nashville, Tennessee, with such movies as *Wild Wheels* to her credit, Beams was clearly not the first or only woman besides Imelda to have made claims on Marcos' attention. "Marcos," declared a Jesuit priest who knew him well, "was a goat." As Ambassador Byroade explained, "He didn't have any vices at all, except for women. He didn't smoke, he didn't drink. But he liked American blondes." Primitivo Mijares, an intimate aide in the 1970s, went so far as to devote an entire chapter to "The Loves of Marcos" in his long expose, *The Conjugal Dictatorship*, published shortly before Mijares mysteriously disappeared en route to Guam in 1977. The President's adultery, he wrote, was well-known throughout Manila. By his account— to be sure, an often hysterically vengeful one—Marcos' affairs included not only Carmen Ortega, with whom he said Marcos had four children, but "international beauty contestants, young movie actresses, and prominent young society matrons." Mijares went so far as to list initials of some of the more prominent paramours, including the "daughter of a one-time movie idol," a Blue Lady whose husband had contributed to Marcos' campaigns, and a statuesque nightclub singer, whom Mijares said Imelda once tried to slug when the two met in a San Francisco apartment.*

"No prize or price is too high to pay by the President or by his

---

*The slugging-at-the-singer story is an old favorite in Manila, with many different versions in circulation. The broad plot is that Imelda missed when the singer ducked, causing the First Lady inadvertently to knock over a Philippine National Bank official who happened to be standing to the singer's side. While the stories vary as to the name of the official in question, most have him being promoted shortly thereafter.

procurers in the matter of satisfying the presidential genitals," opined Mijares. "It could be a fat government contract, an unsecured multi-million-peso loan or anything of valuable consideration."

By other testimony, Marcos' obsession drove him to the extent that he would interrupt games of golf with friends at the Wack-Wack course to jump over a fence on the third hole and be driven off for a tryst, often while Imelda waited for him in the clubhouse. "The cover story was always golf," recalled a Philippines armed forces colonel, who, as part of the fifty-member presidential security command, was assigned to providing security for Imelda and the three children. The colonel said Marcos maintained a "system of safehouses" for meeting women in the capital's green and wealthy enclaves. "Ma'am [as Imelda's underlings called her] hears things and tries to confirm," he recalled. "But the President always denies."

That pattern might well have gone on calmly, the *querida*, or concubine, system being socially accepted, and Marcos' deniability genteely preserved, had not Beams come along with her incontrovertible public evidence. Once she did, the affair radically changed the Marcos marriage, and, consequently, Marcos' politics. Beams' cassette tapes of the President making pillow talk and singing Ilocano love songs were bootlegged by reporters and played for three days running in 1971 by dissident students over commandeered loudspeakers at the University of the Philippines. (Troopers called in to retake the radio station were seen repeatedly doubling over in laughter.)

Beams arrived in Manila in Christmas of 1968, a 38-year-old woman who claimed to be 23, and whose liberal use of mascara made her look like a kind of nubile Raggedy Ann doll. She had been hired to act in a movie called *Maharlika* about Marcos' wartime exploits. Soon after her arrival, she was introduced to a man called "Fred," with whom she "established great physical and spiritual rapport," as author Hermie Rotea recounts in his book on the affair with Marcos. By and by, Fred revealed his true identity as the island nation's president. He told Dovie that he and his wife had been sexually estranged for a long time, which "sort of took off the sting," wrote Rotea, "and they both felt better." The affair lasted nearly two years, and Marcos' friends have confirmed it was the most serious of his flings. He set Beams up in a house in the wealthy capital section of Greenhills, where he also kept his supply of Brut cologne, hair pomade, and nose spray. She would sit him on the floor and feed him fried chicken ("He had the cutest little dimple," she later recalled), while he taught her how to shoot a Thompson machine gun and secretly financed *Maharlika*. But the student unrest that followed Marcos' reelection put a damper on the romance, as the President grew more and more moodily withdrawn. Moreover, Imelda had become suspicious after seeing Dovie's full-length, bikini-clad picture on the cover of the *Free Press* ("Dovie Beams—A Lovely Argument for Special Relations") and hearing innuendos from her aides.

"It had reached the point where even the angels in heaven were beginning to hold their noses," said Imelda's bodyguard colonel, whose duties in late 1969 and 1970 occasionally extended to guarding Beams' Greenhills "safehouse" in the President's absence. Imelda remained his principal charge, however, and day after day, he would accede to her demands that he drive her through the streets of Manila to look for her husband. She rarely spoke on those long drives, only sat with folded arms and furrowed brow in the back seat, staring out the window. But her searches were always in vain, said the colonel, since Ver, who rarely left Marcos' side, could track Imelda's movements with his radio. Imelda by then was often ignoring Ver in public, despising him for what she knew was his role in the intrigues. (A cousin of the President, Ver was so loyal that in one interview he earnestly agreed that if Marcos were to order him to jump out a window, he would answer, "Yes, sir. Which floor?" Ver began his career as a criminal investigator, worked briefly as Marcos' chauffeur, and by 1971, at the height of the Beams scandal, received his promotion to general and was put in charge of the nation's vast intelligence network, known as NISA.)

Overwhelmed by pity, Imelda's bodyguard said he finally approached Imelda with a few of his colleagues and "volunteered to take care of the girl." At the time, he said, Imelda did not respond. But Beams later claimed to a Philippine-American newspaper in Los Angeles that she narrowly escaped an assassination attempt in Hong Kong by Imelda's henchmen.

Marcos was already seeking to abandon the actress by the time their affair reached public notice. A packet of letters left behind in the 1986 flight from Malacanang showed the last stages of the romance marked by Beams' entreaties for his help in extending her visa and seeing that she got paid for her work in *Maharlika*. In lieu of either of these, said author Rotea, she received first a $100,000 bribe offer and then a death threat from Imelda—relayed through the U.S. Embassy, which Beams claimed was seeking to contain the scandal.

Ambassador Byroade, in retirement in Maryland, recalled a different version of events, in which neither bribes nor relayed death threats played any part. "I spent a lot of time on that case," he said. "God, it was awful." At one point, he conceded, he intentionally "scared the hell out of" Beams, telling her she had to "get the hell out of the Philippines, because she was going to get killed.

"I don't mean that Marcos would do it," he explained to Beams, "but you've got to remember he's surrounded by a bunch of Ilocanos, and they're going to protect the boss, by God, no matter what. And they're going to get you, because this is causing trouble." Distraught, Beams replied that she intended to check into a hospital. "That's the easiest place in the world to get to you," he snorted. "One stick with a needle..."

The actress chose to ignore the warning, at least for the next few weeks, and on October 19 of 1970, registered under her maid's name at the Manila Medical Center, from where she mailed her letters of complaint to Marcos. In early November, embassy officials finally persuaded her to leave the Philippines, but before she did, she gave a press conference—for her "protection," she said—and played her famous tapes. Hounded by immigration agents and harassed by Marcos' thugs up to the day she left the country, it is nonetheless a testament to Filipinos' regard for face that Beams received a fragrant lei and official compliments on her departure.*

---

*Beams eventually moved to Los Angeles and married a nightclub owner named Sergio de Villagran. In the fall of 1987, at the age of 55, she was sentenced to eight years in jail for forty counts of fraud and other crimes. The charges stemmed from $18 million in loans she and her husband had obtained by claiming thousands of dollars in nonexistent income and equity. During her trial, Beams' attorney argued that she was innocent of fraud because she had been rendered mentally incompetent by exposure to the AIDS virus, possibly during an ulcer operation, and a long history of other physical and psychiatric ailments.

Though Beams has often claimed to be writing her memoirs, the only published versions of her story in 1988 were a collection of news reports and a book published in 1983 called *Marcos' Lovey Dovie* by Filipino news reporter Hermie Rotea. In addition, a long, unpublished manuscript which she apparently dictated had been commissioned from a ghostwriter by an anti-Marcos Filipino executive who said he once planned to use it to blackmail the President. Beams initially cooperated with Rotea, who promoted her story as "the torrid love triangle that shook the world." Later, however, she referred to him as "this little weasel," and tried to sue him for allegedly stealing her diary, an unfinished manuscript, and a tape recording. (A cult classic among students of the Philippines, Rotea's final product nonetheless disappoints as erotica. An example: "Dovie screamed with joy. Then she developed a headache.")

In the tense weeks leading up to that day, Imelda had been stoic, defending Marcos to her friends to the point of offering elaborate alibis on his behalf for the occasions on which he was said to have been with Beams. The rare times on which she broke down were days when Byroade came to the palace. Then she would intercept the ambassador on the way to Marcos' study, lead him into another room, and start to cry, insisting there couldn't be any truth to the affair. For Imelda, who was deeply sensitive about her race and status, her husband's liaison with a blond foreigner was worse than any mere adultery, and though she had already suspected it for several months, she put off acknowledging it for as long as she could. After hearing the tapes, however, she took the offensive, and began spreading the word that her husband had been set up, and that Beams worked for the CIA.

Reading her comments in a Manila newspaper, Byroade was galled. He picked up his telephone and started calling around the city in what history must record as one of diplomacy's more bizarre stratagems. More to the point, it was one of what would be many occasions in which Imelda led U.S. officials to the seemingly cheerful surrender of their dignity. "My telephones were tapped then, and I knew it," Byroade explained. "And Marcos knew I knew, so I used them every once in awhile to get a message to him. . . . And I was so damn mad, I called about six guys in a row and just blew my top and I ended each one of them saying, *'I'm getting screwed by Imelda and I didn't even have the fun of a good fuck!'* And I could hardly keep from adding, 'Hello, Imelda.'"

Marcos soon smoothed over the matter through the more conventional overture of claiming his wife had been misquoted. From Imelda, he was said to have sought forgiveness by "giving" her the new San Juanico Bridge, linking her native Leyte to the island of Samar (it became known as the "love bridge").*

And indeed, there are suggestions that the Marcoses enjoyed a reconciliation in 1971 and a revival of the strange but apparently deep

---

*Begun in 1969 and completed four years later, the $21.9 million bridge is one of the Marcoses' most famous white elephants. Said to be the longest bridge in Asia, it connects two of the Philippines' least developed areas—linking jungle to jungle—and it remained virtually unused for years. In yet another example of the prevailing black humor, however, Filipinos named a torture after it: undergoing the "San Juanico Bridge" meant being tied in a horizontal position to two chairs, and whipped.

bond that underlay their long marriage. A poem the President wrote to his wife that year, entitled, "You are Still a Dream," referred to her as, "the Muse, the Maria, Malakas and Helen/For whom I would launch a thousand ships...For as long as I have lived, you were my Muse...." And in an entry in Marcos' diary from May 2, 1971, which he wrote aboard the presidential yacht, the President described sitting in bed with Imelda that morning reminiscing about all that had happened since their marriage and agreeing "we had been well-blessed by God." The next sentences hint at what may have been a factor in his obsessive womanizing—his desire for another son, which Imelda seemed to have been unable or unwilling to give him.

Imelda, he said, "was concerned about Bongbong going to England and how we would miss him. When I laughingly asked her what she would do if he brought home a child with an English mother, she said seriously and intensely—'keep the child but not the mother.' She thought that we would then have a child to play with. I jokingly asked why she felt that way about her son but not about her husband [and] she said, 'I love you so much I would be willing to allow you to have a child by another woman if you wanted it so much, but I have to be there and you must do so not because of love for the woman.'

"Of course we both laughed the thought off with unanimous assurances of love," Marcos concluded.*

Another note found in a secret stash of papers two years after the Marcoses fled hinted at the desperation that Marcos may have felt—or at least expressed—at the prospect of losing his wife's affections:

"To Imelda my love—" it began, in handwriting sloppier than most of his other entries. The next line, "I have lost my world," was crossed out, and below it written:

> *My soul crawls in the nightmare of my long night*
> *Yet there is darkness when you are away*
> *I have lost the light in my world*
> *Please return the sun into my life.*

---

*Why Imelda had no more than three children remains unclear, but Beams' accounts suggest she was physically unable to do so, while Rotea's book paints Marcos as obsessive in his efforts to have another son. While it was never proven, physical incapacity to have children may have explained Imelda's mysterious surgery in 1968.

It was signed, "Andy."

While Marcos was patching things up with Imelda, he was striking back against Beams in the *Republic Weekly*, which he controlled, and which in February of 1971 began a series of ten scathing articles, accompanied by nude pictures he had taken of her in friendlier times. "Just who was Dovie Beams?" asked the introductory piece, "A latterday Mata Hari, a troubled soul who had been wronged, a plain adventuress in search of fortune, romance, and kicks or just a pitiful psychiatric case who belonged more inside an asylum than outside it?" After gravely invoking its journalistic "higher purpose," the *Weekly* chose the last option—and then proceeded to heap on Beams every conceivable kind of calumny.

The series began with some truly damning public records—from Beams' 1962 divorce case in Nashville. In particular, it cited a Tennessee psychiatrist's deposition in the case, in which he said Beams suffered "many schizoid traits." The series moved on to quote Beams' former Filipina maid, who allegedly claimed she had helped the actress somehow forge the Marcos tapes, and that she had seen Beams on several occasions "dazed and drugged" after "orgiastic nights." The writers went on to insist Beams had previously claimed to have had "carnal relations" with John F. Kennedy, Edward Kennedy, former British Prime Minister Harold Wilson, Howard Hughes, and a sheik of Kuwait.

Though it wasn't for lack of effort, the articles couldn't prevent the spread of political damage from the scandal, which included a Philippine Senate investigation and more popular articles in *Graphic*, based on interviews abroad with the outraged actress (one entitled "Beams Claws Back"). The repercussions were to last past 1986, when a California state senator charged that Beams' thirty-room Pasadena mansion (with its swimming pool rimmed by a 2-inch band of solid gold) had been bought for her by Marcos. But the scandal did its worst damage in 1971. Marcos was already facing a stagnant economy, rising crime, and continued student protests. By the spring of 1970, he had also begun to be criticized abroad for his failure to cope with a small but reviving rural insurgency. (The guerrillas numbered less than 350 poorly armed members, far below their 1950s peak. But their potential was clear, boosted by prevailing distrust of the government, which had yet to make any credible reforms. The insurgents also drew encouragement from oppositionist politicians, chief among them Senator Aquino.)

Even before the Beams scandal, Marcos had complained that governing the Philippines was "like fighting the Viet Cong." And his paranoia had long ago reached the point where it was said he had hired a palace food taster. But in the wake of Beams' departure, it was clear he was losing control. Firearms were everywhere around the capital, some stolen from the U.S. Clark Air Field, some filtering back from Vietnam. Gangs of teenagers toted carbines and light machine guns through the streets at night, and politicians rarely appeared without phalanxes of bodyguards. "When I visited Saigon, after leaving Manila, I was amazed at how peaceful and civilian it seemed in comparison," wrote a visitor. Nor had corruption abated: the press carried daily stories about friends of government officials receiving huge public contracts or funding for worthless projects, while farmers in the provinces couldn't get small loans for fertilizer. Conventional dissent had been stifled when critics vanished from Congress after the 1969 elections, and the pent-up political tension was palpable. Students and clergy were beginning to travel through the rural areas to try to organize landless peasants. A transportation strike paralyzed the capital for several weeks as 1971 began. "The conditions in this country make it riper for upheaval than any other I have ever served in," a foreign diplomat told a reporter.

Amid all these troubles, Marcos' need to appease Imelda ranked high. Her popularity in those years at times seemed greater than his own, and he continued to tap into the political appeal of the marriage. "Each man has an ideal," he told a Philippine newspaper in 1969, "who embodies all of the graces in form, in mind and in spirit. It is not often given to a man to find that ideal...but I have had that fortune. How can I look for anything more?"

Still, Imelda had been changing ever since she learned of Dovie Beams. In the years leading up to the affair, she was known for her impulsive warmth and generosity, consoling friends when relatives died and giving loans when they were broke. "But she got harder and harder," said her priest. "Her personality couldn't seem to handle it: She had held onto this fairytale vision of romance, this lifelong dream of hers, and now it seemed she had decided to trade in that dream for another."

The other dream was power. Imelda soon learned to make the most of her husband's continuing indiscretions, winning specific concessions of money or new privileges almost every time she managed to catch Marcos "outside the mosquito net," as Filipinos call it. "It appears clear that whenever she went abroad, his movements were documented," said Francisco Tatad, then the palace press director, in a 1987 interview. On her return, Imelda would produce photographs or detailed accounts of Marcos' transgressions, and then fly off to Leyte in a rage, refusing to return until her husband proposed a peace offering. It was in this way, said Tatad, that Imelda earned her two most important appointments, governor of Metro Manila and minister of Human Settlements.

Nonetheless, it was unlikely that Marcos was merely responding to blackmail. He had reasons of his own to boost his wife's clout as he began to notice rivals emerging in his cabinet. "He consciously built her up as a weapon," said Ronald "Ronny" Zamora, the President's moon-faced attorney, confidant, and assistant executive secretary, in 1987. "What he always told us, many times, even fifteen years later, was that he needed something to make sure Congress understood he was no lame duck president. That he had powers beyond retirement. This power was to put up Mrs. Marcos, to make her win. . . . She was meant to show that he still had it."

The two theories behind Imelda's rise weren't mutually exclusive, and it was never really clear who was using whom the most in the Marcos marriage. What was obvious, however, was that Imelda's political stature and personal freedom rose markedly after Dovie Beams shattered Marcos' deniability.

Imelda promptly used her new freedom to leave Manila—something she had rarely been able to do by herself before 1970. But starting that year she began a series of international journeys that took her to sixteen nations in the next half-decade alone. Like Magellan, she circumnavigated the globe, and by dint of the skilled advance work of her brother Kokoy, she was received virtually everywhere with honors normally reserved for heads of state. She met kings, queens, presidents, and premiers; toured ruins; and shopped with her Blue Ladies. Increasingly, she also performed diplomatic missions for her husband, who didn't like to travel and who found her absences convenient. This led to a strange contradiction. While personal trust between the Marcoses had eroded almost completely, the President was placing more and more faith in his wife as his political ally and stand-in. The foreign officials she dealt with had to acknowledge her as his emissary, and her prestige grew accordingly.

In June of 1970, she toured the Expo in Osaka, Japan, an eight-day sojourn that was launched with a pair of demonstrations. The first was a not-so-rousing send-off from a peevish diplomatic corps (alongside government workers frantically waving "Happy Trip!" placards), whom she had summoned in full force to the airport farewell ceremony. The second was a protest by a dozen Filipinos opposed to the trip's vast expense, as well as its timing so soon after Marcos had called for austerity and denounced the "profligate rich who waste the nation's substance, including its foreign exchange reserves." As the first group disbanded, the second was hauled off to jail. "Austerity is only for the poor," remarked the *Free Press*.

Unfazed, Imelda answered her critics by declaring she meant to promote Philippine tourism. And three months later, while rumors escalated about Marcos and Beams, she was on the road again, this time for a round-the-world voyage that lasted a full month. She began with a stop in Italy, where she had a private audience with Pope Paul VI and went to mass at St. Peter's Basilica. Then it was on to Great Britain, to enroll 12-year-old Ferdinand "Bongbong," Jr. in a private boys' school called Worth Abbey in Sussex, and to visit London, where, to her delight, Queen Elizabeth interrupted her vacation in Scotland to receive her at Buckingham Palace. She continued to Portugal, where she prayed at the shrine of the Lady of Fatima in a pilgrim town outside Lisbon, and returned through Washington, where she met briefly with President Nixon. The newspapers noted that she remained overseas on September 11, Marcos' birthday, and that she brought a private camera crew along with her.

At a women's lunch in her honor given by Nixon's wife, Pat (the dessert was mousse Leyte), Imelda wore a pale pink terno and was remembered for her elegance on a day in which the main news was the Republicans' starchy annoyance at Joan Kennedy's choice of outfits (a silver leather midi-skirt and see-through blouse). "I thought Imelda was the most beautiful woman I'd seen," said Bonnie Swearingen, the stockbroker wife of Standard Oil chief executive John Swearingen.*

After the lunch, the Philippine and American first ladies climbed into a helicopter and flew from the White House to visit an electrical

---

*The Swearingens later grew quite close to the Marcoses, whose politics they found harmonious with their own. Asked, for instance, during the late 1970s energy crisis if his conservation proposal to hike gas prices 30 cents per gallon would hurt the poor, Swearingen answered, "For heaven's sake...what is a man on relief doing owning an automobile? Let's not let our sympathies run away with us."

coop and dairy farm in Manassass, Virginia, where Imelda impressed American reporters with her "nuts and bolts" questions. "We think they are two of the most attractive ladies in the world," Nixon declared as the two women left the White House. "Also, they are smart."

Nixon had acknowledged his guest's stature by inviting her to stay at Blair House, the White House guest quarters usually reserved for visiting chiefs of state. Never before had the spouse of a national leader stayed there alone. But as it turned out, Blair House was being renovated during the week of Imelda's visit, so Nixon offered to host Imelda at any of Washington's hotels. She chose the Madison Hotel's presidential suite, where her bill for five days came to $1608.87, paid for by the U.S. State Department.*

Another sign that Washington recognized Imelda's rising power could be found in the bulky, blue-eyed form of Jim Rafferty, who since his arrival in Manila in 1967 until he left six years later was frequently seen in her presence. Rafferty claimed to be a protégé of General William "Wild Bill" Donovan, founder of the Office of Strategic Services (the precursor of the CIA), and he liked to hint that he belonged to "the Agency," remarking, in a 1987 interview, that, "It's best you don't know who I was working for." But in fact he had no CIA links, according to the four U.S. ambassadors under whom he served. Instead, his role was more unusual: Byroade called him "my after-midnight man-around-town" who "knew what was going on in the bedrooms, which was good." He was especially prized for his ability to endure the capital's grueling social schedule of four or five major parties a night, culminating with brunch-to-nightcap marathons on Sundays.

At first, Rafferty took on odd jobs requiring special discretion: before opposition leader Sergio Osmena ran for president, for instance, Rafferty supplied Osmena's bodyguards with armalite machine guns, according to Ambassador Blair. (Blair said the favor was justified since the candidate-to-be had been a "close ally" who had received anonymous threats—and whose compound was next to Blair's residence.) Shortly after Marcos' 1965 victory, Rafferty also dropped in on Father James Donelan, the new director of the Jesuit Ateneo Univer-

---

*The deal was a good one for Nixon, according to subsequent disclosures by Rafael Salas, Marcos' executive secretary from 1966 to 1969. Shortly before his death, in 1987, Salas told author Ray Bonner that the Marcoses gave more than $1 million to Nixon's 1972 reelection effort.

Imelda as a child on her
confirmation day.
*(Malacanang Palace)*

"DAUGHTERS OF MOHAMMED" OPERETTA
ST. PAUL'S COLLEGE - TACLOBAN
FEB. 11, 12-14, 1949

Scenes from the St.
Paul's yearbook, 1949.
*(author's collection)*

Eating American-style food with friends. Imelda, in a white dress, is at right.
*(author's collection)*

Imelda's father, Vicente Romualdez.
*(author's collection)*

Imelda as a young
beauty.
*(author's collection)*

Imelda arriving in Madrid.
Franco's wife is at
right.  (*Associated Press*)

U.S. Vice President Hubert Humphrey at President Marcos' inauguration,
1965.  (*courtesy of Ambassador William McCormick Blair*)

Imelda and Ferdinand with U.S. Ambassador William McCormick Blair.
*(courtesy of Ambassador William McCormick Blair)*

Imelda and Ferdinand in front of a map outlining the defense of Southeast
Asia during World War II. *(courtesy of Ambassador William McCormick Blair)*

A portrait of Imelda
inscribed to her sister
Belarmine.
*(author's collection)*

To dearest sister Belarmine,
For all best wishes & my
love Th a dear, dear sister
of mine! Imelda

Looking for turtle
eggs on Fuga Island.
Ambassador Henry
Byroade is behind
Ferdinand.
*(author's collection)*

Imelda dancing with Governor Ronald Reagan in 1965.   (*Andy Hernandez*)

Dovie Beams,
Marcos' mistress, at a
Manila pool during
the height of her
popularity in the
Philippines.
*(Hermie Rotea)*

Imelda considering
Joan Kennedy's silver
leather maxiskirt and
see-through lace
blouse at a White
House luncheon
hosted by First Lady
Pat Nixon (standing
second from left) in
January 1970.   *(UPI/
Bettmann Newsphotos)*

Imelda's Santo Niño shrine. *(author's collection)*

Imelda about to be stabbed in an assassination attempt in Manila in 1972. *(AP/World Wide Photos)*

Imelda dancing with President Lyndon Baines Johnson in Manila, October 1966. *(Larry Burrows, Life magazine © 1966 Time Inc.)*

With Prime Minister Cesar Virata, looking over some of the prized Murrah buffaloes that were being distributed to farmers by the Bureau of Animal Industry. *(author's collection)*

Imelda kissing Pope John Paul II's ring. *(Associated Press)*

Imelda greeting admirers.   *(Andy Hernandez)*

Ferdinand and Imelda with General Fabian Ver.   *(author's collection)*

With Juan Ponce Enrile, whose defection eventually led to the Marcos' ouster.
(*Andy Hernandez*)

Future President Corazon Aquino pouring coffee for her husband Ninoy in exile in Massachusetts, November 1980.
(© *1980 Charles Steiner*)

Imelda kissing her mother-in-law and rival, Dona Josefa Edralin Marcos. *(Andy Hernandez)*

Imelda with her friend George Hamilton, tossing coins as part of the blessing of a new building in 1984. *(Andy Hernandez)*

Arriving at the airport on the island of Cebu in November 1985. *(Karen T. Borchers)*

The Marcoses
campaigning
in 1985.
*(Karen T. Borchers)*

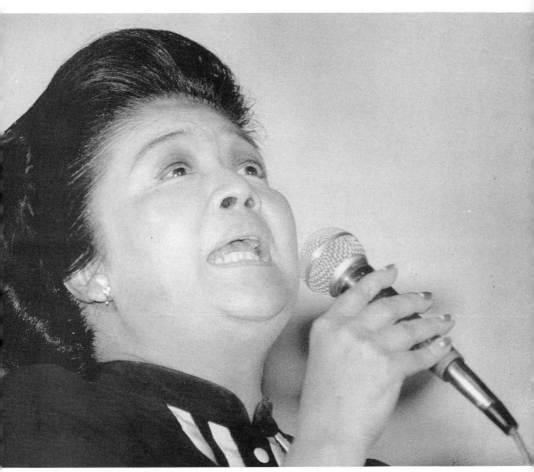

Singing wasn't as effective as a campaign tool for Imelda in 1985 as it had been in 1965. *(Karen T. Borchers)*

The fabulous,
infamous shoe
collection.
*(Karen T. Borchers)*

Some of Imelda's gowns that were discovered at Malacanang.
*(Karen T. Borchers)*

An idealized portrait of Imelda at Malacanang.   *(Karen T. Borchers)*

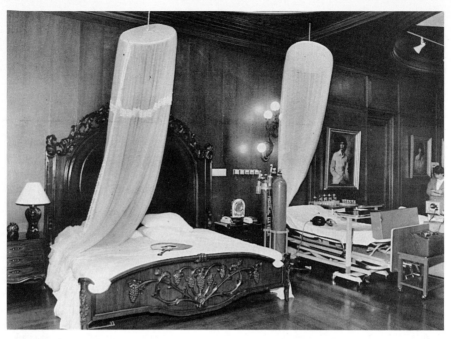

Ferdinand's palace bedroom, complete with medical equipment.
*(Karen T. Borchers)*

Imelda's bedroom.　*(Karen T. Borchers)*

The Lindenmere Estate on Long Island, one of the Marcos' alleged property holdings worldwide. *(© Charles Steiner 1985)*

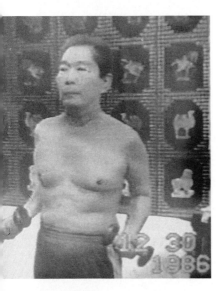

A still from a seized videotape of Marcos working out in exile in Hawaii—in anticipation of a comeback? *(Karen T. Borchers)*

Marcos loyalists demonstrating in front of the U.S. Embassy in Manila in May 1987.   (© *Charles Steiner*)

sity. "He asked what we needed most in the Philippines," Donelan recalled. "He certainly gave the impression that he came from the U.S. government, and he acted as if he could provide whatever money was required." Donelan replied that education was the most pressing need, but said he never again heard from Rafferty.

Soon afterward, the emissary's assignment had boiled down to "keeping Imelda happy," as Lew Gleeck, the consul general of the late 1960s, phrased it. When Imelda needed medical attention in 1968, Rafferty got her into Washington's Walter Reed Hospital. He escorted her on trips, poured her drinks, and even did some of her shopping. Keeping Imelda happy became more and more important to Washington as it grew clear she simply could not be avoided. Marcos increasingly was using her as a buffer and message-carrier, and it was obvious that as much as he belittled her in private, he listened to and weighed her impressions. It was decided that Imelda must be coddled, and it was Rafferty's job to do the coddling.

"You'd see him in the PX, pushing a shopping cart around to buy pretzels or chocolate," said Frazier Meade, a foreign service officer in Manila. "It was kind of bizarre, but I guess it had some merit." U.S. intelligence officials have claimed that Rafferty even purchased pornographic movies for Imelda from Copenhagen. To this, Rafferty, in an interview, angrily responded, "I was set up," saying that a man who worked for Imelda had made the request, but refusing to elaborate.

A cultural precedent for Rafferty's role could be found in the appointed village go-betweens once essential to Philippine society. Calming feuds and brokering marriages, their strength, like Rafferty's, was that they could carry embarrassing requests or messages back and forth without risking loss of face for either side. "It was easier for the Marcoses to say things to me than to the ambassadors," Rafferty said. "'I'm unhappy with the aid,' for instance. They said that quite a bit."

As Imelda's power grew, Rafferty's job became more demanding. In November 1970, he helped arrange Dovie Beams' trip out of the country, and from that time on said he watched Marcos make more and more concessions to his wife. Through most of his dealings with Imelda, Rafferty was an admiring audience. "She put her husband in power," he said, "and I was convinced she had the interests of her people in mind. She was interested in representing them on the national stage, proving they were just as good as anyone."

By the time the Beams affair was resolved, U.S. officials were not alone in considering Imelda as worthy of special attention. The archipelago's constitution limited Marcos to two terms in office, but he had shown no signs of willingness to release his grasp. Imelda's high-profile travels drew the first speculation that he might be grooming her to replace him. Why else, asked Filipinos, did her Washington trip include a conference with Federal Reserve Bank officials and a planned briefing (which she failed to attend) with the commander-in-chief of the U.S. armed forces' Pacific command? Why else did her limousine in London fly the Philippine flag? (When British protocol officers protested that she wasn't entitled to do so, not being a head of state, their Filipino counterparts reportedly replied, "You don't think so, huh?") And why else did she and the President always take separate planes when they flew to the same destination?

For those of the capital intelligentsia who took such questions seriously, the only possible answer was an Imelda presidency in the planning. Not a few found the notion horrifying. In a letter to the *Free Press* shortly after Imelda returned from Washington, a behavioral sciences professor at the University of the East tagged Imelda with "obsessive-compulsive" behavior, "over-aggressiveness (which is definitely masculine)" and "over-motivation," all of which "do not speak well of her and does not create a favorable image of Filipinos, especially of our men in the government service.

"The cabinet members her husband appointed might as well resign and let Mrs. Marcos do what they seem unable to do," the letter continued. "Then taxpayers like me will just have to spend for the salary of one Superwoman rather than pay the salaries and allowance of a whole army of technocrats, bureaucrats and the ubiquitous technical staff that goes with them." Despite its seeming air of male affront, the letter was written by a woman. The *Free Press* editor jocularly accused her of cattiness, and added that he "wouldn't mind having Superwoman for president."

Humor, in fact, was still the prevailing response to hints of Imelda's power lust in the fall of 1970. (The *Free Press* wrote of "the joke that Malacanang is actually being run by a woman," adding, "that's a joke, of course.") Weighing more on people's minds was the approach of the "Con-con," which was how Filipinos referred to the Constitutional Convention scheduled for the following year. Pressure had long been building for a revision of the 35-year-old constitution, which had been all but authored by the American commonwealth rulers. It was a central goal of the rising nationalist movement, and had been a major issue in the protests of the First Quarter Storm. Moderates such as former Senator Manglapus were hoping a wholesale revision might loosen the grip of the two major parties on Philippine politics, making room for other voices besides the moneyed elite. Congress had finally called for a convention to be held in the spring of 1971, and its 320 delegates were to be elected that November.

In her conversation with Nixon in Washington the previous fall, Imelda had warned that "communists" would win a majority of the vote. It had become her signature to use such red flags in her dealings with Americans, and in this case it was particularly baseless. The "oligarchs," as Manila's vested rich were known, unsurprisingly gained the upper hand among delegates, just as they had done for years in the two houses of Congress, where one newspaper claimed a full forty-nine millionaires held seats. In October of 1970 the Philippine *Free Press* described the more realistic threat—that the delegates would simply guard the status quo—with an editorial decrying the "scandalous allowances, concessions, franchises, retainers and other means of enrichment in office to have and to hold—and to protect against true reformers in the Con-con."

Yet as the delegates assembled, they seemed eager for change—at the very least in the tenants of Malacanang. There was talk of a ban-Marcos (for reelection) move, which referred to both Marcoses, and debate about defining the future role of the First Lady, who after all, it was said, was not an elected official, but who seemed to be turning into a de facto vice president. "Men will do anything for domestic tranquility," reasoned Adrian Cristobal, a cabinet member of those years, "and what Marcos did was let Imelda play politics. She had the run of the various ministries for her projects, and you didn't check with Marcos if she wanted something done, because he'd always authorize it." The de jure vice president, Fernando Lopez, was increasingly pushed to the side, widening the rift begun in 1969 between his powerful family and the Marcoses.

By the time Lopez resigned his cabinet post, on January 14, 1971, he felt it was all he could do to salvage his pride. He was finally chagrined at how embarrassingly irrelevant he'd become to the Marcos couple. "I knew they were trying to keep from me what they were doing, who they saw, where they went," he said. Still, business interests seemed to be at the bottom of the Marcoses' gradual suppression of Lopez. One newspaper hinted that allies of the nouveau riche Marcoses had been eyeing a possible takeover of the silver-spoon Lopezes' financial empire. Marcos replied in the press that the real source of tension was the Lopezes' continual pressure on him to grant them special concessions such as approval of a new lubricating oil factory. He also accused the family of supporting the 1969 street demonstrations against his government.

The mild-mannered Fernando largely kept out of the quarrel, whose main antagonists were his brother Eugenio, who was the family patriarch, and Marcos. Their personal feud turned most publicly nasty with a series of cartoons in the *Chronicle* that began soon after Fernando left government. Each day in the drawings, a grinning, bespectacled teacher standing in front of a blackboard would ask a different question of his class. "Who is the richest man in Southeast Asia?" was one. And: "Who buys dresses from Nina Ricci at $3800 each?" And: "Who is the ONLY oligarch in the Philippines?" Eugenio Lopez took the gloves off in February 1971, however, when the smiling male teacher was replaced with a long-haired blond woman, who was, as one young cartoon student whispered to another, "an American lady who's become quite famous lately." The new teacher asked questions such as "Who has just bought a whole floor in a condominium apartment building in New York City?" and (pointing to a picture on the blackboard) "Who is the owner of this fabulous diamond necklace?"

As the early months of 1971 went by, such "lessons" dealt more and more with Imelda, and with her ever more obvious steps to become Marcos' successor. Once more, she was gearing her efforts to the provinces, where her less-than-subtle appeals were still received with enthusiasm. After typhoons and floods, she flew to disaster areas in her helicopter, dropping enriched buns supplied by the United States from the doorway. She also passed out candy bars with her name stamped on the packages. And in March of that year, a shipment arrived in the capital of some seventeen crates filled with pictures, for rural distribution, of Imelda standing in a flowing empire gown in an expensive hotel suite. (The *Chronicle* snidely remarked that it was convenient that they came in time for Holy Week, so recipients "might ponder on them and realize that this is what the Almighty brings them for their sins.")

The First Lady also expanded her seed-distribution project, calling it, like the successful rice program before it, the "Green Revolution." That, however, only led Manila's abundance of black humorists to quip that such propaganda ploys could lead to a "Red Revolution." Others angrily noted the source of the Green Revolution's funds: two million pesos from the sale of Japanese rice donated to typhoon victims, plus five million more from the Department of Agriculture.

At last, that September, Marcos sent out a feeler—beginning, as usual, with the audience he saw as most crucial to his interests. In a conversation with *New York Times* reporter Henry Kamm, Marcos said he was determined to stop Benigno Aquino, whom he called a communist, from winning the presidency in 1973. "If all else fails," he said, "then probably the First Lady would have to come in." Soon afterward, Marcos declared that there was a strong move within his party to draft her, and that while she was naturally reluctant to run, he personally felt that if she did, she would "run away with the elections."

His suggestion brought on a huge, outraged reaction. In May, the *Free Press* published a half-page cartoon drawing of a jewel-bedecked, bulging-bosomed First Lady, with an accompanying text that began by listing her measurements: "36-inch bust, 27-inch waist, 35-inch hips, which make her an enticing package, indeed, an alluring woman with the dreamy, sexy animalism of a Sophia Loren...." Growing fiercer, it then noted Imelda's academic preparation amounted to singing lessons. Her morality, it continued, was "controversial, [her] executive training for management: none...personality: very effective." Asking finally, "are you willing to entrust your country's Marcos-ravaged future in the hands of another Marcos?" the *Free Press* recommended a BIG NO.

Imelda was undaunted. Capital newspapers, as it was estimated, reached no more than 2 percent of the Philippines' population, and while their editorialists carped, the crowds she met at rallies still cheered her. Talk of her candidacy lasted more than a year, though at times it seemed even her husband sought to stifle it. In May of 1972, the office of the President insisted Imelda had been misquoted in a long *Manila Times* interview in which she said: "If the people want me, I'll run for the presidency." But the next month, the *American Parade* magazine championed her cause, calling her "the most beautiful woman in the Orient...infinitely more popular than her spouse," and surmising there was no reason she couldn't follow Israel's Golda Meir or India's Indira Gandhi. In private, Imelda herself told U.S. Embassy officials in October of 1971 that she and Marcos meant to stay in office "until the communism issue was licked." If that meant Marcos had to extend his term of office, he would do so, she said. Or if it required her to run as president, she could do that, too.

Communists seemed increasingly on the Marcoses' minds, serving more than anything as useful tools of leverage in dealings with Americans. Much like Nixon, Marcos was anticommunist in his rhetoric, and yet led his country in an unprecedented, if mostly symbolic, rapprochement with socialist countries. Within four months of becoming president, he had lifted the ban on travel to communist countries, and by March of 1972 established trade relations with the Soviets. Imelda reinforced the latter tie by traveling to Moscow and Leningrad from March 14 to 19. After a two-hour meeting with Prime Minister Aleksei Kosygin, she reported that he had assured her that the Soviets were ready to extend all forms of aid to the Philippines.

This diplomatic mission again drew criticism in Manila, even though Marcos downplayed her trip as mostly concerned with cultural matters. At the same time, and to the distress of professional Filipino diplomats, Manuel Collantes, the acting foreign secretary, defended her as "uniquely qualified" for such missions. As for Imelda, she enjoyed herself thoroughly. She warmed to Kosygin's praise, as she later repeated it, that, "You are businesslike and to the point, yet all woman and beautifully feminine," and she pressed $1000 in "fun money" on a friendly television news reporter accompanying her, advising him to "eat all the caviar you can, because you won't get this at home."

Homegrown communists, of course, were regarded more harshly. While outside analysts still saw the threat as overstated, communists were routine candidates for blame at each new stage of the nation's evolving crisis. The most notorious example of this was the August 1971 bombing of the Plaza Miranda, a crime that may well remain forever unsolved, but in which American intelligence officials have said they have ruled out any communist involvement.

In the heart of metropolitan Manila, the Plaza Miranda was "more of an institution in the Philippines than Hyde Park ever was in London," wrote Manuel Martinez in The Grand Collision, a book about Marcos and Benigno Aquino. Campaigns began and ended there, every two years; bombastic speeches lasted all day, "reputations [were] built and ruined, ambitions established and smashed." But the twin grenade explosions at the Liberal Party rally the evening of August 21 transformed Plaza Miranda from a symbol of democracy into a symbol of dread.

Ten people were killed and seventy-four wounded after someone tossed the grenades near the front of the rally stage at approximately 9:15 p.m. Included in the wounded were eight of the opposition party's senatorial candidates, who had been waiting to speak to the crowd of 10,000. Among those murdered were two news photographers, a 10-year-old cigarette vendor (who witnesses said had picked up one of the grenades just before it exploded) and a 14-year-old hawker of garlands of sampaguitas, the national flower. One of the injured candidates, Jovito Salonga, was permanently blinded in his left eye and deafened in his right ear, while his arms and fingers were torn apart. Sergio Osmena, Marcos' rival in the 1969 election, suffered shrapnel wounds in his lungs and miraculously survived after arriving at the hospital without a heartbeat. As chance would have it, the only candidate on the slate who was not incapacitated was Senator Benigno Aquino, who had planned to arrive late, since he was scheduled as the last speaker. According to Martinez, Kokoy Romualdez took advantage of the coincidence and spread the word that Aquino was the mastermind of the bombing. This so outraged the young Senator that he carried a submachine gun around Manila the next day, "looking for a fight," as he visited his wounded colleagues.

The *Chronicle* quickly joined those who put the blame on Marcos, charging him at least with setting "a tone of intransigence" in the campaign. Senator Jose Diokno also publicly charged the President with complicity, claiming the terrorists were either in the military or military-trained. But Marcos just as quickly accused the Communists. Warning of an "armed insurrection," he suspended the writ of habeas corpus for all those accused of rebellion, and rounded up nine people he said were suspected Communist conspirators. "This is a time of national emergency," he thundered in a television and radio address. "I will impose martial law if necessary."

Few really believed the Communists threw the bombs—they had nothing to gain from the killings, nor did they ever claim credit—and until the newspapers were shut down, thirteen months later, they carried daily counts of the days that had passed as the killers remained free.*

Intrigue and confusion lingered: at one point, a man who had

---

*On their revival, after martial law was "lifted" in 1981, Philippine newspapers used the same tactic in reminding readers of Aquino's assassination, another crime that seemed likely to remain forever unsolved.

confessed to throwing the grenades was embarrassed by two prison guards who testified he was with them watching television at the time of the bombing. Yet not everyone blamed Marcos. One theory, advanced in *Oui* magazine, held that a Liberal ex-mayor of Manila had hired two convicts to rough up his party rivals and was later shocked to discover how generously they had interpreted his orders.

In any case, it was soon clear that the bombing had done the Marcoses no good. At Rafferty's suggestion, Byroade drove around Manila, visiting the wounded campaigners in the hospital and infuriating Imelda, who accused him of showing too much support for the opposition. And three months later, the Liberals swept the Senate elections—a victory greatly aided by the emotional appeal of candidates who campaigned in wheelchairs, their limbs and heads swathed in bandages.

In the month before the voting, Imelda had made a curious decision for someone so clearly consumed with domestic politics. She left the country for more than three weeks, during the campaign's important home stretch, to travel to Iran, Great Britain, and America. With criticism already building at home over her government-funded travels, it seemed both destructive to her public image and hostile to her husband, whom she had supported in every previous campaign. But Imelda was becoming intent on a constituency outside the Philippines, where few knew her background and admiration came easy. The welcome she received from world leaders, who treated her as one of their own, was intoxicating.

She first made a brief stop in New Delhi, where, accompanied by her small private press corps, she had a friendly chat with Indira Gandhi. Her scribes, including biographer Polotan, also served as her briefing team, shouting questions to her from the porch outside her room as she earnestly prepared, while dressing: "She wanted to know the volume of trade from cottage industries; it might come up," Polotan wrote. "The birthrate—had there been no drop since family planning?" From there, however, Imelda and her entourage traveled on to a more entertaining stop: Persepolis, for the 2500th anniversary of the Iranian empire.

Knowing in advance what the festivities would entail, Imelda at first had seemed reluctant to attend. The subject of dynasties was already sensitive in her country. But the Iranian empress insisted, and the Philippine First Lady yielded, walking clear-eyed into her worst public relations blunder to date. Prior to that time, she had already been gaining some fame for extravagance, but in Iran she was to meet and mingle with world masters.

The celebration, held in 1971, had been ten years in the planning. It was unrivaled in modern times in ostentation, evoking comparisons to a Cecil B. DeMille spectacular or a story from the Arabian Nights. Some 5000 guests, among them fifty political leaders (including Soviet President Nikolai Podgorny, Emperor Haile Selassie with his tiny dog in its diamond-studded collar, Vice President Spiro Agnew, and assorted kings, queens, and princes), were quartered in air-conditioned blue and white tents stocked with Baccarat crystal and Limoges china and arranged in a star-shaped city constructed around the ruins of the old Temple of Darius. Invitees feasted on roasted peacock, quail eggs stuffed with golden imperial caviar, and 25,000 bottles of fine wine. They played golf on an imported nine-hole course with grass flown in from France and watched a parade of hundreds of camels and water buffalos. Ministers of the Iranian court wore $4000 uniforms of black wool designed by Lanvin and embroidered with a mile each of gold thread. The entire affair was estimated to have cost at least $100 million, all of which came from the treasury of a nation whose per capita income was no more than $350. In an echo of Imelda's alibi for her trip to Osaka, the Shah said his party was certain to encourage tourism.

Imelda brought her daughter Imee, who was then 15, and an aide who minced behind her with a cream lace parasol. Welcomed at the airport by Abdu Reza, the Shah's younger brother, she stood on a carpeted, gold-pillared platform with the Philippine flag to her right, the Iranian flag to her left, and 400 soldiers standing at attention before her as an army band played the two nations' anthems. Then she was whisked off to the tent city in a black Cadillac, as the Philippine flag was replaced with that of the next guest in line. On the road from Shiraz to Persepolis, the government had built a wall to block views of a slum. Closer to the new city, it had simply uprooted tribes of impoverished peasants for "security," and whitewashed buildings to make them look quaint.

Predictably, Imelda was blasted in the press at home for her attendance at the Shah's party. Writing for the *Bulletin*, columnist Amelita Cruz particularly delighted in a story about how Imelda had ordered little jeweled crowns to be made in Amsterdam for her and

Imee and sent directly to Iran in an effort to avoid publicity at home. (Cruz by then was winning high readership by devoting most of her columns to Imelda, whom she coyly referred to as "You-know-who.") Yet even the wild Philippine press made no mention of the most scathing, widely circulating rumor about the trip. That had to do with Imelda's growing friendship with Mrs. Henry Ford II, the former Cristina Vettore, a beautiful and audacious blond Italian who had shared the First Lady's tent in Persepolis.

Imelda and Cristina had met the previous year, when the Fords visited Manila to see if they might open a plant there. Cristina, a woman of earthy yet haughty glamour, was immediately taken with the Marcoses, whom she found, "very gay, very simpatico." She regarded the President as "the most intelligent man I've ever known," and would spend several hours at a time discussing politics with him over the palace lunch table. "One day I asked, with whom do you identify yourself?" she recalled, "and he said Kemal Ataturk, who brought Turkey to the modern age." As for Imelda, Cristina saw her as "a woman with a big soul, big, big, big. She put the Philippines on the map."

For her part, Imelda had long ago decided that she loved Italians. "They are people," she enthused in 1969, in an interview following a trip to Rome. "If they want to cry, they cry; if they want to laugh, suddenly they laugh. If they feel like singing... they sing right in the middle of the street. I go out sightseeing and someone comes up and gives me roses. Or somebody will stop and say to me: "I like your face." For several years, she seemed taken with Cristina, whose abandon she admired and whose flattery she enjoyed. Still, their friendship was far from a sturdy prop. At times, during Malacanang dinners, Cristina could be seen snickering as Imelda sang or expounded on politics. Nor were Imelda's passions unrestrained. As always a thorough researcher of the backgrounds of those she sought to influence, she gave orders to the presidential security command to keep Cristina away from public fountains on her visits to Manila. "Ma'am had heard she liked to jump into them in Europe," recalled one of the guards.

Cristina had married Ford in 1965 following a five-year affair which caused him to leave his wife of twenty years. The daughter of a widowed factory worker, she, too, had already been divorced. According to Ford's biographer, Robert Lacey, Cristina "made her way in the world on the strength of her exotic, wild, and untamed personality and animal magnetism." She was 45 when she first came to Manila, but looked nearly a decade younger.

In a very short time, the two women were behaving quite intimately with each other. Cristina called Imelda "bombola" for "little doll," while Imelda referred to her as the "bambina." Thus when Cristina decided to show up at the last minute in Persepolis without a reserved tent, it was natural for her to turn to her new friend. "I was going to have to stay in a room with cots and four women, since there were no hotels," she recalled in 1987. "So I called up Imelda, and I said, 'Help, help, I want to be by myself in a room.'" Imelda readily promised to make space for her in the two-bedroom tent she shared with her daughter Imee.

Cristina wore a backless white dress, her long hair falling straight, and an enormous diamond and emerald necklace at her throat. Imelda dressed in a white terno ("like a vision," Cristina recalled. "A man who saw her told me, 'I could not sleep'") Cristina recalled the trip as a "dream for three days" in which kings, queens, and ministers formed the splendid backdrop for her endless conversations with Imelda. On arriving back in Grosse Pointe, however, she was shocked to find her husband suggesting they'd shared more than a tent and talk. She later blamed all the rumors on the woman who became Henry Ford's third wife, a young model named Kathleen DuRoss, whom she would only refer to as "Miss Porno." Besides, she insisted, Imelda was basically uninterested in sex with any gender. Still, the rumors continued to thrive in Manila for years, as if lesbianism might explain the cloying friendship, or Imelda's unsettling ambition.

From Persepolis, Imelda traveled to London and then to Washington for another meeting with Nixon. She told U.S. Embassy officers in advance that she would be carrying a letter from her husband, and that she sought to gauge their support for him. (Shortly before she left, Marcos was overheard telling her, "You better get it straight this time.") She also had a list of others she wanted to see, among them the director of the CIA.

Arriving before her in Washington, Kokoy arranged for some of the meetings with an air of mystery bordering on the ridiculous. "He would always check into hotels under assumed names," recalled Byroade. "He had a kind of old-fashioned idea of Washington, as if he could see the right people and get things done if he'd only check

into hotels with a fake name after midnight." He insisted on dealing
directly with Philippine Affairs director Richard Usher, refusing even
to inform his own embassy of Imelda's plans to visit until shortly
before her arrival.

She stayed in Washington nearly three days, after a meeting with
the United Nations' U Thant in New York and a short trip to see the
Fords at their home in Grosse Pointe. Kokoy lobbied for her to stay
at Blair House, and a State Department memo supported him, citing
"the possibility that she might some day herself be a candidate for
the Presidency of the Philippines." This time the chief of protocol
objected, however, and Imelda, with her entourage of aides, maids,
Blue Ladies, and Rafferty, checked back into the Madison. She was,
however, given secret service protection, on the State Department's
urging that it would be "extremely embarrassing for Philippine-American relations" were she not to be protected during any anti-Marcos
demonstrations.

Her trip went smoothly and inconsequentially. Once again, both
with Nixon and at a lunch with Montana Senator Mike Mansfield,
her theme was the threat of Filipino Communists. She was still enjoying unusual access on Capitol Hill, which reassured the Marcoses
and bolstered her own dreams of succession, but American cables
going back and forth between Manila and Washington demonstrated
that she had begun to be regarded as a problem. Secretary of State
Rogers referred to her snidely at one point as "her usual charming
self," while other officials dubbed her, "the formidable Imelda."

Barely two weeks after her return, Imelda shared with her husband
the huge setback of the November 1971 election results. Six of the eight
Liberals had won the Senate, while the Liberal Party had made startling gains in Marcos' province, Ilocos Norte (the heart of the "solid
north") and won Imelda's province of Leyte. Marcos "cannot possibly
have any doubt now about what Filipinos think of him," wrote the *Far
Eastern Economic Review*. The opposition had finally campaigned on
issues, of which there were plenty, including soaring prices, soaring
crime, and plummeting government credibility. And now they had
two new weapons in the public's alarm about the Plaza Miranda
bombing and concern over Imelda's expensive travels and increasingly prominent role.

The elections had made 1971 an abysmal year for the Marcoses,
but 1972 was much worse. Foreign investors and tourists who had

not already grown weary of the street riots, crime, and corruption were frightened off altogether by a wave of random, unsolved bombings that began in the early spring. Many of the explosions came at night in empty office buildings in the capital's financial centers. In most cases injuries were spared, but a woman was killed and forty-one others hurt when a bomb went off at 9 p.m. on September 5 at Joe's Department Store. City water mains were also blasted, the new airport building was burned, and on one occasion grenades were tossed in the midst of a provincial fiesta. Like quite a few other major crimes in the Philippines, the bombings were never solved, but oppositionists later claimed and the wide belief persisted that they had been carried out on Marcos' orders, as rationale for his later declaration of martial law.

While reeling from this man-made chaos, the economy was knocked out by a subsequent series of natural disasters of Biblical dimensions, including major landslides, fires, an earthquake, and more than forty days of flooding. The torrential storms that struck central Luzon and Manila that July were the worst in Philippine history, bringing nearly 70 inches of rain in the capital area in July alone. The flooding caused 400 deaths from drowning and cholera and ruined the harvest in Luzon's "rice bowl." For several weeks, water damage to Manila's power plants left large areas of the city in darkness through the nights. Street surfaces were washed away and traffic jolted over debris and potholes. By the end of the year, two-thirds of the country was a disaster area, and the GNP had fallen by 3 percent.

The most immediate threat to the Marcoses, however, came not from the skies but from the halls of parliament, where the Constitutional Convention was assembling. In the convention's early stages, aides to Marcos said he had been confident that he could manipulate the delegates into extending his term in power. But he soon found that many instead seemed intent on turning the meetings into a tool to bring down his government. Even Primitivo Mijares, the palace insider turned critic, later blamed the "rapaciously wealthy" delegates for their failure to unify on any issue other than attacking the President, and for letting the convention run out of control to the extent that it turned Marcos into a "cornered rat" who felt justified in declaring martial law. Yet it wasn't just the criticism that forced Marcos' hand. By the end of May, he was faced with a major scandal when an aging delegate named Eduardo Quintero, a respected former ambassador to Japan, shocked the nation by charging Imelda with trying to bribe convention members.

Senator Aquino called it a "Florentine conspiracy." Marcos called the accusations a "vicious concoction intended to smear the First Lady." The *Free Press* put out a SPECIAL PAYOLA ISSUE. The 72-year-old Quintero, who came from Imelda's Leyte, almost immediately succumbed from the stress of his own revelations and was hospitalized for hypertension and advanced diabetes. Convention sessions were held in his sickroom from then on. In a poignant interview from his hospital bed, he confessed to reporters that it had been Doña Trinidad, Imelda's own grandmother, who first taught him the value of honesty and following "the straight path."

In all, said the papers, Quintero claimed to have received nearly $3000 in bribes from delegates, as well as presents, distributed at palace dinners, including a Ronson lighter and a wallet with a stamp reading "Greetings, President and Mrs. Marcos, December 25, 1970" (backdated to hide the date of delivery.) Finally, in his affidavit, he named four different delegates who he charged had told him the money came from Imelda.

The President struck back by accusing Quintero of bribery, blackmail, and consorting with young girls, adding that witnesses had seen him ask the Marcoses for money in the past. Government agents raided the old man's home and made a show of their discovery of nearly 400 pesos ($100) in cash in an unlocked drawer. But the damage to the Marcoses was clear; something else had to be done; the newspapers were carrying huge headlines about Quintero's detailed revelations, and graffiti around the city declared, "Mabuhay, [or, Viva!] Quintero!"

Then something startling occurred. Four days after the delegate signed his affidavit tying Imelda to the payoffs, the *Chronicle* carried a three-column-wide, front-page photograph of Imelda being wheeled into the hospital by nurses, a grim-faced Marcos walking behind her, over the announcement that the First Lady had suffered a miscarriage the day before.

Press Secretary Francisco Tatad declared the baby had been lost at 1 a.m. Saturday while Mrs. Marcos was aboard the presidential yacht, *Ang Pangulo*. Just a few hours later, after Imelda checked into the Makati Medical Center, her obstetrician, Gloria Aragon, told reporters she blamed the miscarriage on Imelda's distress over newspaper reports of the payoff scandal and the ban-Marcos proposal. For the next three days, the miscarriage continued to be front-page news, with bulletins about Imelda's recovery, her cramps, and her depression. A miniature funeral was held for the fetus, which was buried in a tomb outside Tolosa in Leyte, and Marcos vowed to reform the "sick society" which had been harsh to Imelda in her pregnancy.

Privately, some delegates suggested even then that the miscarriage may have been a *palabas*, and Imelda may never have been pregnant at all. Few dared to be so ungallant as to say it in public at the time, and yet fifteen years later, Tatad's assistant, Sol Vanzi, maintained their suspicions were correct. "Tatad and I wrote the press releases [about the miscarriage], wincing," she said. She added that she didn't know who came up with the idea, but that several government employees knew of the fraud.*

It nonetheless worked, taking the life out of Quintero's charges. At the same time it stood as an eloquent example of both the Philippines' public-private nexus and the lengths to which Imelda would go—or her husband would push her—to support him and her own ambition. Marcos then set to work and managed, with tremendous effort, to get the convention narrowly to reject its ban-Marcos proposal and to agree on a new constitution calling for a parliamentary government.

The changes had begun to seem cosmetic, however, in view of the havoc outside the halls of Congress. Adding to the tension within the legislature, Aquino in a speech on September 15 claimed that Marcos for months had been planning emergency decrees to stay in power while orchestrating the violence that would give him an excuse. The speech proved prophetic. One week later, Marcos' Defense Minister, Juan Ponce Enrile, revealed that he had narrowly escaped injury in a spectacular ambush of his car—an event he conceded in

---

*When I located Imelda's obstetrician, Dr. Aragon, in Manila in April of 1987, she took extreme steps to avoid conversation. First she told a friend who had called on my behalf that she would be out of town. When I found her in her office anyway on the day she said she would be gone, she had her secretary tell me first that she was too busy to speak to a journalist, and then that she had left by a back door. Since it seemed no back door existed, I waited for about fifteen minutes in the lobby. Suddenly she burst out of her front door and took off, half running in her high heels toward the elevator. I never got the opportunity to explain what I wished to ask, but I left with the impression that she already knew.

1986 had been staged. At the time, however, Marcos once again blamed "communists" and within six hours—on September 22, 1972—at last followed through on his threats to impose martial law.

"Imelda agrees with me," Marcos had written in his diary the preceding May, "that we must gather all the wealth and security, prestige and power we have acquired through the years and wager it on a single throw of the dice of fate for the sake of the people and the Republic."

Publicly, he declared he was issuing the emergency decrees because "the hour of the communist revolution had come." Yet he added that he meant to take advantage of martial law to reform the nation's institutions; end inequities, corruption, and crime; and develop the economy. The goal, he concluded, was to create a "New Society."

Imelda called it "martial law with a smile."

# 9

# THE MAGIC LAMP

*Mrs. Marcos may be ready for the world, but is the world ready for Mrs. Marcos?*

—U.S. Ambassador William Sullivan
in a memo to the State Department, 1975

On the afternoon of September 22, 1972, tourism minister Manuel Elizalde called each member of Manila's foreign press corps to invite them to a party. The First Lady might drop in, he said, and it might be something special. That was enough for most of the reporters, who showed up as invited around 9 o'clock that evening, at a museum in a quiet suburb several miles outside the city center. Imelda arrived soon afterward, in a terno and elegant upswept hairdo, surrounded by Blue Ladies and security guards in khaki uniforms. She stayed until midnight, but neither she nor Elizalde ever announced the reason for the dinner and the Portuguese rosé. Sitting down at one of the banquet tables, she simply rambled for a while about democracy, and how only the Americans could afford it. Then one of her guards briefly whispered in her ear, and she got up and abruptly left.

Grumbling over the anticlimax, the journalists straggled home to sleep. But within a few hours, most were awakened by startling phone calls, forcing them groggily to confront the biggest Philippines story in years: the declaration of martial law, the arrests of scores of thousands, the authoritarian smashing of America's "showcase of democracy." They rushed to their offices and found there were no longer any overseas phone lines.

131

It had all happened swiftly and decorously, with the minimum of noise or witnesses. Police cars raced about the capital, their sirens silent, in the hours after the 2 a.m. decree, which wasn't made public until the next evening. Barricades blocked dark intersections, with soldiers checking each passing car. Within weeks, some 30,000 people were arrested, including not only suspected leftists but labor leaders, politicians, and journalists who had criticized the government.

The first to be jailed was Sen. Benigno Aquino, whom Marcos accused of conspiring with Communists.*

Days later, a warrant was also issued for Amelita Cruz, author of the "you-know-who" columns on Imelda. Cruz was charged with insurrection, rebellion, and subversion, on orders she was told "came directly from the music room," Imelda's palace study. The story circulated that police who came to pick her up had called from outside her door, "It's you-know-who!" But Cruz's arrest was no joke: she surrendered after a week in hiding for fear she might otherwise be "salvaged"—the Filipinos' ironic word for "killed." She was imprisoned for three months and put on parole for four years, but, like all but very few of the others, never was tried for any crime.

Congress was abolished; the right to strike was suspended and the newspapers were shut down. Police enforced a midnight-to-4 a.m. curfew, and even the popular pastime of rumor-mongering was outlawed. Dictatorship had come overnight—and the startling thing was how widely it was welcomed. The natural disasters, bombings, corruption, and crime had all pitched the nation's morale so low that any dramatic change seemed promising. *Disciplina ang kailangan* ("We need discipline") had been a common lament, with at least one prominent senator yearning for an even more extreme remedy. "We need a blood bath," the politician told *The New York Times* anonymously shortly before the decree. "No country has become great without a civil war."

Martial law, however, brought no warfare nor tanks in the street—only the eerie silence of a capital stunned into tranquility. Half a million guns were voluntarily turned in; one alleged heroin dealer was executed by a firing squad, and for several days no major crimes were reported. While that owed at least partly to the new censorship, many

---

*Aquino, according to Filipino author Manuel Martinez, had in fact previously advocated martial law, saying a system such as Park Chung-Hee's rule in nearby South Korea was necessary to improve the Philippine economy.

Filipinos said they felt safer. The decrees, if not that feeling of well-being, were to last nearly nine years.

American executives were also initially pleased, as Marcos firmly reversed what had been the country's nationalist drift. In one of his first decrees, he vetoed supreme court decisions that would have ended special privileges for U.S. investors. Combined with a ban on strikes and extremely cheap labor, the changes made the Philippines economically irresistible. The U.S. Chamber of Commerce in Manila sent a telegram of effusive praise to Malacanang. Dollars poured into the islands, and GNP growth hit 10 percent in 1973. In the meantime, oil was still cheap; exports of copper, sugar, and wood were higher than ever; the insurgency remained minuscule, and the country prospered.

"It was a bright and shining moment, we all thought—we all hoped," said Ateneo University director James Donelan, a tall and courtly Jesuit priest from New York who had lived in Manila since 1946. "Father Jim," as he was known, credited the Marcoses, in whom he saw "a touch of greatness," and to whom he gave support through the late 1970s.

Donelan was always closest to Imelda, and his relationship with her became an example of how thoroughly the Marcoses co-opted their friends—and how easily the line was blurred in the Philippines between church and state. For more than a decade, the prominent priest wrote several speeches, briefing papers, and letters for the First Lady. He also danced with her, traveled through England to find a school for her son, and occasionally wore a jacket she had given him that had "Imelda" stitched over one front pocket. He said the only compensation he received for his work was the use of a small government Toyota. "Naive as it may seem, I thought I was serving the country!" he wrote me in a letter in 1987. "How could Camelot change into the Gulag Archipelago?"

Back then, however, he felt martial law was like "a breath of fresh air. There was no garbage in the streets, no drugs, no crime." Conveniently for the Marcoses, there were also no critics, all known dissidents being either in jail or in hiding. That created unprecedented freedom for the couple, and that freedom had its most momentous effect on Imelda. In the next few years, she made her greatest contributions to the Philippines, speaking out for birth control (an urgent need long stalled by the politically powerful Catholic Church), sponsoring the country's rural electrification program, and tirelessly promoting native handicrafts and tourism. At the same time, she did her country and herself tragic damage with her escalating number of vendettas, frivolous projects, and relentless personal use of public funds. "Martial law is what ruined Imelda for good," said Donelan. "With no controls, she went berserk."

Martial law had its impact to be sure, as did Marcos' continuing adultery. But so also did a momentous event that took place near the end of 1972: the attempt on Imelda's life by a knife-swinging assassin.

All that winter, Marcos had rarely appeared in public. It was said he had withdrawn for "security reasons," and he told friends he'd uncovered a full five plots against him. He grew dependent on his wife and aides for information, and usually left it to Imelda to keep up appearances outside the palace. In the process, she became even more clearly identified as a national leader, and Filipinos grew used to references to the "conjugal dictatorship." (Or, as former Marcos aide Mijares wrote in his unique style: "The long dark night that descended on the Republic has now disgorged its monstrous two-headed offspring.") Her new status was gruesomely confirmed on the afternoon of December 7, when a killer who supposedly had meant to strike the President chose his wife as a stand-in.

While thousands of Filipinos watched in horror, the scene played out on live television: a slim, middle-aged man in a dark suit rushed up to Imelda as she stood in a receiving line to thank workers in one of her beautification campaigns. Her security guards froze, stunned, as the man pulled a foot-long bolo knife from his sleeve and began swinging. "I noticed him just as he was on the last step of the stairs leading up to the stage," Imelda said later. "I thought, 'Oh, he is going to do something wrong to somebody!' But I didn't think it was me. Then he looked at me—a very fierce, deranged look, a crazy, mad look, and I thought, 'It *is* me!'"

Imelda fell backward across a table and thrust up her arms, pushing the blade away from her. Spectators screamed as her assailant rushed forward, slashing, tearing open the front of her dress and splattering blood onto her bra. "I fell back and kicked at him, pushing him back with my feet," she said. "Since both my arms were wounded and I could no longer use them, I slithered back away from him by using my elbows." The man kept swinging even after her guards sprang to life and shot him through his cheek. They then shot him several more times until he fell dead. He had severed tendons in both of her wrists and nearly cut off her fingers—requiring seventy-five stitches in all—but Imelda's parrying saved her life.*

As Imelda lay on a stretcher, her beige terno soaked with blood, she called out to General Ver to cover her, pleading, "I don't want Sir to see me in this condition." The next morning, however, she was preening for television cameras in a silky, frilly hospital gown unlike any her attending doctors had seen. At her side was Republican Senator Charles Percy, who had flown in immediately from Singapore to tell Imelda and the world how terrible it all was.

For the rest of the week, the government-controlled television station played and replayed its gory tape of the assault. Marcos immediately announced that Imelda's attacker, identified as an engineer named Carlito Dimaali, had been part of a right-wing conspiracy to kill both the President and his wife. He ordered police to arrest Eugenio Lopez, Jr., Jesus Cabarrus, Jr., and Sergio Osmena III. At least two of the suspects happened to be from families that held some political threat: Lopez was the son of the feisty owner of the *Manila Chronicle* and Osmena, a Cebu entrepreneur, the son of Marcos' challenger in the 1969 election. Cabarrus was a wealthy executive and pilot.

From Los Angeles, Dovie Beams suggested Marcos himself had been behind the plot to kill his wife, so that he would be free to marry her. That seemed unlikely, however, since neutral witnesses said Marcos was not only visibly shocked by the attack but immediately upgraded the arms carried by Imelda's guards. He also moved his presidential offices, along with dozens of security officers, next to her hospital suite for the entire time she stayed there. That said, the early years of martial law were not marked by great affection between the Marcoses. They lived in separate wings of the palace and often went for days without speaking to each other in public. Nor, reportedly, did they even share a food taster. Moreover, on emerging from his isolation, Marcos continued to enjoy the company of attractive young women, mostly up-and-coming starlets who hung about his chair on afternoons he spent waterskiing with foreign diplomats off the presidential yacht, *Ang Pangulo*.

---

*Dr. Robert Chase, a Stanford University hand expert flown in to consult on Imelda's surgery, said he believed the First Lady survived due to her expertise at Ping-Pong. "She was actually extremely agile," he said. "She threw her arm up and danced back when he came forward, and that was part of her Ping-Pong capability."

Marcos did admire his wife's bravery, however, while on her part, her survival of the bolo-knife attack raised her sense of mission to a Nietzschean extreme. For long after it was no longer necessary, she kept her arm in an elegant gold-chain sling, and years later said she never did recover the full use of her right hand. "This is my second lease on life," she would tell reporters in hushed tones. "My personal life is over. There must be a reason for my second lease on life."

Marcos certainly shared Imelda's sense of exalted mission, and probably schooled her in it. Entries in his diary—especially in the year before he declared martial law—are full of his sense of weighty purpose. On March 7, 1971, for instance, he writes of coming home from a golf game at Fort Aguinaldo and feeling, "some kind of melancholy at all the people waving and smiling to me as if to say, 'We depend upon you to protect us. We know only you can do it. We trust you.' The "mute demands," as he describes them, echoed the constant "message" he deduced "from the visions I see asleep and awake."

The visions told him, he writes, that: "'This is your principal mission in life—[to] save the country again from the Maoists, the anarchists and the radicals.'

"'Subordinate everything to this,' God seems to be saying to me," he continues.

"'And you are the only person who can do it,' He says, 'Nobody else can.

"'So do not miss the opportunity given you.

"'And if you do, it will mean not only your death but that of your wife and children and of the wives, children, and friends of men of equal persuasion.'"

*          *          *

As Imelda's own devotion increased, so did her impatience with bureaucratic hurdles, as well as routine compensation. She came to view government as a kind of private "magic lamp," as U.S. foreign service officer Frazier Meade put it. "Just rub it, and it gives you anything you want."

She and her husband were encouraged in that view by a long line of international bankers made giddy by the late 1970s' abundance of "petrodollars." As late as 1979, when the Philippines' overseas debt was gauged at $9 billion, the bankers were bullish on the Marcoses. "Our portfolio is very good," Chase Manhattan's vice president, R.N. Earman, Jr., told *Fortune* magazine that year . "The jumbo loans are going into the right places. You might not agree 100 percent, but we don't think the money is being squandered."*

Another factor making both Marcoses look good in the 1970s were "technocrats"—the new scores of confident, skilled young professionals recruited during martial law. Technocrats could get things done in a week, it was said, that once had taken a year. And their feats were magnified with a public relations budget that rose from three million to 68 million pesos (roughly $17 million) in the first eighteen months after September 1972. For propagandists, the Marcoses coopted Manila intellectuals such as prominent essayist Carmen Guerrero Nakpil, who wrote several of Imelda's speeches. Nakpil and her peers gave the couple an aura of legitimacy, while the haughty, attractive writer voiced her tempered zeal for the couple with her assessment that "in a country where men had no balls, Marcos had seven of them."

The Marcoses also had American support; Byroade, the U.S. ambassador, had known of the martial law plan days before it was decreed, and said he had warned the President that Washington wouldn't be pleased. Yet Marcos had already discussed his idea with President Nixon, who offered no objection, according to Ray Bonner's *Waltzing with a Dictator*. And since Filipinos weren't protesting, neither did the U.S. Congress, which remained preoccupied with Vietnam.

"I desperately didn't want Marcos to do it in the beginning," said Byroade. "But I've got to admit it was the best government the Philippines ever had." Byroade said there had been "some thought" to cutting aid in response to Marcos' authoritarian move, but in fact the United States did just the opposite, stepping up military assistance from $80.8 million in the four fiscal years from 1969 to 1972, to $166.3 million in the next four years, a large hike even considering inflation. In the same period, Marcos tripled the armed forces' ranks and boosted their budget by 800 percent.

A CIA study written shortly after the declaration of martial law noted how Marcos, at the same time, was massively enriching himself with public funds. And by 1975, *Cosmopolitan* magazine had called Imelda one of the ten richest women in the world, and possibly the

---

*Citibank's vice president Daniel Jacobsen added that the Marcos government could continue to borrow on favorable terms, praising the administration for being "very skillful at managing their debt." Within just six more years, however, the debt had nearly tripled, reaching $26.5 billion, and by 1987, the new Aquino government was threatening to stop payments.

richest, bar none. Yet in those early years, the couple still had their glow. The countryside was targeted for more funds, and land reform was once again promised—though this time, with landowner politicians hogtied, it had some initial success. A sweeping plan went into effect for all rice and corn holdings over about three acres. Before it bogged down in the mid-1970s, roughly half of 450,000 eligible rice and corn tenants had been issued certificates and 15,000 had become mortgage-paying owners.

A new population control commission made similar progress, aided by Imelda's "direct, personal, and public interest in it," according to Fred Schieck, Manila director of the U.S. Agency for International Development (AID) in the 1980s. Bolstered with her leadership, and with $70 million in U.S. assistance, the commission provided pills, condoms, and intrauterine devices in an overdue reply to one of the Philippines' most serious problems, the one million new infants born every year. For a time, shortly after martial law, the archipelago had one of Asia's strongest population programs, and the birth rate dropped from its all-time high of 3.01 in the previous decade to 2.71 from 1975 to 1980.*

"[Imelda] makes things happen in a country where not much happens," enthused George Suter, who was then president of the American Chamber of Commerce. Chiefly, however, she was making things happen for the rich. By 1975, she was filling Manila's skyline with showy, western-style high rises, with almost every new building controversial for its cost or purpose. She added fourteen tall luxury hotels in preparation for the 1976 International Monetary Fund Conference, spending nearly $500 million in government loans allotted by presidential order—in the same year that the government spent merely $13 million on badly needed public housing. She built a multimillion-dollar Nutrition Center in Manila, which displayed in elaborate audiovisual demonstrations its "Nutrinoodles," "Nutribuses," and "Nutripaks" of food supposedly distributed to the poor. Meanwhile nutrition programs foundered in the countryside, and children in the depressed outer islands grew bloated bellies from malnutrition. Imelda also commissioned

---

*In mid-1985, a year before the Marcos government fell, Schieck said Imelda told him she would continue to help behind the scenes, but had to withdraw from her public advocacy of birth control, since the Philippine Catholic Church "was looking for too many things to use against us." And two years later, AID officials complained that the Aquino government had returned to ignoring the problem, "kowtowing to the Church," as one described it, despite worrisome signs that the population rate was once again on the rise.

a grand state-of-the-art Heart Center for Asia, with only 100 beds, in the capital of a nation where malnutrition and tuberculosis remained leading causes of death.

Ronny Zamora, Marcos' attorney, said the President rarely had advance notice of his wife's building projects. "The hospitals, the lung center, the kidney center—all those things she built, the President would wake up one morning and find out. She'd call the budget ministers in, and work out the whole thing behind his back. . . . He never left the palace, so these things would be going up around the city and he'd never know."

More often than not, Marcos' underlings avoided telling him about his wife's costly projects, or, indeed, about anything unpleasant, unless they had no choice. "Marcos had a short memory," said Zamora. "She had a long one. You could cross the President. You couldn't cross the First Lady. She would remember, and people would lose jobs, influence." Zamora's viewpoint, of course, was highly partisan. In fact, Marcos' memory was probably no worse than in his youth, when he'd dazzled his classmates and aced the bar exam, and through most of the 1970s, his mind was as keen as ever. He'd simply stopped using it to pay much attention to his wife. His concerns had shifted long ago to history, sports, and young girls. And it was that very inattention that drove Imelda the hardest. While she outdid herself with ever grander projects drawing ever more public attention, she could win neither approval nor rejection from the man who remained the most important person in her life. Still, it didn't stop her from trying.

Manilans joked about Imelda's "edifice complex," while workers on the overnight shifts she required for her many rush jobs lived in fear of her unannounced 3 a.m. inspections. But Imelda defended her projects as a source of national pride, "to show the world that, see, we have a pretty face." Manila indeed became her mirror, with its thin veneer of showy western luxury. When foreign visitors came to town, she simply steered them past the miles and miles of winding alleys of crowded slums that flooded each winter and reeked every summer to the grand, pristine row of her prize buildings, on land reclaimed from Manila Bay—the Cultural Center, the Folk Arts Theater, the $65 million Convention Center, the $40 million Plaza Hotel. There they could not fail to be awed.

Even as dedicated a liberal as former United Nations Ambassador

Andrew Young was apparently deeply moved after touring Manila in
May of 1979, years after the Marcoses' glow had faded amidst increasing reports of corruption and human rights abuses. "My only problem
with this visit to the Philippines is that I have been so impressed," Young
told U.S. Ambassador Richard Murphy. In a toast to the Marcoses at
Malacanang Palace, where Young and his wife stayed at Imelda's invitation, he added, "You can't...come to the Philippines without being
terribly impressed with the tremendous experience of development that
meets you from the very beginning of your move down the Philippine
streets." He gave particular praise to Imelda's "Metro Manila Aides,"
the thousands of red-and-yellow uniformed streetsweepers who day and
night tended the capital's wide main thoroughfares (the ones tourists
frequented),* and told Murphy that his wife had been highly impressed
by Imelda's Nutrition Center.

Imelda was proud of her prominence in the mid-1970s, and her
speeches strongly encouraged her fellow Filipinas. "Think big," she said,
in one address to women, written by Donelan. "Think that there is not
a task that you cannot undertake, not a position that you cannot fill,
not a challenge that you cannot meet." By then, she was also habitually
speaking of the government in the first person plural, and sometimes
the singular. "When we proclaimed martial law it was not to destroy
democracy but to keep it going," she told *Fortune* magazine correspondent Roy Rowan. "As leaders of a country, you know, you have a
flock. Some are going too much to the right. Some are going too much
to the left. You have to be like a cowboy as a leader to whip them to
the center. What is the center? Me. Who is me? Imelda, Filipino."

Imelda, Filipino, still had other goals besides democracy, however. Chief among them was revenge. She soon found that martial
law could provide the crowning blow in the class struggle that continued to consume her. One of the first things she did in the wake of
the decree was to eliminate the newspaper society columns, telling a
Blue Lady friend that she thought they "diverted the eye of the poor."
Soon afterward, the Marcoses were busily dismantling the corporate
empire of their chief rivals, the Lopezes, who until that time employed more than 10,000 people. The first step was a presidential
decree lowering electric rates by 25 percent. Once that sent stocks

---

*Imelda ordered that t-shirts of some of the aides be stamped "CIA," meaning, as she told
me, "Certified Imelda Admirer."

plummeting for Manila Electric's holding company, Meralco, Kokoy Romualdez bought the firm from its desperate owners with a $1500 down payment. Finally, Marcos took over the Lopezes' ABS-CBN media conglomerate, renaming it, inevitably, "Maharlika."

Throughout these maneuvers, Eugenio Lopez, Sr.'s son remained in jail, "held hostage," as Eugenio, Jr., later described it, "to keep my father quiet and neutralized, and to get our properties away from us." He was still in jail in 1975, when his father, in exile in San Francisco, died of cancer. The old man had assumed his son would be returned once he sold his company, and family members said his health quickly deteriorated once he realized that he wouldn't.

Primitivo Mijares, who in those years was close to Marcos, believed Imelda was far more dedicated than her husband in crushing the Lopez clan. Not only did she personally resent their wealth and status, which they'd flaunted for years, but she smarted at the memory of having to beg Fernando to run as her husband's vice president. Said a diplomat then serving in Manila, "She hated the Lopezes with a passion." And as Imelda later told the story to Roy Rowan, she did pressure Marcos to agree to let her brother buy Meralco. "Lopez, can you imagine that man—God is not sleeping, I always say— can you imagine that man, he came to me in Hong Kong...to beg me after martial law for the government to take over Meralco," she said. "And in my desire to patch up a dog fight, I went to the President, and I said, Oh come on, I don't like all of this hullabaloo and fight, I said; What can we do to buy Meralco? What can we do to buy Meralco?...And I said, OK, we will try to get Kokoy to get the Meralco." Kokoy didn't just get the Meralco: the Lopezes were also forced to lease out the Manila *Chronicle*'s presses, which he used to publish the slavering *Times-Journal*.

Meralco was a prize, but it came with a high price: it created in Steve Psinakis, Eugenio, Sr.'s tall, Greek son-in-law, the regime's most voluble enemy. Not long after marrying former Blue Lady Presentacion Lopez, Psinakis began his passionate quest to restore his in-laws' fortunes and see the Marcoses overthrown. The swaggering, bearded engineer became an expert media manager: Calling himself "the number-one enemy of Marcos," he hung on the phone day and night from his comfortable San Francisco home with reporters throughout the United States, urging them to meet with exiles or passing them documents to do with a constant stream of governmental misdeeds in Manila. He also wrote a book, called 'Two Terrorists' Meet, based largely on a long conversation he had with Imelda in New York.

Twice, Psinakis himself became the story. The first time was when he orchestrated the daring and well-publicized September 29, 1977, prison break for Eugenio, Jr., and Sergio Osmena (involving forged passports, an Israeli pilot, and pliers smuggled into the prison in the underwear of Eugenio, Jr.'s wife). Three years later, he was targeted in a U.S. grand jury investigation into alleged violations of the U.S. Neutrality Act.*

While Imelda was making enemies, she worked hard to win friends. Beginning soon after martial law, she built a palace coterie distinct from those who owed their first loyalty to her husband. She determinedly wooed several members of the military, including her old nemesis, Ver, taking them or their wives with her on her travels, buying them watches and slipping them money. It was an uphill struggle; the military brass hadn't ever had much affection for her, and some members held a long and bitter grudge after she had several of them dress in women's clothes for a fashion show. But gradually she won over some of the men, chief among them Colonel Luther Custodio, who soon became a general and one of her principal bodyguards.

A decade later, the Agrava Commission investigating Benigno Aquino's murder said Custodio had "presided over the whole clockwork-like proceeding." Another military leader enjoying Imelda's patronage—and also prominently implicated in Aquino's killing—was General Prospero Olivas, who became commander of the metropolitan police.

Imelda put equal energy into keeping up her Washington contacts. After Nixon was reelected, and to the distress of the State Department, she insisted on coming to town, uninvited, for the week of his January 20, 1973, inauguration. Her brother Kokoy told Ambassador Byroade she had planned to come anyway that week for a medical appointment. Byroade warned Foreign Affairs Secretary Car-

---

*In 1982, FBI agents raided Psinakis' home after claiming they found 600 feet of detonating cord in garbage bags outside. Psinakis claimed he had nothing to do with any manufacture of explosives, and after the Marcoses were overthrown, the Justice Department said it would no longer pursue the investigation. In 1987, however, Psinakis was arrested in connection with the inquiry as he passed through San Francisco on the way to his new home in Manila.

los Romulo that it was a busy time for Nixon, that it was U.S. policy not to have heads of state at the inauguration, and, further, that Imelda might be offended in the case of "special treatment less than she would expect." But Romulo smilingly answered that he would leave that problem with Byroade.

John Sharon, an attorney active in Democratic politics, offered to help out as Imelda's host, providing seats on the platform beside himself and his wife for the swearing-in ceremony, tickets to the inaugural ball, and a box for the symphonic concert at the Kennedy Center. (Sharon ended up providing both the tickets and some legal work he did for Imelda free of charge; though he submitted some $30,000 in bills, he was never compensated.)

Despite the perquisites she enjoyed, it turned out that Byroade's concern was well-founded; Imelda left Washington thoroughly upset by her treatment. At a lunch at the Madison Hotel, she complained to Richard Usher, the State Department's director for Philippine Affairs that her feelings had been hurt by the choice of her seat at the swearing-in ceremony and concert, saying the treatment hadn't been appropriate for a First Lady from a friendly country. "She then went on at some length about the honors which had been accorded her on the occasion of her visit to Moscow last year," Usher wrote in a secret memorandum on the conversation. He said he had sought to calm her down, telling her that Nixon had intended to meet with her before former President Johnson's sudden death preempted his schedule, and reminded her of the treatment she had enjoyed on previous trips. But though she brightened briefly at the memories, she continued to seem wounded.

Talk then turned to Philippine affairs, and Imelda grew more animated: she defended martial law, cited the danger of communist guerrillas, and reminded Usher that "President Marcos was the best one for [the] U.S. There is no one else who could handle the Philippine situation satisfactorily." She pleaded for more U.S. aid to support land reform and the military, and put in a bid for any surplus army equipment that might be left after the Vietnam war. She also vowed that she and her husband had no wish to remain in power indefinitely. They only wanted to get the country to the point where it might operate constitutionally again, she said, and when that was done, they would retire. "We do not want to have our throats cut," she told him, drawing her index finger across her throat for emphasis.

A CIA profile of Imelda in December 1975, however, took a far different view of her goals. Calling her "ambitious and ruthless," it concluded she "clearly hopes to exploit her enhanced power to build a political base that would enable her to take over in the event of her husband's abrupt departure from the scene." With Kokoy the principal manager of her political advancement, her followers, the memo said, included media workers, executives, a few politicians, and military officials, most of them, "sycophants needing protection."

Indeed, by the winter in which the memo was written, the Marcos regime's balance of power had shifted. On November 6 the President had given his wife her first official position, appointing her governor of the newly created Metro Manila region. With five cities and thirteen municipalities, the capital region was the Philippines' most populous (5.5 million) and prosperous area, and historically the leading beneficiary of most of the national resources. Imelda set to work and saw that her region got even more. She improved public transportation with new taxis and sky blue, air-conditioned "love buses," and added new slaughterhouses, markets, and composting plants. She also tackled the capital's estimated 1 million squatters, bulldozing the packing-crate shanties along the brown and sewage-clogged Pasig River and trucking former inhabitants to relocation sites 30 to 40 miles outside the city.

Foreign Minister Carlos Romulo was soon openly referring to her as the "de facto vice president." Within three years, in the fall of 1978, she had won her first elected office, a seat in the interim assembly, and had been appointed by her husband to his cabinet, as head of the far-reaching and liberally funded Ministry of Human Settlements. (With its motto, "Man, the center of things," the "superministry" quickly grew to have more than two dozen corporate offshoots, more than $1 billion in assets, and the power to annex resources of both private firms and other government budgets. Its mission made it the ideal political platform, since it touched the life of every Filipino in its quest to provide for the so-called "eleven needs of man," including not only water and food but recreation and ecological balance. It also supervised the spending of some $200 million in U.S. aid for new schoolhouses and roads. Not one rural schoolhouse was built after 1978 without displaying Imelda's name next to her husband's, on a prominent plaque informing readers in much smaller print of America's shared participation.)

Still, even in 1975, Imelda was wielding profound informal influence by sharing decisions on political appointments to the point where high officials came to be referred to as either "his" or "hers."

One official indisputably "hers" was Conrado "Joly" Benitez, a chain-smoking, pedigreed Manila technocrat (whose family head founded the Philippine Women's University). Benitez held a Stanford University Ph.D. in education and had a narrow face that resembled that of the young Marcos. He was first Imelda's general adviser, then her deputy at the Human Settlements Ministry. In Benitez' opinion, Imelda was "everyone's Pygmalion [*sic*]," but his particular influence on her was profound: the two often spent as much as eighteen hours a day together, talking over development strategies or touring projects in her black limousine. Imelda soon picked up his obtuse "technocrat" jargon as well as his habit of doodling circles, arrows, and graphs on paper tablets to illustrate his arguments. It wasn't long before she fell into the habit, for instance, of drawing large, complicated world maps during interviews with foreign correspondents to emphasize the strategic importance of the Philippines' location. (Her meticulous artwork, in which she portrayed threatening countries as daggers, was one reason her interviews always lasted so long.)

Imelda eventually produced an entire large book of her doodles for distribution to foreign guests, describing her "plea for a new international human order." It became a collectors' item among diplomats who received them and found amusement in her red, blue, and yellow stars, hearts, infinity signs, and happy faces. The substance of the plea, for a "more explicit recognition to the transcendental nature of man, his well-being, congruity with the environment, and his role in the planetary system and cosmos" was presented as a resolution to the thirty-seventh session of the United Nations General Assembly, which voted to study it further.

In those same years, Benitez inspired some of Imelda's most controversial projects, among them a $40 million "University of Life," a lavish but ultimately vastly underused campus even he conceded was "disappointing." ("We never really got the programs developed," he said in a 1987 interview. "It was a funny way to do it; usually you develop programs and then build the buildings. But I think Imelda couldn't wait...and then I never had time to develop programs. There were so many other things to do.")

While Imelda was boosting Benitez, she managed to eliminate her chief internal rival, Executive Secretary Alejandro Melchor, whose wide powers had led some to call him the "little president." Melchor was fired at the end of 1975, after he helped orchestrate a purge of more than 2000 corrupt government officials, including some of Imelda's protégés. The purge had taken place in September, while Imelda was out of the country, and on her return she was furious. Within a month, the "little president" was gone, and U.S. analysts believed Marcos had been forced to retreat from his support of a desperately needed housecleaning. As for Imelda, Melchor's departure and her warmer relations with Ver left her free to deal with her sole remaining opponent of any significance: her husband's defense minister and attorney, Juan Ponce Enrile.

Unlike Ver, whose loyalty precluded ambition, the wealthy, Harvard-educated Enrile fiercely wanted to be president. He expressed his hopes in little ways such as by traveling with a security contingent more suitable in size for a vice president than a cabinet minister. Marcos' continual boosting of his wife as a potential successor unnerved Enrile, as Marcos no doubt meant it to do.

Marcos was still nurturing his wife's hopes in 1975. He would often say things in front of her and others like, "After me, we need someone to unify the country." More tellingly, documents found in Malacanang after the couple fled showed Marcos had prepared a handwritten presidential decree, signed June 7 of that year, that named Imelda head of a commission of cabinet members whom he designated to take over were he to die or become incapacitated. There are those, including Zamora, who say even the decree may have been just another tactic to encourage Imelda to fight for the team. But Imelda that year had little reason to doubt her husband's sincerity, and she dedicated herself to hunting out and thwarting potential rivals of both Marcoses.

Enrile topped her enemies list. A shrewd and very wealthy attorney, he often squinted with the painstaking air of weighing generations of political consequences attendant on each utterance. He had many admirers among Manila's journalists and soldiers, and spent much time cultivating them. That made him a powerful threat in the eyes of Imelda and Ver, according to the minister's fragile and theatrically blond wife, Cristina. "Slowly they started to chip away at his powers," she told me in an interview. In *Breakaway*, a 1986 book written in close cooperation with Enrile, Filipino author Cecilio T. Arillo also accused Imelda of "a systematic sowing of intrigues

...designed to oust Enrile." Her intrigues seemed to do the trick; from beginning as one of Marcos' most trusted aides, the defense minister was pushed to the sidelines, even as he held onto his post.*

Although his involvement with Marcos was ebbing, there was certainly plenty Enrile might have done with his time and remaining influence. Within just a few years after martial law, the once professional Philippine army was quickly becoming unmanageable. By 1975, after the first delegation from the human rights group Amnesty International was received in the Philippines, independent reports of systematic torture of political prisoners, mostly in safehouses during interrogations, began filtering back to Washington. Amnesty counted 6000 political detainees that year, among them Catholic priests and former beauty queens. There were also persistent reports of "disappearances" and unlawful government-ordered killings, most often in the countryside, where soldiers felt more free from central control. By the late 1980s, Enrile was styling himself as a military reformist, but there was little evidence it meant much besides political posturing.

The early feud between the defense minister and First Lady was aggravated by a separate rivalry between Imelda and Enrile's wife. A former Blue Lady who disdained and occasionally snubbed Imelda in public, Cristina, as a private joke, named her pet poodle "Adlemi"— "Imelda" spelled backward. "I had to show respect, so I couldn't call it Imelda," she explained in 1987, as she sat beside an enormous tiger rug on the patio of the couple's vast Manila compound, which included several guesthouses and its own private chapel. "And after all, it wasn't such a personal offense. I named my pets after things I saw in the newspapers. I also have a turtle named Payola." Beginning as early as 1970, however, Cristina said palace politics became too much for her, and she

---

*Enrile's alienation had two important impacts on the Philippines. Primarily it sapped his competence in dealing with the growth of the NPA, the communist New People's Army. But eventually it also inspired his successful 1986 revolt with his loyalists, which virtually installed the new president, Corazon Aquino. By that time, his peevish isolation had long been clear to both Filipinos and Americans. After 1981, when Ver was made armed forces chief of staff, U.S. intelligence officials said they weren't sure what the defense minister did all day besides politicking with military officers personally loyal to him. "He used to tell us, 'Look, since 1981, I'm out of it,'" said a high-level U.S. intelligence official in Manila in 1987. "He wasn't making any decisions on the NPA. He'd been deprived of all control of the military except for [weapons] procurement, and it had been nine years since he'd been to Mindanao (the seat of some of the strongest rebel factions)."

would constantly urge her husband, "Johnny, it's time to leave. When, when, when?"

*         *         *

While Imelda's feud with the Enriles was annoying, it paled nextto her dealings with a much more powerful adversary, the new U.S. ambassador, tall and white-haired William Sullivan, assigned to Manila in the spring of 1973. Unlike Byroade, Sullivan had no trace of admiration for Imelda, whom he adamantly sought to avoid and peevishly refused to call the "First Lady"—"She was no lady," he said. In his memoirs, he described her as having a "shrewd native intelligence, a certain physical charm...but a limited education." Imelda sensed his patronizing and hated him for it, obsessively. She frequently railed against him, warned underlings to "watch out for...the white *datu*," or ruler, and ordered that he be tailed.

Sullivan, vigorous and aggressive, had only recently left a post in Laos, directing the CIA's secret war. He had little patience for the ceremonies Imelda enjoyed, and he bristled at her practice of summoning the entire diplomatic corps to serve as backdrops for state occasions. "We called ourselves the potted palms," he recalled, wincing, years later. He rarely missed a chance to twit her in return, and pointedly left by his plate the expensive party favors at Malacanang dinners (on one occasion, he said, these were pearl pins worth at least $300). The ambassador had more serious cause to dislike Imelda, however; his embassy was building files on palace corruption that he said showed "the Mafia pales by comparison to what they did." "They" almost always meant Imelda—along with a wealthy palace crony named Eduardo Cojuangco, the first cousin of Corazon Aquino, whom Marcos later put in charge of the Philippines coconut trade. Using either Cojuangco or Kokoy as the "muscle man," said Sullivan, Imelda frequently in those years was demanding stock shares, gratis, from many of the Philippines' leading companies.

"The Philippines is a very porous society," said Sullivan. "And the American Embassy was one of the two main institutions people would tell things to—the other one being the Church." Back in Washington, he said, "there was never any doubt about her operations. Marcos was the more subtle one, and his deals didn't come out for years."

Like his predecessor, Byroade, Sullivan said he worried about corruption and kept track of it, but he never really made it an issue in his dealings with the Marcoses. Both men felt the U.S. aid programs were audited well enough to have remained generally unscathed. As for the rest, corruption was an old story in the Philippines; it seemed wrong—they said—to meddle in internal affairs, and higher priority always went to dealing with U.S.-Philippines relations and particularly the U.S. bases agreements. Yet while Sullivan said he tried to stay aloof, he couldn't avoid several run-ins with Imelda.

Their first open clash came soon after the ambassador's arrival, when he was quoted anonymously in a *Newsweek* profile on Imelda. In the article, Sullivan conceded that Manila's First Lady was popular, but added that Manila's intellectuals couldn't stand her. Imelda guessed the identity of the "western diplomat" and got Sullivan to confess to his quote. Three days later, the ambassador was summoned to a dinner at 8:30 p.m. the next day at one of the capital's most elegant French restaurants. He arrived at 9 p.m., he said, since he knew Imelda would also be late: he'd earlier watched her motorcade career past his home in another direction. After being greeted by Carmen Nakpil, the speechwriter, he recalled, "I walked into the room, and there were some 50 Filipino professors. They'd all been summoned at 7:30 p.m., and they'd all been drinking heavily, sitting around this big, horseshoe-shaped table."

Imelda made her entrance shortly thereafter. In tow was the Egyptian minister of culture, who was visiting with the King Tut exhibit. She gave no clue as to the evening's program until everyone had finished their dinners, whereupon she began to summon the professors, one by one, to sit in a chair before her in the middle of the horseshoe. "She sat there with her briefing cards and called, say, for the professor of astrophysics," Sullivan recounted. "She'd ask a question and he'd answer, and she'd say a few sentences to show she understood. It was all an act, a command performance, all put on for my benefit."

Later there was dancing, but at 11:30 p.m., with the midnight curfew approaching, Nakpil clapped her hands peremptorily and led the professors away. Imelda's bodyguards handed out curfew passes at the door. Sullivan was astounded. "Here she'd summoned these professors, stood them up by two hours, got them half-crocked, and left them with curfew passes and no way home," he recalled. "I felt it was a keen insight into just how far her pride would take her."

Intrigued as he was with her psychology, however, Sullivan believed Imelda's power in the mid-1970s was limited—she had no impact on trade arrangements, the insurgency, or policy concerning the U.S. bases. He refused to take her seriously and in the strongest signal of his lack of esteem, he fired Rafferty soon after he arrived. "I told him his position was redundant and he went home," he said.

Still, State Department cables show Sullivan devoted much time to tracking Imelda's dealings overseas. Her travel schedule picked up considerably in the mid-1970s, after Marcos announced plans to bring a "new balance" to Philippine foreign relations. It was the same tune Marcos had played a decade earlier, when he opened trade with Eastern Europe, and it never amounted to more than some small-scale, tentative business ventures and several symbolic shows of independence from the United States. Imelda, for instance, went to Moscow once just a few months before martial law was declared. She went again in 1978, at the height of the Carter Administration's human rights pressures, and again just before the "snap elections" of 1986, when American insistence on reforms was at its all-time peak. The gestures, each time, proved a weak counterweight to Marcos' domestic practice of catering to American security and business interests—but they routinely elicited concern from Washington, where State Department officials scrutinized each trip.*

Marcos found Imelda the natural candidate for such journeys, since he trusted few others and recognized her mastery of high-profile symbols and shows. And Imelda, who loved to keep busy, thrived on the bustle that came with each new trip. Between 1974 and 1980, she traveled three times to the People's Republic of China, twice to Libya, and once to the U.S.S.R. She also managed stops in those years in Mexico, Algeria, Bolivia, Burma, Egypt, and Nepal. Everywhere she went, she shopped and hobnobbed, giddy with the pomp of third world receptions—the finery, the long vacuous toasts, the martial music. She seemed happiest of all, said her friends, in the anticipation, planning her trips far in advance. "Mrs. Marcos may be ready for the world," remarked Sullivan in 1975, a year in which she shuttled overseas almost every other month, "but is the world ready for Mrs. Marcos?"

---

*Typical of the Marcoses' way of asserting their "independence" was Imelda's conversation with Henry Kissinger on *Ang Pangulo* in December of 1975, as recounted in Manila's newspapers. Imelda said, "We are between two world powers. Across the China Sea is China. Across the Pacific is the United States." Kissinger interrupted, "Now, tell me, what are you going to do? Play us off against each other?" Imelda bowed her head, smiled, and said, "Thank you very much, Mr. Secretary. You've given us an idea."

Imelda, in interviews, never downplayed the importance of a trip. But with characteristic deference to her husband, she told journalist Roy Rowan in 1979, "In this country, where there are more crises, the stronger one keeps house...and the smarter one. The other one runs the errands for the boss."

She went to Iran several times to discuss the oil crisis and met with Fidel Castro in Havana in 1975 to discuss normalization of relations and ways of avoiding competition in the marketing of sugar. In 1974, she led an extremely high-profile trip to Peking that so filled her with enthusiasm that the CIA believed her responsible on her return for speeding up the Philippines' establishment of ties, one year later, to the People's Republic.

Of course, not all of her trips were so serious-minded. In 1975, Imelda flew sixty guests to Katmandu for the King of Nepal's coronation on a leopard-skin-covered golden throne. Her entourage arrived on four government jets, one of which returned to Manila to pick up more food, and included Cristina Ford; Christiaan Barnard, the South African heart-transplant pioneer; a military aide; and a corps of bodyguards. Like the Shah's party, the ostentatious gathering of the world's ultrarich was distinguished by its glaring insensitivity, since it took place amidst one of the world's poorest populations.

Imelda spent much of the time pursuing Britain's Prince Charles, whom she deeply admired and often showered with costly gifts and invitations to visit Manila. Friends said she had hoped for years that he would one day marry her daughter Imee. During the ceremonies, she found her way to a seat by his side, after which a British correspondent quoted in *The New York Times'* account noted: "She's certainly keeping Charles amused. She keeps talking and Charles keep saying, 'Really? Really?'"*

Diplomats and journalists were dazzled by Imelda's skill at monopolizing the limelight: at a moment when the press corps seemed most bored, for instance, awaiting the King's arrival on an elephant, she threw open her white parasol like a peacock's tail, and took a short promenade with Japanese Princess Michiko, instantly drawing photographers.

---

*Stephen Barry, the prince's valet, later wrote in his memoirs that Imelda's gifts and attentions frequently made his charge uncomfortable. "I can remember him staring at a huge volume of some beautifully bound but obscure books," he wrote, "and saying, 'What can I give her this time?'"

Imelda's favorite destinations remained Washington and New York, which she visited at least once a year to shop and lobby, almost always insisting on meeting with high officials and often hand-carrying messages from her husband. To the extreme irritation of U.S. diplomats who spent untold hours trying to keep up with her, both she and Kokoy constantly refused to provide details of her schedule or entourage size in advance, yet invariably took lapses of VIP courtesies as a national affront. (U.S. cables are peppered with worried pleas from Manila diplomats to afford her various perquisities.) She always traveled in royal style, in a Philippine Air Lines DC-8 jet furnished with beds, showers, and even a grand piano, and with a squad of Blue Ladies who would sleep in shifts so that the ever-alert First Lady would have round-the-clock company.

One of Manila's more cherished scandals involves the government takeover of Philippine Air Lines (PAL) from owner Benny Toda. Marcos, having heard that his wife owed PAL nearly $6 million, approached Toda in church with Imelda at his side to demand that he send a bill. Toda did so after some reluctant hesitation, finally deciding to cut the charges to $3 million. Soon afterward, a Manila daily, the *Evening Post*—published by Imelda's official biographer, Kerima Polotan—began printing a series of articles about alleged PAL management abuses. Another paper, the *Times Journal*—owned by Kokoy Romualdez—echoed the charges, which reportedly had some basis but oddly enough had been ignored until then. At last Marcos called Toda to the palace to suggest that he transfer control for a mutually agreeable price. Toda did so, but has said he was never paid.

Among Imelda's most controversial trips were those she made to Libya in 1976 and 1977. Both times, her aim was to personally persuade Muammar el-Qaddafi to stop shipping guns to Philippine Moslem separatists—specifically the Moro National Liberation Front (MNLF)—who had been fighting the central government since Spanish times in the southern island of Mindanao. Before her first departure, she told Sullivan that she had been reading as much as she could about Qaddafi and found him "fascinating," being particularly struck by his "incorruptibility." (To a more trusted friend, who promptly relayed it to the U.S. Embassy, she confided her amazement that the Libyan hadn't taken any personal shares of his nation's vast oil revenues.) Sullivan concluded a cable to Washington before her departure by noting, "It remains to be seen whether Mrs. Marcos will be able to work her wiles on the ascetic

Libyan colonel, not to mention the MNLF leadership. But she will certainly give it the college try."

To say the least, it was rather unorthodox for a president's wife to go as an uninvited supplicant to a head of state who had virtually declared war. And it had mixed results at best, with overtones of downright tawdriness. But Imelda, through sheer single-minded moxie, established it in the national memory as one of her most spectacular feats. And as in her journeys to Mayor Lacson's office twenty-two years earlier, she managed to win herself a title for her efforts. In September of 1978, she was nominated for a Nobel Peace Prize by four prominent Filipinos (among them the grateful labor secretary, Ople, and a supreme court justice) who praised her for having "traveled more than 20,000 miles and braved the danger of the skies to meet an unknown man in the middle of the desert of Libya for the sake of peace for 44 million [Filipino] people." The nomination came in the middle of a bid by Marcos loyalists to have Imelda named as deputy prime minister, the strongest attempt yet to put her in position to succeed the President. Imelda won neither the prize nor the post, but did receive the gratifying tribute of associate Supreme Court Justice Ramon Fernandez, one of those nominating her, who declared her "the greatest woman in the world today."

On her first visit to Tripoli, Imelda was kept waiting by Qaddafi for two days, a rather substantial slight. And when the meetings finally began, they soon deadlocked, apparently hopelessly, until, as the Philippine press reported, Imelda mustered her persuasive talents and pleaded, "I am being spit upon by the big powers. Don't let me be spit upon by the small powers too!" They seemed to be the right words: after two more days, she returned to Manila in triumph with the Tripoli Agreement, which held the promise of future MNLF peace talks, rough plans to normalize Philippine-Libyan relations, and a set of leather-bound volumes of the Koran that the Libyan had given her.

"'You are a good woman,'" she said Qaddafi had told her. "'Why don't you become Islam? [*sic*]'" She in turn offered to teach him to dance, while her camera crew filmed the scene. In a rare honor for Imelda, Qaddafi took her to his desert home to meet his father. He also broke diplomatic precedent by inviting the wives of the diplomatic corps to a state dinner for Imelda, hosted by one of Qaddafi's three wives in a tent in her backyard. There, Imelda met Qaddafi's mother; "When I saw their relationship, everything became clear," she later told friends. "Qaddafi had a messianic obsession with trying to find God because of his subservience to his mother." U.S. Embassy officials in Tripoli cabled that her visit "can only be described as a diplomatic success." And for weeks after her return, palace aides said Qaddafi would call her to discuss religious philosophy. "He was head over heels in love with her," insisted Zamora. "They would talk for hours."

Imelda thrived on the attention, and did her best to use it to make her husband jealous, talking about how handsome "the Chairman" looked in his black and gold burnoose and how white his teeth were. In the blush of her victory, soon after she returned, she ordered a new mosque to be built in Manila. ("We may yet see artificial sand dunes in back of the Cultural [Center] in Manila Bay," noted Sullivan in his cables.) Imelda soon toned down her rapture, however, telling some of her friends that she was certain Qaddafi was gay, and others that his secret was that "he was just a frightened mama's boy."

Mama's boy or not, Qaddafi continued his arms shipments not long after Imelda's return. The only really lasting effect of the much-touted journey was lingering intrigue over her dealings with Qaddafi. The encounter attracted such irresistible interest that a CIA station chief in Manila once asked Imelda point blank and very gravely after a party if she had or had not slept with the Libyan. At first, he said, Imelda evaded the question, but finally murmured, "I was never alone with the Chairman." Added the station chief, however, who had long experience in the Middle East, "I can't imagine he didn't try. From the perspective of his culture, he must have thought it relevant that a woman was sent to him."

Using his wife as a sexual lure was simply one of the more extreme examples of Marcos' creative diplomacy. In other, more substantive ways, he found her the ideal emissary. "A First Lady is very convenient," Imelda later explained to Roy Rowan. "A First Lady has no official position, yet she is official, [so] you can be ambivalent." Since she carried messages from her husband, she usually won direct access to chiefs of state, she said. And in her own conversations, she could float ideas and test reactions without any risk of committing her government. "Marcos can always say, 'She made a mistake,'" she said. "You know, 'My wife talks too much.' He can always fall back on that." Sending her also saved money, she noted proudly, since while ambassadors stay in hotels, governments faced with first ladies "always put you in the guest house."

Marcos claimed to have kept a firm grip on the proceedings, briefing Imelda before her trips, preparing "shopping lists" and jargon-free memos easy for her to understand, and speaking to her on the phone from Manila two or three times a day. He also insisted on minute by minute accounts, not only of her whereabouts and whom she met, but of weather conditions and flight patterns for each of her trips.

"We have agreed on certain formulas," he said. "She may use the following words, 'I do not know if I read the President right, but I heard him say....' Then she will add, 'This, of course, will be subject to a confirmation. But I heard him say that if it were as follows, possibly it could be considered....' With that kind of a formula, she can tell me what the reaction is. Or if the reaction is a counterproposal, she calls me up and tells me. Then I tell her what to do...I tell her exactly what to do....And of course, how can you say no to a lovely woman like that?"

With the developing nations seen as increasingly important in those years, few international leaders indeed wanted to slight Imelda. One of the best examples of her talent at exploiting this reserve of goodwill was her spectacular trip to Peking in 1974.

At the time, the Philippines still recognized the Republic of China on Taiwan, but in the wake of Nixon's trip to the People's Republic, Marcos was eager to follow suit, and Philippine foreign policy experts had already started laying the groundwork in Peking. Imelda and her husband decided she would seize the opportunity for a splashy foray that September. She came as Marcos' special representative, on what the Philippine government said was a "goodwill mission...with a view toward eventual normalization of relations." Her invitation came from Premier Zhou En lai, with whom she had an hour-long meeting, but the rest of her trip was taken over by Zhou's leading government rival, Madame Mao Zedong, or Jiang Quing.

Drably dressed in her Mao suit and hat and thick spectacles, and fourteen years Imelda's senior, Jiang Quing lavished attention on her Filipina visitor, attired much more gaily in a print dress, black suede coat, and jaunty silk scarf. She took her to schools and communes and a "model community" she had created in a hamlet of 600 peasants she had organized into a production brigade: a "tiny utopia of proletarian culture" as Jiang Quing's authorized biographer, Roxane Witke, described it, in which the peasant subjects produced proletarian poetry, fiction, song, dance, and opera. Jiang Quing also staged an enormous reception in which thousands of children, workers, and students were called out to wave flowers and chant welcome slogans in her political stronghold of Tientsin. Imelda, plainly thrilled, extended her stay by five days. She later said she had feared Jiang Quing would live up to her reputation as a "radical ideologue," but had found her, instead, to be "soft-spoken, very feminine." As Sullivan described it in his memoirs, Imelda "unwittingly but inevitably" let herself be exploited.

The speed with which Imelda and Jiang Quing became friends should not have been surprising. Their backgrounds, personalities, and goals made them natural soulmates. Jiang Quing's childhood, even more than Imelda's, was marked by chaos and deprivation. Her mother was a servant and prostitute, and Jiang Quing learned early to fend for herself. At 14, she became a "jade girl," or actress in a traveling theater group, according to Ross Terrill, author of an unauthorized 1984 biography. Married three times by the age of 24, she met Mao, who was then almost twice her age, in the Communists' cave headquarters in Yenan after the Great March, on her flight from the Japanese invasion of 1937. Determining to win him, she seduced him and became pregnant (they eventually had two daughters), after which Mao threatened to go home to become a farmer if party leaders failed to grant him a divorce from his third wife. This they allowed only on the condition that the new Madame Mao stay out of politics for thirty years—a limit she agreed to, but which hugely frustrated her.

When her enforced isolation elapsed, at the beginning of the Cultural Revolution of the mid-1960s, Jiang Quing sought her revenge on the leaders who had opposed her, as well as anyone else who dared to slight her or her husband. She won a seat in the Politburo in 1969, and became known as one of the most fiery defenders of the purity of Maoism. As did Imelda, she fiercely denied her own ambitions, even as she struggled to replace the dying chairman: "Everything I did, Mao told me to do," she would later insist. "I was his dog; when he said to bite, I bit."

As the head of the far-left Gang of Four, Jiang Quing made wild public vendettas and feminist speeches—saying at one point, "Man's

contribution to human history is no more than a drop of sperm."
Such sentiments and such ambition hardly endeared her to China's
entrenched patriarchy, which, led by Zhou En lai, determined to defeat her. It was at the climax of their struggle that Imelda chanced to
visit the Chinese capital.

While Imelda was still in China, Sullivan sent a cable to Washington and his colleagues in Peking declaring himself fascinated by
the "ultra-close identification" developing between her and Jiang
Quing. "That formidable old schemer," as he called Madame Mao,
had taken over Imelda's visit "lock, stock, and barrel," as a challenge
to Zhou En lai, who, though then ailing, had earlier made it clear he
viewed the visit as significant. Jiang Quing continued to court Imelda
even after her return, sending gifts every few days, Sullivan noted,
"mostly in the form of delectable foodstuffs."

Imelda was inspired. While some Chinese leaders were repelled
by her frivolity—the foreign minister, in a speech the following May,
called her a "product of a corrupt capitalist system, under which cap-
italists toy with women"—Jiang Quing had treated her as a worthy
colleague in the dramatic shared struggle of development. Imelda's
rhetoric rose to the occasion. "Our own people share certain memories with yours," she declared at a Peking state dinner. "We also
overthrew a colonial power only to be overcome by another."

The trip had profound and lasting influence on Imelda, especially
since it came at a time when she felt disparaged by her erstwhile
American friends. Describing her mood in a memo to Washington
the following November (when Imelda again was on her way to the
American capital), Sullivan said she had grown "increasingly critical
of the western system of things, particularly as currently being man-
ifested in the U.S." She was furious at American reporters, not only
for their slights to her but for unseating her friend Nixon, and having recently taken some losses in the American stock market, she let
Sullivan know she feared U.S. economic "disorder."* She also worried about western moral decay. Having just sent her increasingly
rebellious daughter Imee to Princeton, she fretted that Imee was "surrounded by faggots."

"Given all this background, Imelda is in a slightly touchy state,

---

*Imelda visited the Nixons, whom she told reporters were "old friends of the Philippines
and of the Marcoses" in November of 1974, as the ex-President was recovering from pneumonia in Long Beach. She brought him a huge bouquet of flowers, praised his record in
office, and confided, "In the East, there is a saying: 'Love is the most potent of medicines.'"

and a small offense or an untoward incident could spell lasting damage," Sullivan wrote. "It is hard to prescribe exactly what is needed, beyond much cotton batting and a dose of good luck."

The ambassador had good cause to know just how touchy Imelda was, since the two had only recently had their most emotional of run-ins. The scene was an annual party to commemorate McArthur's Leyte landing in that province's seaside town of Olot. There, Imelda had recently constructed an immense "ancestral home," on the scale of a large country club, with a swimming pool, chapel, and several coconut-log cabanas on 24 acres of palm-lined coastal land. (The emblems of her taste there ran from the exquisite to the garish; dotting the grounds were supposedly genuine Javanese temple artifacts alongside concrete pedestals topped with bowls of neon-colored plastic fruits.) Summoning Sullivan to her table, he said, she remonstrated that the United States was making a serious mistake in seeming to favor Zhou En lai's "small clique" over Jiang Quing. There was no question, she said, that when Mao died, his widow would be China's new ruler. She coyly added that she had established an "excellent working relationship" with Jiang Quing and would be pleased to serve as a bridge between her and the U.S. government.

"I should probably have just thanked her very much...and said that I would relay it faithfully to my government," Sullivan conceded. "I guess the devil made me do an unchivalrous thing." He told Imelda that he thought she was wrong, described Jiang Quing as one in a long sequence of "deviants" from the mainstream of the Chinese Communist Party and predicted that she would soon be wiped out.

Imelda listened carefully, then burst into tears and left the table. Her priest, who had been sitting near her, went to comfort her and returned to inform Sullivan that she had taken his remarks personally, as indicative of the attitude the United States would take toward her should Marcos die in office. "I assured the priest I had meant no such inference, [sic]" Sullivan wrote in his memoirs, but "my relations with her never recovered." Two years later, after Mao had died and his wife had been arrested, just as Sullivan predicted, the ambassador again encountered Imelda at the annual Leyte ceremony, although this time he was determined to stick to trivial conversation. To his chagrin, however, his Australian colleague raised the subject, whereupon Imelda swiveled around to face Sullivan and launched into what seemed to be a prepared speech. Jiang Quing had not moved quickly enough, she said. When Mao died, she should have seized the center of attention and the role of authority. She should have placed herself in charge of the funeral and issued all instructions and invitations as the inheritor of her late husband's mantle. She should never, for instance, have permitted herself to be photographed as part of the official mourning group, occupying not the first, but the fourth place of honor. That was a very serious mistake.

Sullivan changed the subject as soon as he got the chance, and as he did so noted the relief of the Philippine officials around him, who he said "were aware that their President was not immortal and did not choose to dwell publicly on the probable manner of his succession."

The Philippine press naturally treated the Peking trip as another heroic achievement, with front-page photographs of Imelda wearing a Mao suit and playing with infants at a people's commune. Her prestige was also boosted by the revelation that she had signed a contract to buy a million barrels of cheap Chinese crude oil. Yet the oil deal was a bad bargain; the crude was of such poor quality that refining was nearly impossible, and two years later, the government found it was costing 15 cents more per barrel than oil from the Middle East.

*   *   *

Even apart from the government-controlled press, Imelda continued to have a way with reporters. In her mid-40s, she was still beautiful and retained an aura (at least) of charming candor that made strangers want to protect her. She granted coveted access in marathon blocks of eight to ten hours to a few, mostly male, foreign journalists. The anxiety that later gave her what one Filipino photographer dubbed "the eyes of a secret service agent" was not yet visible. She looked straight into her interviewers' faces, speaking in emotional, quotable bursts, in dramatic contrast to her husband, who would gaze off into the distance, his gestures stiff, his talk rambling and legalistic. Combined with exquisite luncheons and breathtaking trips through town in her black limousine (license plate IM777), Imelda's interviews were often sufficiently head-turning to result in positive publicity. She was not unaware of her attraction. "Not everyone who comes here at this time is ours," she told Philippine television news reporter Felipe

"Jun" Medina, one of her favorites, in Tagalog late in 1972. "But we will use them."

After an interview in 1977, William F. Buckley raved about Imelda in his syndicated column, calling her "that exquisite woman [whose] determination to help her people has an elemental force." Though she traveled with "an enormous security staff," he noted, "she seems to be hugely popular." In her conversation with Buckley, Imelda lavished praise on Mao Zedong, the world figure she and her husband admired more than any other, and of whom she said, "I have known three popes...I tell you there is nobody who irradiates the kind of ...holiness...that flowed out of Chairman Mao." She quickly followed that up by telling Buckley she saw resemblances between him and the Chinese Chairman.*

Subtlety was never Imelda's strong suit. In 1982, when Roy Rowan was writing her profile for *Life* magazine, she called him from Manila just before midnight at his Connecticut home and talked for nearly an hour, "trying to pry about the tone of the story," Rowan recalled. "I couldn't think of anything to get her off the phone, so finally, I said, look, tomorrow's my wedding anniversary, which it actually was." The next morning, a delivery truck rolled up to his home and rendered forth one of the largest floral bouquets Rowan had ever seen. It had come from the Waldorf-Astoria's floral shop in Manhattan, with love from Imelda, and looked, as he recalled, "like something you would throw around a horse."

Of all the American reporters who grew close to Imelda in those years, one of her favorites was *Newsweek*'s former international editor Richard Z. Chesnoff. Then 39, Chesnoff admired her in return. Imelda met Chesnoff soon after he arrived in Manila. Chesnoff and Richard Smith, then *Newsweek*'s Asia editor, interviewed President Marcos, and asked Marcos to arrange a separate interview for them with the First Lady. The two men were granted an interview with Imelda that same day. Richard Smith wrote a *Newsweek* profile of

---

*Mao was more or less an acquired taste. Imelda's most heartfelt enthusiasm went to more mainstream heroes such as Mohammed Ali and Elvis Presley. Of Presley, she once said, "He was ahead of his time, because he had deep feelings. He had the privilege of deep feelings because he was deeply loved by his mother, Gladys. He was able to appreciate deep, profound beauty in sounds. And he started a musical revolution. They say all revolutions start from love."

Imelda called "First and Foremost Lady," which was published in the February 1976 issue. The correspondents' actual interview with Imelda appeared as a sidebar to the profile, with Smith's and Chesnoff's names under the questions and answers. Eight months later, Chesnoff resigned from his *Newsweek* job and embarked on a variety of writing projects, including two that had to do with Imelda and the Philippines. Chesnoff traveled with the First Lady on her first trip to Libya and became a frequent visitor at Malacanang.

Chesnoff also did the writing for an extraordinary color photograph book on the Philippines. The original editions were collectors' items: Bound in blue and gold Philippine Ikat tribal weavings, they were nearly 2 feet by 1 foot, weighed more than 10 pounds, and cost more than $50 each. The text combined historical and sociological observations with praise of the Marcoses' accomplishments. At the end of the book, Chesnoff thanked both the Marcoses and several members of the Philippine army and air force, who had shuttled him and the photographers around the country for several weeks. Press Director Francisco Tatad said each government department later was informed how many copies they had to buy.

Chesnoff next began work on a biography of Imelda, but that project had less success. It remained unpublished in 1988. While he declined to elaborate, Adrian Cristobal, who became the palace spokesman in 1981, said the Marcoses dropped the idea of a third biography after Cristobal reviewed the first draft. Chesnoff later took a job as Paris correspondent for *U.S. News & World Report.*

Shortly after the publication of the lavish coffee table book about the Philippines, there was a surge of productivity by Imelda's publicists. *Golden Quotations of Our First Lady* was published in 1978, and was rapidly followed over the next two years by *Selected Speeches of Imelda Romualdez Marcos, The Ideas of Imelda Romualdez Marcos* (a two-volume set), *A Direction to Growth, The New Human Order,* and *A Humanist Approach to Development,* all under her name. (Her turnout paled when compared to her husband, however, whose books— *Marcos Speaks, The Marcos Wit, The Marcos Mind, Democratic Revolution in the Philippines,* et al.—filled shelves.) In addition, two more flattering biographies appeared, *A Biography of Deeds,* by her press secretary, Ileana Maramag, and *Heart of the Revolution,* by Isabelo Crisostomo.

The books were meant to counteract the picture of Imelda as the "Steel Butterfly" many Filipinos by then had dubbed her. While she could still inspire adoration in crowds of poor country folk, her image suffered in the city from reports of her overseas spending sprees and frolics with rich Europeans. When the *Manila Bulletin* conducted a 1978 poll asking Filipinos whom they most admired, respondents ranked Imelda sixth, after her husband, who placed first; Benigno Aquino, who still was in jail; and Communist Party chairman Jose Maria Sison. She was so vexed by this that she had a palace aide call the paper and halt distribution of 300,000 copies. The fact that Jesus Christ placed ninth didn't seem to appease her.

A more pointed slight had come on her forty-fifth birthday, in 1974, when three Filipino university students staged a play entitled *The Coffin of Cinderella*. It presented the rise and fall of a character clearly recognizable as Imelda, who was raised from poverty by a handsome prince, killed him as he stood in her way, and was finally chased off her throne by her indignant subjects. Police closed the play down after three wild performances, and the writers went into hiding. (The actors and actresses avoided jail, since they were children recruited from an orphanage.)

Imelda still refused to restrain herself. On New Year's Eve of 1976, she threw a three-day party for thirty celebrities headed by Gina Lollobrigida, on a floating casino rocking in Manila Bay. In 1977, a Honolulu columnist marveled at how Imelda bought $40,000 worth of clothes and gifts there in a single shopping spree without trying anything on. In 1978, a Cartier representative in Hong Kong said she had put together the world's largest collection of gems. In 1979, when she hosted the opening of a new beach resort, she sent a plane to Australia to ship in extra loads of white sand.

Her friend Donelan suggested that she try to "dress down" a bit, eschew the jewelry and sequined ternos, maybe even copy Jiang Quing. But she told him he didn't understand Malay culture. "The people want to see me in diamonds," she said. Later, she expounded on the theme in one of her most frequently cited quotes to reporters: "I am my little people's star and slave," she said. "You have to be some kind of light, a star to give them guidelines. You have to show them how to be a star, how to be good, how to make beautiful things. You are some kind of model. This is very important, especially in a developing country. Everybody is in the gutter. Everybody's poor.

Don't tell me we should go there and all look poor. It's ridiculous."
She said she always told her American friends, "Hey, you're nice
people, but why are you such masochists? You're always ashamed
of being wealthy, white, tall, good-looking people. What's wrong with
that?"

Nor could Imelda be persuaded to see less of her "jet set," as
they had come to be called, of idle socialites and nobility and wealthy
entrepreneurs. Cristina Ford moved into the palace guest house and
stayed for months at a time during the late 1970s, after her husband,
Henry Ford II, was discovered to be having an affair and then left
her. "I felt secure there, after my tragedy," she said, adding that the
Marcoses, "were like family... calling all the time after my separation, trying to do everything to save the marriage."

She said Imelda "gave me Filipino advice about Henry," which
she added she did not follow. "She said to pursue him very much.
If you pursue him, show him so much love, he can't be indifferent,
she said."

Cristina remained intrigued by the Marcoses, though she said she
often found Imelda aloof. "I knew my limits," she said. "The President had his friends that he'd trust very much, but her, to tell you
the truth, in my experience I didn't see which ones she trusted entirely. She was always aware of her position and knew, always, people can betray you. I think that was often on her mind."

Imelda publicly admitted to feeling isolated, telling one Filipino
interviewer, "There can be a terrible, intense loneliness here, and I
am always afraid of being intensely lonely." Yet at least on one subject, she was more frank with Cristina than with others: "She used
to say, well, Cristina, the destiny—she believes very much in destiny—if destiny brings me to be president I would do a good job,
because my knowledge is so big about it, I would be just like the
President."

Besides Mrs. Ford, Imelda's closest non-Filipino friends were screen
actor George Hamilton, pianist Van Cliburn, and investment banker
Mario D'Urso. On Van Cliburn, Imelda conferred the Philippines' first
International Artist Award in 1973, declaring, "He has charmed the savage breast of discord with the unifying power of his universal art." The
award entitled Cliburn to a monthly cash stipend for the rest of his life,
as well as insurance and a state funeral. For Hamilton, Imelda reserved
other benefits: the Marcoses' attorney, Zamora, said he once heard her

call a friend in New York to ask that he deliver $150,000 to the actor on the pretext that "he could buy a bullet-proof limo for the President. But we both knew that was bullshit."

She lavished so much affectionate attention on all three men and was so often seen with them that there were inevitably innuendos. Marchers in antigovernment rallies in the 1980s went so far as to wear t-shirts reading, "Marcos, You Are Not Alone," with a picture of George Hamilton on the back. Yet Imelda's Filipino confidants insist the three friendships were inspired mostly by her sense of decor; she simply liked the look of tall white men around her.

"She called them the Three Stooges," said one of Imelda's closest aides during the martial law years. "She'd tell me, 'Now, look. You go to an Italian restaurant in New York. You need an escort, right? Now, who would the average American look up to?' George Hamilton may not have been a brilliant actor, but he was glamorous.... Anyway, she always had a big chip on her shoulder. She'd say that she always dreamed of having white valets, white busboys, and white waiters."*

Of her western male trio, Imelda doted most on Hamilton, who, like Cliburn, almost always visited Malacanang accompanied by his mother. Hamilton also often met Imelda on her trips to New York and Rome, where he was studied by her snickering bodyguards, who called him "Dracula" because of his large white teeth. Tall, suave, and perennially tan, he made, as Imelda often said, the perfect dancing partner. She couldn't seem to spend enough time with him, as an excerpt from her 1983 social schedule, describing a Honolulu visit, suggested: "Breakfast with G. Hamilton, lunch with G. Hamilton, shopping with G. Hamilton, disco with G. Hamilton, midnight snack

---

*Indeed, Marcos never seemed jealous of the trio, while his private notes show him actually fond of Van Cliburn, whom he called, in a letter to his daughter Irene, "such a nice engaging and very charming person."

In the same letter, however, written on June 18, 1973, Marcos describes a "sour note" during an evening cruise with Van Cliburn to Bataan on the presidential yacht. The boat ran into rough seas, and "was not only rolling and pitching but it was going around in circles. It was rolling so much that Van Cliburn laughingly told us when we all met on the heli-deck at 6 a.m. he could not sleep...and he was thinking of the Titanic...and he collected all his valuables which, of course, for him meant only his decoration which we had given him as International Artist...plus one big leg of beef which he said he tucked under his arm ready to supply his friends who would be in need of food if they should be close to him swept into the sea in the event of sinking."

Faced with this distress, Marcos wrote, Imelda "and the Blue Ladies as usual like a couple hundred of nannies [were] all wanting to take care of poor helpless little Van Cliburn—height 6 ft. 4 inches and whose appetite is endless and ravenous."

at the gazebo with G. Hamilton, and back to Makiki Heights with G. Hamilton."

"He was relentless in his pursuit of style," said an *Esquire* profile of the actor in 1980. As a 13-year-old, he learned to mix perfect martinis for his mother's parties and began to "live," as he said, "in a dinner jacket." His home was a mansion once owned by Douglas Fairbanks, Sr. He drove a 1939 Rolls-Royce that had been built for King George VI. His social schedule was a paparazzi's dream: among his dates were Angie Dickinson, Vanessa Redgrave, Lynda Bird Johnson, and "Dynasty" star Catherine Oxenberg. He named his son from a former marriage "Ashley," and even had what one writer called, "a pet for success": a Lhasa apso named Nietzsche. He once told a reporter, "People seem to be embarrassed by glamour. I never am. It's always been a part of my life." Imelda trusted not only in Hamilton's glamour but in his business acumen; her New York real estate agent, Joseph Bernstein, later said the actor served as a personal adviser to her on financial affairs and sought out at least one property for her to buy. (There have also been published reports suggesting that Imelda may have sponsored Hamilton's purchase of a $1.2 million house in Beverly Hills in 1982.)

On another occasion, a prominent Filipino executive recalled, Imelda sought him out at a wedding party early one morning in 1983, to advise him to "talk to George" about the executive's troubled company, since "he makes a lot of money from movies." Said the executive, "I felt like an ass. There I was explaining my business problems to George Hamilton at 2 a.m. to the beat of disco music. He listened, but I felt like an ass."

Like Hamilton, D'Urso, a Naples-born partner in New York's Lehman Brothers (before it merged with Shearson American Express), had the right look and right connections: lean, tall, and elegantly European, he was often spotted in those years sharing cocktails with Henry Kissinger or Marietta Tree, or jogging through Central Park in a red velour running suit. He arrived late to work, took long lunches, and could be heard saying things like "molto chic." He met Imelda in April 1973 when both were in Spain for the wedding of Franco's granddaughter, and found her "terribly attractive, full of life, very dynamic, intelligent, and interesting." For the next decade, he would visit Manila three or four times a year, and escort Imelda on her yearly trips to Rome, as well as on other junkets, to the point where some of his colleagues took to call-

ing him a Blue Lady. He set up office in Manila and said he became
Shearson-Lehman's main contact there, arranging development loans
for government organizations such as the Central Bank and the long
distance telephone company, and managing some of the Central Bank's
assets.

D'Urso maintained that he never handled the Marcoses' "private"
accounts, although that distinction became less meaningful in the
course of their relationship, as the Marcoses gradually merged private with public. D'Urso said he did often discuss Imelda's overseas
investments with her, however, and considered her "a very, very
shrewd investor in the stock exchange, [and] in property," who had
worldwide business contacts and a good sense of markets. In 1978,
he said, Imelda told him the Marcoses needed overseas assets because of threats to their power, communist or otherwise. "They were
scared that there could be, not a revolution in the Philippines, but
some sort of takeover, where they would have to counteract, and if
there was a new election and so on, they needed some funds for
them to go back in power," he said. (Six years later, a U.S. Senate
report said Imelda's personal fortune was believed to run into hundreds of millions of dollars, much of it invested abroad.)

D'Urso said he used to tease Imelda about her shopping sprees.
"I was very critical," he said. "I'd say, here you'd see a big, big shopping bag and behind it, a little Filipina." But to all indications, he
enjoyed the perquisites of the friendship. One of the Marcos family
videotapes, later seized by the new Aquino government, shows him
rocking with Imelda and Cristina Ford in the Marcoses' private New
York disco. In addition, color slides in the private collection of one
of the presidential bodyguards include a shot of D'Urso mugging with
diamond bracelets and tiaras aboard *Ang Pangulo* in Manila Bay.

Imelda's bodyguards said Manila expenses for D'Urso and the rest
of the jet set were routinely and completely taken care of by the Marcoses. The bodyguards hated Imelda's western friends without exception. "They'd get up at 10 or 11 a.m., throw temper tantrums if
the butter was too hard or the air-conditioner was too warm, watch
videotapes, and go out for dinner," groused one of the stewards,
Captain Ricardo Morales, who was later to join the anti-Marcos forces
at a critical moment.

It was D'Urso who brought Gina Lollobrigida to Manila, in 1975.
The 48-year-old Italian actress had recently begun a career as a photographer, and had just finished a magazine assignment on "the most

interesting men in the world." Like Chesnoff, Lollobrigida wanted to produce a picture book on the Philippines, and also like Chesnoff, her efforts to do so were supported with government resources. The Marcoses, said D'Urso, gave her a house, access to a plane, and the aid of high-ranking government officials. "But Gina was very naughty," he added. "She came for a week and stayed nearly a year. Imelda got bored with her." There was one other problem. Another "naughty" photographer took a picture of Lollobrigida and Marcos jogging together alone on the beach of the lovely, isolated island of Borocay. It was widely circulated in foreign newspapers and cackled over for months in Manila coffee shops.

A more peripheral member of Imelda's jet set was Bonnie Swearingen, the blond, stylish wife of Standard Oil's chief executive. In addition to visiting Malacanang two or three times, she accompanied Imelda in 1981 to see King Hassan of Morocco in his palace in Rabat, where the entourage enjoyed festivities including a banquet, shopping tours of the bazaar, games of golf, and entertainment by a 100-piece orchestra. Swearingen said Imelda worked hard to bring business to the Philippines and "was constantly trying to promote my husband's business" there. Each time she came to Manila, she said, Imelda proudly insisted she tour historic sights, such as the island of Corregidor and the trail of the Bataan Death March. "Some people thought it was a bore, but I adored it," she said. To her mind, Filipinos loved their First Lady. "Every time we stepped off a plane, there were hundreds of people to greet her," she said. "The feeling for the President was more respect, but for her it was affection. The people of the Philippines considered her their role model."

Swearingen was so taken with the Marcoses that she did her best to help them in 1982, when they were angling to be invited for a state visit to Washington. "I wanted her to be invited at that time," she said. "It was very important for them." So she lobbied, in her own way. Dancing with Ronald Reagan at a White House affair, she said, "Did you know that Mr. Marcos was in the Bataan Death March? He told me the way he [survived] was by jumping under an alligator and breathing through a reed!" Whether or not her revelation did the trick, the Marcoses did get their invitation.

*     *     *

Despite Imelda's growing public relations problems, Marcos had trust enough in her appeal to stand her off against Benigno Aquino in elections for a new "interim assembly," to replace the old bicameral legislature.

The elections, the first since martial law was declared, came after a spate of criticism in the American media and mounting pressures for reform from the new Democratic administration of Jimmy Carter. In one instance of that pressure, in April of 1977, Carter's assistant secretary of state, Richard Holbrooke, visited Manila and was asked to join a cruise on *Ang Pangulo*. (Ambassador Sullivan was pointedly not invited.) In between some serious talk, Holbrooke enjoyed a little waterskiing—simplified by the yacht's powerful motor and a team of frogmen who helped guests to their feet—and partying, during which he joined cabinet ministers Enrile, Carlos Romulo, and Estelito Mendoza in watching Imelda sing and dance by herself almost until dawn, and long after Marcos had retired.

Holbrooke said he wanted to get the Marcoses to talk about human rights and the bases, and particularly about Aquino, who by then had spent five years in solitary confinement, where he'd undergone a religious conversion and acquired worldwide fame as a symbol of the Marcoses' abuses. The Marcos-controlled courts had charged him with murder, possession of firearms, and subversion, while Marcos had personally accused him of being both a communist and a CIA agent. At the mention of his name, Holbrooke said Imelda "got very agitated, and said he was a communist." Said Marcos, more calmly, "If we let Aquino go, you will lionize him." Holbrooke answered that he couldn't predict how Congress or the press might treat Aquino, but that the administration would not give him undue honors. The Marcoses, he said, seemed to think it over, but the former senator would remain in jail for three more years.*

---

*From his conversations with Aquino and observations of the Marcoses, Holbrooke by then was convinced that Imelda had influenced Aquino's long sentence. More generally, he blamed her as "absolutely ... the instrument of (Marcos') undoing." With a different wife, he maintained, Marcos would have been more conciliatory to the Americans. But the President wouldn't tolerate criticism of Imelda and remained to all appearances dependent on her. A procession of U.S. diplomats were as mystified as Holbrooke by that dependence. David Newsom, who followed Sullivan as U.S. ambassador, recalled an occasion that winter when Imelda suggested the United Nations General Assembly hold its meeting in Manila. "We didn't want to set that precedent; it would just be too expensive," he said. He informed Marcos of the problem, and said the President agreed, but added that it was obviously something Imelda wanted, "and could we help him find a way out?" Taken aback, Newsom said he'd try. A few days later, the deputy ambassador gave a speech complimenting the idea but adding that it needed further study. Imelda's attention having already turned to something else, her proposal died quietly.

In 1978, with negotiations pending with the United States on a potentially lucrative new bases treaty, Marcos did agree to loosen up enough to hold the spring elections, and to let Aquino run for a seat in the assembly. That led to one of the more absurd chapters of the long Marcos saga: Aquino campaigning from his jail cell, almost completely deprived of access to the pro-government media, and heading a disorganized group of challengers to a Marcos-sponsored slate led by the First Lady. Before permitting the voting, Marcos guaranteed himself one of the assembly seats, along with the posts of both prime minister and president.

Imelda had at first seemed hesitant to run. Faced with a draft-Imelda campaign in the controlled newspapers, she said, "I have no political ambitions, except to serve the people." But the *Times-Journal*, owned by her brother, printed her reply with the comment, "A dynamic achiever, the First Lady is believed to be the ideal candidate to lead her region's ticket." And Ambassador Newsom cabled Foggy Bottom that her "demure denial is a sure sign that she intends to run."

Newsom was right. Imelda accepted the "draft" days later, in a speech to government backers for which she wore a t-shirt emblazoned with the name of Marcos' newly formed political party, the KBL (its full name, in Tagalog, translated to the "New Society Party"). "I don't know how to campaign for myself, so it's up to you who drafted me to take care of me," she told them. It was a nice *palabas*: Imelda was nothing if not a campaigner. She began addressing daily street rallies, as many as nine a day under record Manila summer heat in the mid-90s. She told off-color jokes, sang love songs, and made veiled threats. She told delighted audiences that she was well aware of the current shortage of toilet paper, and knew what they were doing with her leaflets. "If you vote for our enemies, I will turn my back on you," she then told them. "I won't love you." They nodded and smiled. She advised crowds of ragged slum dwellers that "if the opposition offers you money, accept it. Any of their money is from foreigners, and since they have been milking us for more than fifty years, it's time to pay us back."

Both Marcoses, meanwhile, made full use of their patronage powers, announcing new pension rights for civil servants and new clothing allowances for teachers in the weeks before the election.

The opposition campaigned with desperate enthusiasm. Concentrating their resources, they challenged the Marcos slate only in the Metro Manila region, with twenty-one candidates to champion their new party, known as Laban (Fight). Martial law was the only real issue in the campaign, but it was a subject basic to every Filipino's way of life. Completely apart from the suppression of speech and press, the unexplained murders and torture of political detainees, there was the inescapable fact that most Filipinos had grown poorer. The ban on labor activism had encouraged economic expansion but let wages shrink. Ninety percent of all Filipino workers were paid wages that the government's own Labor Department described as "below the minimum subsistence level." The problem was partly beyond the Marcoses' control: the price of oil had skyrocketed, while chief exports, particularly sugar, had plummeted. But legions of Filipinos had come to suspect that this government's corruption was not like that of its predecessors. This time, it seemed completely out of control.

Aquino, who burned to make these points, was never allowed to leave his cell, but he had two popular surrogates in his seven-year-old daughter, Kris, and a young businesswoman named Charito Planas. "I am Kris Aquino. I am 7 years old," Kris's speeches usually began. "My father is Ninoy Aquino and I have not been able to live with him for a long time. Please help me to get him free." Her squeaky determination never failed to win sympathy. "She had absolutely no stage fright," said her mother.

Planas, plump and fiery, found particular advantage in her gender; while her male colleagues shied from what they feared would be ungallant attacks on Imelda, she felt no such constraint. "I told the people of Imelda's monumental vanity and gave examples of the impulsive mean streak behind Imelda's beautiful, graceful visage," she said. "I showed pictures [of her] with jewelry and tiaras, with huge diamond solitaires." There were striking contrasts between the two women. Unlike Imelda, Planas was highly educated, with a law degree and business background, and came from one of Manila's leading families. She enjoyed telling friends that Imelda had once wanted to marry her brother, but that her brother "did not find Imelda aggressive enough."

Neither of the Marcoses hid their wounds. Imelda was constantly in tears through the campaign, leading her husband to growl, "Everytime my wife cries, I could kill." And indeed, almost everything about the First Lady had become fair game—even including her past association with Mayor Lacson and the question of her daughter Imee's parentage. But there was never any doubt about how the campaign would end. ("It was not an election as you or I would know one," Newsom dryly observed.) There were widespread reports of ballot box-stuffing; large-scale voting by unregistered, or "flying," voters; and forging of tally sheets to suit the New Society Party's needs. Early returns showed some precincts with progovernment margins of as much as 200 to 0. And before any official returns were announced, Marcos appeared on television to declare his wife the winner—conveniently placed in the number one slot in a landslide sweep by all twenty-one New Society candidates.

The elections had been meant to signal a relaxation of the Marcos rule, but it was clear the couple had overestimated their ability to maintain control. When they allowed Aquino to make one television broadcast midway through the campaign, from a makeshift studio set up in his cell, he electrified the capital with his passionate criticism. And when they temporarily lifted the ban on political demonstrations, they unleashed wild bursts of antigovernment rallies—ten a night by the last week of the campaign—including an all-day "noise barrage" of clanging pots and pans and an hour in which Manila motorists kept their fists on their horns. At one of the rallies, some 30,000 people cheered as Marcos was burned in effigy.

The government ended by cracking down harder than ever. Immediately after election day, six opposition leaders and some 600 Filipino students, workers, and nuns were arrested as they marched in protest of the fraud. Planas, who had spent fourteen months in jail after martial law was first declared, went underground and managed to escape to the United States after Marcos' soldiers claimed to have found guns in her home.

The new repression brought on another, stronger, wave of criticism in the American press. *Newsweek* called the election a "charade," while the *Far Eastern Economic Review* said the aftermath "was like a declaration of martial law, part two." In May, more than 100 U.S. members of Congress signed a letter protesting the fraud. The Marcoses in turn became even more intransigent. In June, Imelda took off once again for Moscow, where she stayed nine days and enjoyed standard courtesies: a two-hour talk with Kosygin, an agreement to cooperate in cultural and sports activities, and a seat as a guest of honor at the Tchaikovsky music competitions. She spent her birthday there and gave her Soviet guests a party at which she passed out "Happy Birthday" t-shirts. The *Manila Bulletin* quoted her as saying that the Soviet Union had shown the world, "the noble dimensions of the maximum wholeness which man can achieve." *Newsweek* quoted her as saying, "the Soviet Union, while feared by many, may come out on top, and no one wants to be caught on the losing side."

But Imelda was still hedging her bets. With her thirty-six-member entourage, she flew straight from Moscow to New York, and from there made a side-trip to Washington, where she determined to confront her congressional critics.

She arrived full of her usual confidence, with her private television crew to tape the proceedings. She left humiliated and in tears, having failed for perhaps the first time to win over critics with her usual spirited charm. The fifteen members of Congress, all but one of whom were Democrats, were almost unanimously harsh, peppering Imelda with questions about torture, voting fraud, government nepotism and her own flirtations with the Soviets. One member of Congress said Imelda reminded him of Ngo Dinh Diem. Others had talked to Planas, who was hiding out in Maryland, and repeated her criticism.

Imelda seemed stunned. Asked whether she had spent millions on jewelry, she replied that she considered herself "the number one beggar." She spoke of her Cultural Center, her Nutrition Center, and her population campaign. She called Planas a communist. Her performance was far from convincing. "It was like talking to the Tooth Fairy," California Congressman Pete Stark complained afterward. "She never heard of the charges."

Imelda later told a U.S. State Department official that it was the most difficult meeting she had ever attended. "She seemed shaken in a way which I do not think will ultimately prove to be productive," the official noted in a cable to Manila. "There was a sad, almost tragic quality to her performance, and if, as reported, she is increasing her role and influence...it can only lead to more difficult times ahead."

The cable was prophetic. On Imelda's arrival back home, negotiations on the U.S. bases were abruptly suspended, and there were anti-American protests of youth groups in the streets of Manila, led by the First Lady's daughter Imee. "Imelda had been slapped, and she was getting hers back," said a high-ranking American diplomat. (The talks soon got back on track, however, and Marcos managed to extract a $500 million, five-year commitment in military and economic aid as "compensation" for American use of the bases.)

One month later, Imelda's potential succession once more became an issue, when Marcos floated the idea of her becoming his deputy prime minister. A small positive flurry arose in the press, but soon died, reportedly because of objections from the military, with whom she was still deeply unpopular. All else remaining equal, that should have dampened Imelda's hopes for some time. But things were to change radically within a year.

Diplomats who visited Marcos late in 1978 noted his face often appeared puffy: "He was obviously under a variety of medications," said one American emissary. After long periods in which Marcos didn't appear in public, Manila's active rumor mill began producing stories that he had been hospitalized or died. "Every time a Filipino checked into Stanford University, we'd hear it was the President," said a U.S. State Department official.

By 1979, the CIA had reported that Marcos was suffering from lupus, a disease of the immune system and kidneys. The puffiness of his face noted by visitors was most likely a side effect of corticosteroid drugs used to suppress the disease. For an intelligent health enthusiast, the potential for other side effects must have been particularly depressing: they included weight gain, cataracts, osteoporosis, and psychosis.

In 1982, when the Marcoses returned from their U.S. state visit, the palace coterie was shocked at the President's appearance. "It had all been rumors before that," said Zamora, the family attorney. "But all of a sudden, you could see he was really sick. They were moving hospital equipment into Malacanang at night, filters were being installed, and he looked weak; he was always too hot or too cold, always sniffling. Things got frantic. He was really turning sick. You could sense things were falling apart."

# 10

# DYNASTY

*Large families living in squalor strain the moral sense. Our own experience of greed, graft, and corruption has largely been the consequence of large ... families. ... Aggression comes from pressure, and population pressure, indeed, arouses the aggressive instincts of men.*
—Imelda Marcos, in a keynote address to the
First Asian Regional Conference on Family Planning,
Philamlife Auditorium, January 7, 1974

*Under martial law, everything is relative. You have to be related.*
—Manila joke, circa 1978

Family life was central to Imelda and Ferdinand Marcos, as it is in a distinctive way to most Filipinos. But in the Marcoses' case, the scruple of providing for one's heirs—and kin, in-laws, godsons, goddaughters, and highly trusted friends—became, with the opportunity of their long reign, the dream of a dynasty. That dream eventually helped cost them their rule. It stacked millions, maybe billions, of dollars onto the national debt, disheartened would-be legitimate entrepreneurs, left the poor even poorer, and pitched official credibility to a new low.

It started with a vacuum. Once Manila's leading "oligarchs" were ruined and oppositionists chased out of public office, the Marcoses installed trusted allies in their stead. Imelda's brother Kokoy won the best share of the spoils: He took over the fallen Lopezes' Meralco firm and published his newspaper, the *Times Journal*, on their printing presses. He also bought out the nation's largest land transportation company after the government drove it to desperation by stalling approval of rate hikes. The company's original owner was Corazon Aquino's increasingly outraged wing of the Cojuangco family.

Another Romualdez sibling, Alfredo, grew rich from shipping, and was said also to be involved in the $57 million jai-alai industry, which Marcos had taken over from its former "oligarch" owners. Imelda's sister Conchita for eight years handled millions of dollars in remittances to the Philippine National Bank from Filipinos working abroad. Marcos' sister, Elizabeth Marcos Keon, served several years as governor of Ilocos Norte, until the President's son, Ferdinand, Jr., took over. By one report, the President's brother, Pacifico Marcos, controlled fifty corporations.

Still, it was the doings of more distant relatives and friends, known as "cronies," that led to unprecedented criticism in the foreign press. In January 1978, soon after the President called for the assembly elections, a flurry of articles appeared in leading U.S. newspapers about "crony capitalism" and its damage to the economy. While the Philippine media remained muzzled, the government endured western scrutiny of several Marcos family favorites who had made millions of dollars from preferential government loans, contracts, or guarantees—often, it was understood, in return for a cut of the profits or a share in control of the ventures. Many of the beneficiaries had direct links to the generous Imelda, who often seemed more ready than her husband to view the treasury as a private gift stockroom. Yet the exposés also detailed what the CIA had known for years: that Marcos, as one U.S. agent described it, was "micromanaging the Philippine economy."

Among those making news was Antonio Floirendo, a trim and graying banana planter in Jordache jeans whose palatial plantation home in southern Mindanao had a swimming pool built around an artificial Niagara Falls. A frequent member of Imelda's overseas expeditions and donor to her projects, he won approval to rent Filipino convicts as cheap labor. Roberto Benedicto, Marcos' fraternity brother, was put in charge of the government-decreed sugar monopoly and the television and radio network seized from the Lopezes. Millionaire Eduardo Cojuangco, cousin to Corazon Aquino but one of Marcos' closest friends, was handed the government's coconut monopoly. The Tantoco family, close friends of Imelda, won a third Marcos-granted monopoly on duty-free imports, while Imelda's Human Settlements Ministry took over $10 million of their debts.

The man who made "crony" a catchword, however, was Herminio Disini, a frequent golfing partner of the President, who had married Dr. Inday Escolin, Imelda's cousin and physician. A stocky CPA, Disini built up a network of more than thirty companies with hundreds of millions of dollars in government loans and investments. His interests were diverse, from charter airlines to cigarette filters. But his most controversial feat was when, as local agent for Westinghouse Electric Co., he helped clinch a deal to build a $1.1 billion atomic power plant in Bataan, some 50 miles from Manila. The plant soon ran far over budget, while Disini's total commissions neared $40 million.

The parade of crony feats through the U.S. press was politically powerful stuff, especially in the early 1980s, when several of the chosen few bungled, went bankrupt, and were bailed out by the government. By 1984, at least 100 companies owned by friends of the Marcoses had failed, according to the *Washington Post*. Yet they continued to flaunt their largesse in a nation where most people survived on less than $55 a month. Their government-sponsored failures played havoc with what was left of the Philippine economy. The foreign debt had lurched from $600 million when Marcos took over to nearly $25 billion in 1983. Jaime Ongpin, a prominent Filipino executive and oppositionist, estimated as much as $7 billion had been wasted on the crony projects. The failures were fairly predictable even in 1979, yet Imelda, as usual, ignored the dark clouds when she made one of her most famous ripostes in an interview with journalist Roy Rowan. Asked how it was that so many of her relatives and in-laws had so quickly reached the top of business and government, she replied: "Sometimes you have smart relatives who can make it. My dear, there are always people who are just a little faster, more brilliant, and more aggressive."

Imelda's quote went down in memory as "Some are smarter than others," which was perhaps a fair enough condensation. And like former Senator Avelino's "What are we in power for?" it capsulized Filipinos' clearly justified and long-lived scorn for their politicians. It also came at a time when defiance was in the air: the opposition had been galvanized by the brief freedom of the 1978 elections, and "Xerox journalism" was beginning to appear on the capital's streets. One of the first, most comprehensive works was a December 1979 pamphlet called "Some are Smarter than Others," listing hundreds of large banks and businesses believed to be controlled by a dozen of the Marcoses' friends and relatives.*

---

*The Xerox journalists included anonymous executives and disenfranchised opposition politicians, among the most active of whom was Juan Frivaldo, a former provincial governor in self-exile in suburban Santa Clara, California. For years, Frivaldo kept up a barrage of freelance editorials and letters of outrage to newspapers and U.S. government offices, including the CIA, urging that they look into Kokoy Romualdez's takeover of Philippine meat marketing, Imelda Marcos' purchases of luxury speedboats, and other skul-

The cronies filled roles the Marcoses surely would have preferred for their children, who had all reached adulthood by the 1980s. But the three heirs showed little of their parents' political or business flair. Family friends tended to blame their mother most for their failures: as much as she knew they needed discipline, she couldn't help but overprotect and indulge them, and they grew up loathing any kind of responsibility. "When they were young, they seemed to have a conscience," said a Manila socialite and former intimate. "But little by little, they stopped questioning their mother....I suppose there was an open account for them. And this is where they lost their sense of values."

Bongbong, mop-haired, soft-spoken, and Oxford-educated, turned 20 in 1978. Two years later, he was elected without opposition as vice governor in Ilocos Norte, where he was given a bachelor's beachhouse with a swimming pool ringed by palm trees and a hotel lobby-sized dining room with turtle-shell chandeliers. With all that, he didn't spend much time there, preferring his friends and the discos of Manila. His major achievements in office were officially recorded as improving provincial slaughterhouses and running sports programs, and he made no secret of his aversion for his post, telling one friend, "I don't want to do a good job. If I do a good job, they will give me a bigger job." He chafed at his lack of freedom, complaining his youth had been "stolen" from him. "I asked him once, don't you like to be the president someday?" recalled another friend, Rodolfo Farinas, mayor of Ilocos Norte's provincial capital. "And he said, 'I don't want my children to turn out like me.'"

What made Bongbong behave well at all was his father, whom he held in awe and in whose presence Bongbong was known to break out in sweats. For his mother, however, he showed subtle contempt. "His father had been telling him to get a wife," said Farinas, who referred to Bongbong as "Bongets." "But Bongets told me marriage is scary, like blackmail.... You have a wife and she gets bored, she wants to travel, she wants to go shopping. It's trouble, especially if

---

duggery by those he jointly referred to as the "Octopus Gang." Shortly after the 1979 Sandinista revolution in Nicaragua, when popular rebels overthrew a similar political and economic dynasty, Frivaldo even wrote junta leader Alfonso Robelo, congratulating him on the achievement and seeking serious advice on how the Filipinos might copy it. Robelo wrote back with thanks and some Spanish generalities about how all popular sectors had participated, but gave the wistful Frivaldo no detailed plan of action he might duplicate.

one is a politician." Bongbong shunned publicity, and his only real fame came after his family fled the palace, when a videotape of a Marcos party was released, showing him wearing a flashing bow tie and leading the rest of the clan in singing, "We Are the World."

Imee, Bongbong's articulate, plump sister, took more naturally to the limelight, though she, like he, complained about the constant guards and "all these boring official things one has to go to." In 1973, she enrolled in Princeton University, where she studied Byzantine literature. She tried twice to stay in a dorm but each time had to move out because of threats to her security. Though she failed to finish her U.S. undergraduate requirements, she later got a law degree in the Philippines. A national assembly seat followed, as did director-ships of a 10-million strong political youth group and the government's experimental film program. Initially, however, Imee resisted politics, saying, "It has just too many responsibilities involved, and I'm not quite ready to shoulder any of them." She took two years off before leaving New Jersey to read romantic and sado-masochistic literature, in what she called her "decadent phase."

Imee's relationship with Imelda was complex and often stormy. "My mother and I terrorize each other," she would tell friends. Yet there was no denying how deeply Imelda influenced her. In her early teenage years, she first sought to emulate her mother, going so far as to surprise Imelda's friends by secretly dressing up in her extravagant jewelry at a beau monde gathering in Spain. Later she rebelled, taking joy in eluding her security detail as often as she could to slip away from the palace and meet friends in the city. In New Jersey, she also spoke out against martial law and palace politics, calling Malacanang a "snakepit." No doubt intentionally, her antics led to running battles with Imelda, who had high expectations for her daughter.*

In later years, it was one of Imelda's most bitter disappointments that she couldn't make an illustrious match for Imee. After her hopes to net Prince Charles fell through, she determined Imee should marry plantation owner Antonio Floirendo's son, Tony, Jr., but he eloped with a former beauty queen. A few years later, Imee would also

---

*With her father, Imee enjoyed a more constant bond. Marcos admired and encouraged her spirit and intelligence, writing in a typically non-self-effacing diary entry on May 22, 1973: "For she is me all over again: sensitive, brilliant, emotional, schizophrenic—searching, always inquiring—never content."

elope—with a man already married. It was an incident which for all its rebelliousness carried echos of her mother's youth, while also leading to one of the worst scandals of the Marcos reign.

The youngest child, Irene, was of the three the most serious, a diligent student of music and anthropology, with the temperament of "an English school mistress," according to Imee. Irene didn't complain like her siblings, but had chronic back pain, which Imee ascribed to "the angst and ennui she's been repressing all these years."

When at 22 Irene chose to marry wealthy businessman Greg "Greggy" Araneta, 35, Imelda piled onto the event all her stored-up but frustrated hopes for her other two children. Though the shy Irene might have preferred a quiet, dignified affair, Imelda again, inexorably, played to the grandstands. With the lavishness of a Hollywood mogul, she transformed the entire Ilocos Norte farming village of Sarrat (with a population of 20,000) into a fantastical rendition of a Spanish colonial town. Millions of Filipinos, most of whom lacked plumbing and adequate food, were entranced by tales of the fortunes in public funds spent on construction, renovations, decorations, food, and entertainment. Three thousand laborers, including soldiers, were flown or trucked in to work on the project. They rebuilt the local airport to accommodate international flights and built a new 250-room luxury hotel and a red brick "People's Center" where guests would share the wedding breakfast.

In the weeks before the ceremony on June 11, 1983, prominent residents reconstructed their homes at government expense, soldiers paved streets, and schoolteachers tied thousands of white toilet-paper blossoms to the trees. Fresh flowers were flown in from Honolulu, and Sarrat's crumbling, seventeenth-century church, which had already been restored a few years earlier for Marcos' sixtieth birthday, was touched up again and carpeted. An oceanliner with 500 first class cabins was moored off a China Sea beach to quarter the 180 members of the national assembly and their wives. There were more than 5000 guests from Manila and abroad, including Cristina Ford; George Hamilton's mother, Anne; the mayor of Shanghai; and the U.S. ambassador, Michael Armacost, all of whom were shuttled back and forth on a series of twenty-four special flights. The total expense of the wedding, not counting the new hotel or airport, was estimated at more than $10 million.

It was the kind of occasion on which Imelda thrived, with days packed full of urgent chores. She saw to every detail. Arriving two days before the event for a final once-over, she noticed a white house that she said stood out awkwardly in the restored barrio. She immediately ordered more workers to make the 250-mile trip from Manila and paste up ersatz red brick over the facade, "to capture the Spanish ambience."

On the morning of the wedding, cardboard fans and t-shirts were handed out, just as they had been at the wedding of Britain's Prince Charles. The fans had glossy pictures of the wedding couple and the t-shirts bore the slogan, "I love Greggy and Irene." Marcos and his wife came to the church in an enormous white Rolls Royce, amid scurrying guards with walkie-talkies and in wilting, 100-plus degree heat. Imelda wore a terno of flounced ivory silk and carried a matching parasol. Villagers climbed trees to catch a glimpse of the bride, with her $20,000 ecru gown and 20-foot veil studded with diamonds. "I hope you will have several children, despite the First Lady's family planning program," Marcos ebulliently toasted his daughter.

There were five tiered wedding cakes, each the height of a tall Filipino, and one in its own gazebo, surrounded by white gauze. During the three days of celebrations the Philippine Philharmonic orchestra played Tchaikovsky; government jets flew in delicacies and Dom Perignon; and movies, concerts, and variety shows played in five outlying villages. Until the last minute, when self-consciousness seemed to take hold, there were plans to broadcast the ceremony live on national television. Even then, the bacchanals left such a deep impression on the native farming families of the transformed village that they later read divine retribution in an earthquake that came a year after the wedding, calling the cause, "the Marcos fault." Others, apparently, were in no mood for jokes. On the eve of the extravaganza, an employee of Imelda's Human Settlements Ministry in Davao, Mindanao, reported that her only child, who had suddenly fallen ill, had died after being rejected by hospital authorities. The reason was her family's failure to pay a deposit of 300 pesos, or about $28.

*       *       *

The arid tobacco- and garlic-growing region that hosted Irene's wedding had long been known as "Marcos-land." By 1983, it had a Marcos University, a Marcos highway, and a town named Marcos, with neighborhoods dubbed Ferdinand, Imelda, and Pacifico, for the President's brother. In Marcos' birthplace, the town of Batac, Imelda built a Marcos Museum, on Marcos Avenue, wherein were stored seven life-sized plaster-of-Paris likenesses of her husband, as well as replicas of his claimed war medals and his favorite faded trousers from grade school.

One might have thought, in Sarrat or Batac, that the Marcoses had reached the peak of their tribute to themselves. Yet there was still room to climb, as was proven in "Imelda-land," on Leyte, and particularly at the Santo Niño shrine. There, near the spot where Imelda said her childhood home once stood, she constructed a grand, two-story red brick and white grillwork mansion in the style of a colonial museum. Technically a shrine to the infant Jesus (a Christchild statue indeed stood on the ground floor, in front of a star-shaped display of flashing disco lights), the structure was more accurately a shrine to its own creator.

Imelda's life story was described in the 18 guest rooms on the ground floor, in a series of intricate dioramas, one in each room, becoming larger and more brightly lit as the story progressed. The first showed Imelda as a young girl grating coconuts on the floor of her family's simple home. Next she appeared as a teenage beauty queen, standing on the beach in a Botticelli Venus-like pose, while the face of her future husband stared down from a dream bubble over her head. Later scenes showed Imelda in presidential campaigns, at the first oath-taking, and in Libya, shaking hands with Qaddafi. But the last diorama was by far the most impressive, an ecstatic culmination of glamour and good works. In the center of a vivid sunny lanscape, she appeared in a pink terno, smiling down at a small group of adoring peasants. All around her were scattered symbols of her contributions to the New Society: her Cultural Center, her Metro Manila Aides and her housing projects, known by their Tagalog acronym, BLISS. To one side stood her husband, smiling at her fondly. To the other was a small group of foreigners, all in apparent states of admiring rapture: Cristina Ford, George Hamilton, Van Cliburn, and Ronald Reagan.

\*     \*     \*

Only one monument to the Marcos dynasty was left unfinished by the time they fled Manila in 1986. On a scenic mountain ridge in

Taytay, 12 miles east of downtown Manila, eight enormous holes were left in the ground—gaping reminders of what was to have been the Basilica of the Holy Infant. Construction plans had included a 29-foot statue of the infant Jesus, fourteen chapels, and a 1600-foot-long sanctuary. But more important, the basilica, on land purchased by Imelda's Cultural Center foundation, had been meant to host the Marcoses' grand remarriage ceremony on their twenty-fifth anniversary in 1979. It was also to be the receptacle of their tombs. Those grand plans were scuttled, however, when Pope John Paul II refused to officiate at the remarriage, even after Imelda flew to Rome for a personal appeal.

The silver anniversary was instead held at Malacanang Palace, starting at 7 p.m. on a May evening and ending twelve hours later. It featured 500 guests, including a planeload of European royalty, music by Manila's symphony orchestra, and dancing until sunrise the next day. Father James Donelan presided over the ceremony. Then he quit the palace for good.

"I looked down and I saw this entire row of European garbage sitting in front of me," he said painfully, eight years later. "And I realized, there were just too many things going wrong. The cronies, the corruption, the human rights abuses. I suppose I had thought I could have had some influence. But too many things were going wrong."

More and more people had been coming to Donelan's university office to tell him about torture. Parents, in tears, would describe what they had seen when they visited their children in jail. Their stories were often so horrifying that the priest at first told himself they were exaggerations, but the tales soon became too repetitive to ignore. Visiting human rights researchers were chronicling the same atrocities. Amnesty International counted 230 "disappearances" alone from 1975 to 1980, while also collecting reports of tortures including electrical shocks, squeezing testicles with pliers, and pouring vinegar and pepper on eyes. The torture and killings in Manila were widely blamed on the spy network Marcos had set up under General Ver. Rural civilians, meanwhile, were terrorized by the paramilitary Civilian Home Defense Forces.

Donelan had hoped he might reach Marcos through Imelda, but to his despair found she wouldn't even listen. Carter Administration officials by then had essentially dismissed the First Lady as a "hardliner" on human rights, which Donelan directly confirmed. When he tried to broach the subject, Imelda simply began to talk and wouldn't stop, and wouldn't hear of interruptions. She would go on for several hours at a time, a technique she had discovered would numb most adversaries into apathy. "That was her defense," said the priest. "It was something you had to see to believe. I've seen her start talking at 3 p.m. and not stop until 3 a.m."

Shortly before the silver anniversary, Donelan had a particularly disturbing visit from the father of a former Ateneo University activist named Edgar Jopson. The priest had deeply admired Jopson, a top-rate scholar in his field of management engineering and a two-term president of the student union. "He was a real hero, back when I was dean; intelligent, an idealist, and a leader," he recalled. Jopson had also led some of the student demonstrations in the First Quarter Storm, and on graduating, joined what Donelan called the "real left"—the New People's Army (NPA). He was eventually captured and jailed, and his father had come to tell Donelan that he had seen clear marks of torture when he visited his son. But Jopson soon escaped, and neither the priest nor his father heard from him for about two more years.

Jopson had been on Donelan's mind when he looked out over his Malacanang pulpit. The contrast of the idealistic young man's sufferings with the Marcoses' self-indulgence shocked him out of his hope that if he just held on a little longer he could influence Imelda to be a force for change. Most of his colleagues had long ago joined the opposition, and Donelan had felt their resentment each time he drove off in his Toyota to visit the palace. But at the same time he felt a special burden: if he left, no one else would even try. Yet finally he came to share his colleagues' cynicism. While he never believed Imelda directly caused the abuses, he found her tolerance just as immoral. "There was just no way I was going to get through to her," he thought.

About a year or so later, the priest got word about Jopson. He'd been killed in a raid by constabulary troops in Davao City in Mindanao. Twenty-one soldiers had surrounded his hideout, cornering him and three other NPA members. Only Jopson had been killed. "It was an execution," Donelan said sadly.

For all his good intentions, all Donelan did was to stop socializing with and writing speeches for Imelda. Other clergymembers were doing much more. Inspired by Latin America's "liberation theology," Filipino priests and nuns were going to the countryside and working, in the gap left by government, to improve the lives of the poorest of the poor. Many grew to feel a bond with the only other organized group who seemed to share the same ideal, the members of the NPA. Some went so far as to join them. Years later, Donelan spoke wistfully of those colleagues. His years of engagement with Imelda had changed little, he conceded, though he, maybe more than anyone, had had the potential to influence her. Whether his own lack of will or her unyielding defenses caused his failure, he never knew. But once he finally left, she never phoned him again, and never really seemed to notice he was gone.

# II

# THE CROSSROADS OF THE WORLD

*. . . Crazed with avarice, lust and rum,*
*New York, thy name's Delirium.*
> —Byron Rufus Newton, Tax Commissioner
> for the City of New York, 1906

In popular memory, Imelda Marcos' name may forever be tied to the image of shoes. But shoes—even 1060 pairs of them—don't begin to capture her ambition, her romantic spirit, or even her greed. Not when another symbol at hand does it all so well. That symbol is New York City's Crown Building.

Towering like a twenty-six-story tiered wedding cake, its gilded crest overlooking Manhattan's ritziest corner (Tiffany's, the Plaza, the horse-drawn buggies trotting up Central Park South), the Crown Building at 730 Fifth Avenue stood for everything Imelda ever wanted, and had for a time. She admired it for its "old world charm" and its art-deco black marble lobbies, but adored it for its location, rising over what she called "the crossroads of the world." She loved to drive past it with acquaintances not in the know, point it out and declare, "Now, that's a beautiful building! Who owns it, I wonder?"

Bought in 1981, and later valued at $51 million, the Crown Building was the star attraction of a New York investment portfolio Imelda methodically assembled after the fall of her friend the Shah of Iran encouraged both Marcoses to stash more funds abroad. It was also, in the best tragic hero tradition, the key to what brought her down. "It was almost as if, being colonized all those years, she turned around and tried to colonize us," mused Mahlen Perkins, one of the

185

American attorneys later assigned by the Aquino government to try to recoup the investments.

Imelda had delighted in owning pieces of four corners of New York, a well-rounded portfolio, as she saw it, in the city she regarded as the center of civilization. Besides the Crown Building, she had claims to a $50 million office building at 200 Madison Avenue; a $71 million skyscraper at 40 Wall Street and the $60 million Herald Center mall, at 34th and Broadway, all bought between 1982 and 1984. In a system long used by drug barons and other corrupt third world leaders, but which the Marcoses raised to an art form, the ownership of all four properties was ingeniously disguised by "shell" partnerships, front men and women of well-compensated (or terrorized) loyalty, and corporations based in such havens of tax freedom and secrecy as Panama and the Dutch Antilles. Lastura NV of Curaçao (later changed to Canadian Land Company) bought the Crown Building; Voloby Ltd. of the British Isles (later changed to Herald Center Ltd.) bought Herald Center; Glockhurst Corp. NV of Curaçao bought 200 Madison, and NYLAND Ltd., also of Curaçao, bought 40 Wall Street.

Along the way, the corporate name changes helped cloud the question of ownership. But two more layers of secrecy were already in place. Each of the offshore corporations was owned by a trio of Panamanian firms—nine trios in all, since one of them owned both Herald Center Ltd. and Glockhurst Corp. These in turn were technically owned by blank or "bearer" shares that belonged to whoever held them. Nowhere did either of the Marcoses' names appear on a document pertaining to ownership of the properties. Only one of the Panamanian firms' names—Excelencia Investment, Inc.—was any kind of giveaway.

Thus safeguarded, Imelda's privacy was threatened only by what computer scientists like to call human error, and for a few years, she and her aides and her Manhattan realtors, Joseph and Ralph Bernstein, managed to avoid it. But keeping secrets was something Imelda could never do for long, and she eventually began to take risks so grand they raised the question of whether she really wanted to be caught. In Center Moriches, Long Island, she made sweeping inspections of her 10-acre estate, called Lindenmere; she held luncheons prepared by her Washington embassy's staff in the sixteen-bedroom mansion, and had her picture taken on the front porch with the general contractor, Ernest Hoffstaeter, who later showed his copy to reporters. She visited the estate no less than eight times, always with a group of thirty to fifty people, and on about ten other occasions her friends Cristina Ford and Anne Hamilton, George's mother, showed up alone without prior notice to spend a night or two. Soon after she bought the Crown Building, she had it refurbished at the attention-getting cost of nearly $15 million, which paid, among other things, for imitation-suede wallpaper and 1363 ounces of 23-karat gold leaf to regild its facade.

Once, in December of 1982, after a party at Imelda's townhouse on East 66th Street (the former Philippine consulate, converted to her private pied-à-terre), the First Lady hopped into her black limousine and brought her entourage and secret service escorts on an impromptu midnight tour of 40 Wall Street, a 70-story, spired skyscraper that is the second tallest building in Manhattan's financial district. After standing and gazing at it for some fifteen minutes from a vantage point across the street, Imelda finally murmured, "It's a nice building. I'm kind of proud of it."

By then she had grown cavalier about her free-spending trips to New York, but she was leaving a growing line of stunned witnesses in her wake. One who would later recount his experiences to Aquino government investigators was Oscar Carino, who in the 1980s was Manhattan branch manager of the Philippine National Bank. In a secret sealed affidavit dictated in Manila in April of 1986, Carino, who called himself Imelda's "protégé," suggested she had used the bank as a personal account, possibly from as early as 1968. After Carino joined the New York branch, he said he would get calls from one of the First Lady's personal secretaries, Fe Gimenez or Vilma Bautista, or sometimes from Imelda herself, telling him to disburse bank funds to people or corporations or the secretaries' private accounts at other banks. For convenience, Carino also created his own firm, Oscarmen Holdings, Ltd., making himself president, and using the firm's account at the Republic Bank to ease the unauthorized transactions. (Recovered documents later showed that more than $9 million of Imelda's New York disbursements, much of which went to pay for the overseas properties, was later charged to the Philippine Intelligence Fund with the approval of Ferdinand Marcos.)

Carino said he sometimes was also tapped to give the Marcoses business advice. In the fall of 1981, he said, the couple asked his thoughts about the potential for the Crown Building, which he gathered they were interested in buying. The conversation showed that Ferdinand Marcos most likely knew of the investment from its earliest stage. Still, palace aides universally and consistently spoke of the New York properties as "hers."*

Among upper-class Filipinos, the line between the Marcoses' friends and enemies was never so sharp as to prevent the free flow of information. There were so few families that "counted," and so many ties between them that each side almost always had a good idea of the other's doings. One wealthy investor who for years was a trusted broker of the Marcoses' overseas investments liked to speak of Manila's "Janus-faced society," offering himself as an example. While he lived mostly in the United States, he kept up neighborly relations "just in case" on trips back home with the New People's Army (NPA) members camped around his province. He also often hosted dinners for close relatives prominent in the opposition. Information was constantly traded back and forth in such ways, maddening the Marcoses and high-ranking rebel and opposition leaders, but ensuring that their mid-level "technocrats" and fighters in the field knew the score.

Given that love of gossip and Imelda's indiscretions, it wasn't long before oppositionists in Manila, San Francisco, Washington, and New York had a good idea of most of Imelda's properties. Realtors, bankers, and government records provided the documentation they lacked, and a scandal over the properties broke out after June of 1985, when I and two colleagues at the *San Jose Mercury News* in California, Lewis Simons and Pete Carey, tracked down and described investments by the Marcoses and eight of their "cronies," in a series of articles titled "Hidden Billions." Philippine newspapers freed by the "lifting" of martial law in 1981 reprinted the series, renaming it, "Hidden Wealth," and soon an impeachment motion was filed in the Philippine parliament charging Marcos with "plundering the nation's wealth." The motion was squashed by the ruling New Society Party (KBL), but the scandal persisted, leading to more American news reports, particularly a detailed follow-up in the *Village Voice*, and eventually a U.S. congressional investigation. The foreign pressures eventually pushed Marcos to his ill-fated call for new elections in the fall of 1985.

---

*Carino consistently declined to speak to reporters who heard hints of his unusual role. When I reached him unexpectedly by a lobby phone at his luxury condominium in New York in the spring of 1985, he stammered, "This is very unpleasant!" and refused to say anything more. Soon afterward, he accepted a post as Philippine ambassador in Toronto. Carino later insisted that his affidavit be sealed, citing concern for his safety. But the details of his own involvement had long been grist for Manila's gossip mills.

\*     \*     \*

In December, at the height of those pressures, Imelda agreed to an interview in Malacanang Palace. She received me in her music room, sitting below a life-sized portrait of her in younger days, rising from a clam-shell and swathed in an aquamarine mist. She spoke nearly without interruption for the next three hours, across a small table which held a vase full of roses and the largest microphone I had ever seen.

"It is very simple character assassination," she declared. "Money has never been my obsession. When the President became president, he put a trust fund for me and the family so that all of our time and our obsession will be to serve the general good for people and country. And what little modest wealth we had we put it in the Marcos Foundation to service deprived children who want a better education."

She wore a vermilion dress with a deep v-cut neckline, pearls and diamonds at her ears, and a small jeweled Philippine flag pin on her breast. By 1985, she had lost the winsome poise and clarity of syntax of her days on the campaign trail, and she rambled in a hoarse voice that alternately suggested sorrow and giddy resolve. Yet she still looked stunning and sounded passionate. She beat her lacquered nails on her breast, saying, "My conscience is clear. If I were corrupt, it would show on my face." She counted her accomplishments of two decades: the new hotels, the Heart Center, the Cultural Center. She then took twenty minutes to draw a map of the world, making her long-lived argument that the Philippines was at the strategic center of the world, and slowly penning in the names of nations—Uruguay, Indonesia, Pakistan—as I gently but vainly protested that I saw her point.

We went back and forth about the buildings. "It is so mundane," she complained, "when here we are, so transcendent." Asked why, then, her name had appeared on a court document linking her with a Long Island estate, she shook her head sadly, saying, "There are many things you can't understand in this world." She then brightened, and added with a Shirley Temple smile, "There are also miracles in this world."

Finally, she sighed heavily and said, "Well, First Ladies have their uses too, to be some kind of buffer for the President. If you didn't have a sense of humor here you would be dead. Let us not wallow in this difficulty. There's so much that can be done. History will be much kinder to me. Once all the passions and emotions will have died down, they will know, this was my first concern: Man. It's a beautiful world. We have some little problems, and they'll be cleared up."

As it turned out, Imelda's real estate investments paled next to the money her husband had been sending to Swiss banks—at least $1.5 billion, according to one suit filed by the Philippine government. But just as the New York properties carried symbolic weight for Imelda, they were powerful symbols for her people, evoking special outrage and making it, finally, impossible to clear up the "little problems."

The paper trail that ended her reign had started with a lawsuit filed in Suffolk County, Long Island—the first tear in the corporate veil thrown over the investments. It was the single instance in which Imelda's name appeared on a document, since the suit was aimed at her, and something at least temporarily out of her control. Before *San Jose Mercury News* reporter Pete Carey came upon it, it had not previously been reported anywhere.

In the suit, New York investor Pablo E. Figueroa, a Filipino doctor, said that he and Imelda and other business partners had bought the Long Island Lindenmere property with plans to expand it into a $19 million luxury resort. Figueroa held a 10 percent share in a firm set up for that purpose and called Luna 7. But Imelda abandoned the plan, the suit said, transferred Lindenmere to another corporation, and began to convert the property into her private estate. In the process, Figueroa claimed, she failed to pay him $1 million she had promised as his share in the deal. A second lawsuit, with a nearly identical complaint, was later found to have been filed by another partner, Augusto M. Camacho, a Filipino architect who also owned 10 percent of Luna 7.

Both cases were settled out of court soon after they became public, and neither the attorneys nor the plaintiffs would discuss them with reporters. But both suits had contained two bald sentences that lingered in the minds of Filipino and American readers. Imelda, the plaintiffs said, "does business in New York state systematically and continuously [including] extensive real estate purchasing, improving, developing, and managing." Moreover, they charged, she had hired "agents, representatives, and/or nominees to keep hidden her personal direct participation and involvement."

The agents in question made valiant efforts to keep up their pretenses. On one occasion, Pete Carey called Vilma Bautista, Imelda's personal secretary, at her efficiency apartment on Manhattan's west side and asked why she was listed as the agent for four luxury condominiums on Fifth Avenue, worth nearly $1 million in all and registered to offshore corporations. She denied knowing anything about them. "This could be another Vilma Bautista," she ventured. Reminded that her telephone number was listed on the deed, she giggled and answered, "There are so many names, so many numbers."

Court papers in the Lindenmere suit identified the law firm of New York realtor and attorney Joseph Bernstein as representing Imelda's firm, Luna 7. And in 1986, Bernstein and his brother Ralph, founders of New York Land Co., admitted to their real estate transactions for Imelda in testimony before a U.S. congressional committee. In a 1985 interview, however, Joe Bernstein denied having known the First Lady. "I wish I did," he said. "Everybody thinks I do.... Send her my way."

Young (in 1981, Joe was 32 and Ralph 23) and aggressive, the Bernsteins were tax haven experts who had begun to build careers helping the world's ultrarich get richer. Joe Bernstein, owlish behind thick octagonal spectacles, took pride in having coined the phrase "Dutch Sandwich" to describe one type of corporate shell. The brothers' Philippine experience dated from childhood: Ralph was born in Manila and Joseph learned to speak Tagalog before he learned English. Their uncle, Jack Nasser, was a textile manufacturer with offices in Manila and with long ties to the Marcos family. By one report, Nasser introduced Joe Bernstein to Blue Lady Glyceria "Glecy" Tantoco, one of Imelda's closest associates, who always wore dark glasses and whose nickname fit her icy demeanor. Tantoco brought the Bernsteins to Imelda. "She was a mean person," said a Bernstein aide who worked with her. "She had the image of a woman who could whip slaves."

Tantoco, whose husband, Bienvenido, was Philippine Ambassador to the Vatican, had for years been profiting from her friendship with Imelda. Owner of the pricey Rustan's chain of Philippine department stores, as well as duty-free shops throughout Manila, she would fly on shopping trips with the First Lady through New York, Rome, and Paris, stocking her stores free of millions of dollars in customs charges. She also bought artwork, jewelry, and clothes for Imelda, charging substantial commissions each time according to Imelda's other friends. Tantoco became the front for many if not all of Imelda's New York purchases. Though it had yet to be proven in 1988, Marcos aides alleged she held the blank "bearer" shares of the Panamanian owner companies and pocketed commissions of about $5 million each on the four buildings.

As the Bernsteins later testified before the House Subcommittee on Asian and Pacific Affairs, they eventually purchased $181 million in commercial real estate for the Marcoses. Joe Bernstein said Marcos had taken him aside in April of 1982, during a party in Manila, to ask him how to avoid U.S. taxes on the Crown Building. In other meetings, Bernstein said, Marcos asked him about drafting trust agreements for anonymous beneficiaries whom Bernstein assumed to be the Marcos children. And in the same month, the President signed a "declaration of trust," giving Joe Bernstein authority to act on his behalf in matters regarding the Lastura Corporation, the holding firm for the Crown Building. The handwritten declaration, on the stationery of the Manila Peninsula Hotel where the two had met, was found in Malacanang after the Marcos' departure, and became one of the single most crucial documents—the "smoking gun," as Representative Stephen Solarz would call it—in unraveling their financial network.

While Marcos remained in the shadows, Imelda showed an obvious, constant interest in the New York properties. From 1981 to 1984, she met with Joseph Bernstein two or three times a year to discuss them. She used code names for the properties and agents in telexes that went back and forth from Manila: the Crown Building was code-named "Ferragamo," for a favored shoe designer; 200 Madison was called "Midtown Cement"; Joe Bernstein was called "Esquire"; and Tantoco, "Saturn." Imelda, naturally, was "Excelencia." But "Excelencia" was the first to drop the subterfuge. Early in her professional relationship with Bernstein, over dinner at a New York restaurant called the Sign of the Dove, she informed her new friend that she controlled a Swiss bank account with $120 million in it. To prove it, he said, "She began pulling out a bank statement and waving it around. It's kind of hard to forget that."

In 1985, after the lawsuit linking Imelda to the properties came to light, Marcos sent his trusted aide Zamora to New York to try to "salvage the situation," as Zamora phrased it. He was to work alongside the President's chief financial adviser, the MIT-educated Manila banker Rolando C. Gapud. "From that point, all of the major purchases were cleared with Mr. Gapud, and never reported to Mrs. Marcos," said Zamora. "If we did, it was a courtesy." Zamora finally also tried to sell the Bernsteins the four Manhattan buildings, which he called "a mistaken investment."*

*          *          *

Wealth has been leaving the Philippines ever since natives traded their gold for iron. In sending their money overseas, especially in the panicked months following the 1983 killing of Benigno Aquino, the Marcoses differed only in degree from many other upper-class Filipinos, who together looted their country of as much as $10 billion in the last years of the regime, according to Filipino economists. Whatever their political differences, these leading families shared a profound distrust in the Philippines' stability, and acting on that distrust helped prove it right. By 1985, capital flight was gouging the remains of the Philippine economy.†

Marcos repeatedly denied that he or Imelda had any investments in the United States, but professed concern about the "hidden wealth" of

---

*The Bernsteins were interested in buying, and offered $235 million for all four properties. As 1986 began, Gapud had promised to relay their offer to the Marcoses, and at the time it must have seemed a reasonable solution. Not only was word leaking out, but properties had long been in trouble. Highly leveraged to begin with, they had begun sucking up money, largely due to a series of tactical errors made earlier by the Bernsteins. Remodeling of the ten-story Herald Center, for instance, which Imelda had envisioned as an upscale boutique emporium, had run a shocking $26 million over budget. Imelda tried to fire the Bernsteins in July 1985, but was dissuaded by her fear that they might publicly contest it. When the time came to buy, however, the Bernsteins stalled, lacking the cash, and within a few months, the properties were embroiled in political struggles and even further out of their reach.

†Defense Minister Enrile, Energy Minister Geronimo Velasco, and coconut czar Eduardo Cojuangco were among the most prominent Filipinos found to have owned significant properties overseas. But one of the most interesting investors was Nemesio I. Yabut, a former police officer who in 1985 had been mayor for fourteen years of Makati, Manila's Wall Street. A devout Marcos loyalist, Yabut employed thugs to terrorize the district's voters during elections. Early one evening that spring, I located him at his $520,000 pink stucco home in San Francisco's exclusive St. Francis Woods district. He opened the door dressed in his pajamas and bathrobe and invited me in to have coffee, while eight stocky Filipino men in dark suits, their hands stuck in their pockets, fidgeted meaningfully around the table. In the course of the next hour, Yabut confirmed real estate records showing he owned not only the two-story home, which was in his wife's name, but a $900,000 apartment building, two condominiums, and the Old Clam House restaurant. "But I'm only a lowly mayor," he added. "I have very little money....I'm small fry." Like most other Filipino investors, Yabut worried over the consequences of publicity about his U.S. holdings, but he assured me that he had done nothing illegal, and had not neglected to pay his American taxes. "I remember the story of Al Capone," he said, grinning. "Al Capone was never convicted of anything but tax evasion."

other leading politicians and executives. He ordered his justice minister, Estelito Mendoza, to investigate, and Mendoza had such "cronies" as Enrile, banana magnate Antonio Floirendo, and entrepreneur Herminio Disini cowering for weeks. Marcos was specifically exempted from the probe, but the questions continued to plague him and his wife. As usual, the taint stuck more to Imelda than her husband, but she managed to maintain her customary cheer.

As 1985 ended, the couple threw their annual New Year's Eve party at Malacanang. Fred Schieck, the Manila director of the U.S. Agency for International Development (AID), was one of the guests, and he caught Imelda's eye at a moment well past midnight, as festivities were winding down. The First Lady was performing a routine holiday chore, handing out 100-peso notes to a long line of servants from a bag held by Vilma Bautista. Seeing Schieck watching, she winked, pointed at the bag, and merrily called out, "Look! The hidden wealth!"

# 12

# IMELDA YEARS

*We must be concerned with the post-Marcos situation.*
—Imelda Marcos during a meeting with
    Assistant Secretary of State John Holdridge,
    September 1982

Lupus is a slow but steady killer, its weapons rebellious antibodies spawned by the victim's own immune system. Instead of defending from disease, these antibodies go on the attack, gradually destroying the body's tissues and organs. Thus lupus became a particularly ironic fate for Ferdinand Marcos, whose best talent was cultivating loyalties.

The disease is capricious, varying targets and tactics in flare-ups and remissions in its course of several years. But it always wears away the kidneys, clogging and straining them with the abnormal blood cells it spawns. Slowly, erratically, and agonizingly, lupus plagued Marcos beginning in at least the middle of 1979. In the next seven years—until the night the sickly President and his family were chased into exile—Imelda had her most profound impact on the Philippines.

"By November of 1985, she was effectively running the government," said Henry Byroade, who made several visits to Manila once his tenure as ambassador ended. His assessment was only partly true. Imelda never held sway over the army, which made that point decisively by overthrowing her the following February. Moreover, there was never a time when Imelda had sole access to Marcos. Even at his most ill, he would also see Gapud, his financial advisor, and the ever-loyal Ver. But as early as 1979, one classified U.S. intelligence study found Imelda was "functioning increasingly as the head of government." And her clout grew tremendously from that point on.

Like President Woodrow Wilson's wife, Edith, who tended her spouse for several weeks after his stroke, Imelda gained passive powers. She screened her husband's visitors, made or canceled appointments, and affected policy by choosing what he might postpone or ignore. But she was much more than Marcos' caretaker. She called cabinet meetings, helped plan election strategy, and continued to serve at least nominally as governor of Metro Manila, national assembly delegate, and Human Settlements Minister.

Just as quickly as she was gaining power, however, Imelda was losing her grip on reality. A journalist had once described Imelda's friend Jiang Quing as "driven by demons"; of Imelda, *Rolling Stone* magazine remarked in 1985 that she was "crazy as a rat in a coffee can." "She was a spacewoman," said a high-level U.S. intelligence official who dealt with her often in those years. "She would talk and talk at you, and by the time you'd try to interrupt, she had said so many things wrong that it was just no use. Sometimes she'd go on for so long and it would be so insane that you would wonder, why am I here?"

Seers frequented the palace in those years, holding seances and making prophesies. One prediction that Imelda held dear said that the next Philippine president would be a woman, who would become the "spiritual center of Asia." Yet there were also more disturbing predictions, warnings of violence sparked by "negotiators in white suits"—though Imelda could not have known then that Aquino would return to Manila dressed in white. Sol Vanzi, her former press aide who had stayed close to the palace, remembered reading Imelda's palm one night in the late 1970s, at the end of a long party aboard *Ang Pangulo,* and being dumbstruck by Imelda's questions. The first thing Imelda had wanted to know, as she sat before Vanzi in her third change of outfits that evening—a brilliant red dress with ruby jewelry, which had followed a green dress with emeralds after a white dress with diamonds—was, "Will I ever be poor again?"

Vanzi studied the soft, pale hand, its curving nails painted in Imelda's trademark oxblood red with tiny white crescents.

"Ma'am, you will be poorer but still rich," she answered.

"Will I die here in Manila?" came the next question. Its answer was even more obscure.

"Ma'am, you'll be coming and going."

Then, finally, "Will I die violently or peacefully?"

"You'll be surrounded by violence," Vanzi began, studying Imelda's blank face as the words sank in. But at that moment, they both saw Marcos approaching, and Imelda burst back into her bubbling party mode, while Vanzi was left wondering over her former boss's broodings.

An undercurrent of mysticism runs through many everyday affairs in the Philippines. That perhaps made it not so striking that planners of Malacanang social events quickly adapted to the First Lady's superstitious tastes. "It was easier to get things done if you played the numbers game," said the Marcoses' attorney, Zamora. "For example, making reservations, you made sure the list reached seven—if you had six, why not throw in a seventh? If there were ten segments to a parade, why not make it eleven? It didn't harm anybody, and after a while, you'd forget you were pandering to superstition."

A mystic particularly close to the palace for a time was a man in his late twenties, known as the "Bionic Boy," who, it was said, could read messages without looking at them and dial telephones without touching them. At one point in 1978, the presidential security command was persuaded to use the Boy to try to track down New People's Army (NPA) leaders. Squinting behind his thick spectacles, he claimed readily to have visualized a leading rebel suspect checking in at the capital's Intercontinental Hotel. A full SWAT team promptly descended on the room the Boy designated, to the terror of the lone occupant, a middle-aged Singaporean executive.

Spiritual advisors were also called in for an emergency exorcism after one of Imelda's rushed construction jobs went awry. The First Lady had commissioned a new film center to be built on the bayfront alongside her other showcase projects. But the history of the project became one of the harshest indictments against her. First, tens of thousands of squatters were forced to move. Then, as the center was being rushed to completion, the structure collapsed, killing sixty-four of the workers. The disaster was later blamed on both Imelda's usual impatience and substandard work by a politically well-connected contractor. When the center finally opened in 1982, there were rumors that it was haunted. Two security guards died under mysterious circumstances, and the projection screens clattered to the floor on opening night. It was at that point that Imelda called for the exorcism, by a specially trained priest, after which the center's programs continued, apparently without further problems.

In contrast to Imelda, Marcos' public image remained sedate and scholarly, yet there were signs he was every bit as interested in the psychic goings-on. In Marcos' diaries, he writes of his "strange capacity to receive messages," the "clairvoyance" he believed saved his life on various occasions, and "the separation of my spirit from my body on occasions, of extreme pain." Local newspapers reported that he was making frequent trips to Baguio to see a man named Jun Labo, one of the Philippines' most famous faith healers. Labo, like others of his school, claimed to perform elaborate surgery with his bare hands and without incisions. Marcos also warmly welcomed followers of the Maharishi Mahesh Yogi, who in 1984 bought a controlling interest in Manila's University of the East, the country's largest university. In a speech to sect members, the President vigorously endorsed what he called "the scientifically tested and proven technology of the unified field" and declared it a "great honor" to have been appointed "founding father of the age of enlightenment in the Philippines." (Imelda was appointed "founding mother.")

Still it was Imelda, in public and private, who continued to distinguish herself in the field of eccentricities. One of her most memorable feats was her entertainment in January 1982 of a visiting delegation from the National Academy of Sciences. The small team of distinguished scholars had come to the Philippines to study ways of conserving firewood. They were summoned to the palace peremptorily just before noon as they were preparing to head out to the countryside to inspect some ipil-ipil trees. Dressed to troop through the forest, in sneakers and blue jeans, they were ushered into a foyer filled with aristocratic-looking Filipinos lounging about in evening clothes, a tableau that, for Rand Corporation consultant Guy Pauker, a team member, recalled what Versailles might have looked like under Louis XIV. Imelda had planned a banquet for 120, and as Pauker and his mystified colleagues were led to the long head table to sit beside her, they heard musicians wearing barong tagalogs strike up violins. There was champagne, red and white wine, and brandy, and a series of entertainments that began with a parade of exquisite young Filipina models and included native dancers leaping over bamboo sticks. Then Imelda, "giggling like a shy ingenue," as Pauker remembered, sang a few songs in Tagalog.

Trying to shake off his sense of unreality, Pauker finally apologized to Imelda for having worn a safari suit to what appeared to be a state occasion. "She fluttered her eyelashes at me and said, 'You are a beautiful man. It doesn't matter what you wear,'" the retired scientist recalled in 1987, adding, "at that point, I suppose I really should have fallen in love with her."

By 5 p.m., the party seemed to be ending, but the academy team leader insisted on discussing the scientists' mission. The scientists and First Lady filed into the cabinet room, where Imelda snapped her fingers, and servants rushed in with a blackboard and video cassette recorder. "The poor devil started again about the ipil-ipil trees," said Pauker, referring to the team leader, "but it was no use. She started talking and wouldn't stop until 8 p.m." At that point, Pauker started taking notes. His records showed that Imelda drew a circle on the blackboard, erased part of it and, pointing, declared to the scholars before her, "These are the cosmic forces surrounding the planet." Then, pointing again: "Here's where the Philippines are." Pointing once more: "Here's a gap, right over the Philippines, a black hole where the forces come down, and that's why we have such strong faith healers here."

That apparently was the debut of one of Imelda's most notorious theories, but she later expounded on it for other audiences. By 1983, she was prevailing on the CIA station chief in Manila to tell President Reagan that the "hole in the stratosphere" directly over the Philippines would be the perfect place in which to operate the Strategic Defense Initiative, or "star wars" system.

Armed forces Captain Ricardo Morales, a tall 29-year-old with preppy good looks and a bashful smile, came to know Imelda's oddities first-hand, after he was selected in 1982 as one of her two chief bodyguards. By then, she was sleeping less than three hours a night, and it was not unusual for her guards to be awakened in the predawn hours with the announcement that she seemed to be preparing to leave the palace. "She would suddenly dress up, and do her hair, and so of course we'd dress up, too, and wonder where she was going," he said. "But then she wouldn't go anywhere. She'd just wander through the halls, looking at her pictures. She was like a little girl, like that...but also a little bit scary."

There was something childlike, too, in how Imelda treated her husband. Though they still often quarreled, she had never really lost her regard for him. She called him "Dente," short for "presidente," and on Sunday afternoons would cook his simple boiled foods, tenderly cutting his vegetables apart on his plate. For her friends, meanwhile, she prepared elaborate pasta dishes, or a specialty, squid *en su tinto* (in its ink). Imelda liked to dress informally at home, and on those afternoons, in the family kitchen without makeup, in her thick cotton "dusters" printed with zoo animals, she looked more like a plump washerwoman than the aging but elegant vamp that was her public persona. "When Marcos was ill, she'd call us over for a meal, and we'd lunch alone in the family dining room," said a friend. "But then, sometimes, a maid would come in and whisper that he was awake, and she'd scuttle around like a little kid, rearranging the dishes to make it look like we hadn't started eating without him. She'd put her finger to her lips and whisper, 'Shhhh! It's Dente!'"

Emerging simultaneously in Imelda, however, was another, surprisingly cruel, side that drew the Marcoses into ever wilder intrigues and that led some U.S. officials then in Manila to judge her "totally amoral"—capable, some soon came to believe, even of murder. The first of these intrigues came in 1982, when her daughter Imee eloped with a man of whom she violently disapproved. Soon afterward, Imelda orchestrated his kidnapping by the military, according to Zamora, the Marcoses' attorney.

Less than two years later, after government troops in broad daylight assassinated "Ninoy" Aquino, a wide range of U.S. and Filipino authorities became convinced that Imelda at the very least had known of the plot, and likely helped envision it. The two events together sealed Imelda's image as a dangerous Dragon Lady and finally thwarted her chances of holding power in her own right.

The government-sponsored kidnapping of Imee's husband could be seen as a prototype for the Aquino murder one and a half years later, but practice did not make perfect. Both crimes were impulsive and clumsy and absurdly blamed on communists. And each, in its time, did unprecedented damage to what remained of the Marcoses' credibility.

The kidnapping, in particular, had followed major efforts by the Marcoses to restore their stature with Filipinos and other world leaders. In May 1980, the couple had finally allowed an ailing Benigno Aquino to leave jail for the United States, where he received triple bypass surgery at Baylor Hospital in Dallas, Texas. Imelda later insisted she had fought to convince her husband to allow it. ("I saved Ninoy's life," she claimed, and Aquino certainly did seem grateful. He gave her a golden rosary, which she kept on display for visitors, and he told the *Christian Science Monitor,* "I doff my hat to her. She has made her mark....I don't think we will have another woman like that in fifty years.")

Then in January 1981, with Imelda weeping quietly at his side, a vigorous-looking Marcos, his disease in remission, told his nation in a broadcast from the palace's Heroes Hall that he had ended martial law. The timing was ideal: Pope John Paul II was soon due in Manila and the decision was also sure to please the new Reagan team about to be inaugurated in Washington. The incoming administration had already shown its warmth. In December, Reagan had met with Imelda in New York, making her the sole exception to his policy of not receiving any foreign leaders before his inauguration. Plans were also under way for a U.S. state visit, Marcos' first in sixteen years, in September.

It became clear quite soon, however, how much *palabas* there was in the lifting of martial law. Marcos had signed a number of private decrees in advance that preserved his broad authority. He restricted the power of the courts, while retaining the right to rule by decree, order arrests without charges, and dissolve the assembly if he chose. About 1000 prisoners arrested under martial law also remained in jail. Yet little by little, the onus of a military regime faded away. Controls on the press and the numbed opposition were loosened. The country seemed to be edging back to normalcy. Yet normalcy lasted less than one year.

The new year of 1982 brought with it the at first seemingly inconsequential revelation that a handsome, 32-year-old basketball coach and professional golfer named Tommy Manotoc had vanished, after last being seen having lunch in a chic downtown restaurant. The news acquired more meaning once word spread that Manotoc had married Imee Marcos in early December in a quick, secret ceremony in Arlington, Virginia.

The palace press director, Adrian Cristobal, used to say of the Marcos children, "It takes guts to date them." Never had he been so right as in Manotoc's case. Not only had the sportsman eloped with the Marcos' first-born child, he was already married, though estranged, to a former beauty queen named Aurora Pijuan, and he had two children of his own. Before wedding Imee, Manotoc had applied for a Swiss annulment and secured a divorce from the Dominican Republic. But divorce is illegal in the Philippines, and the Marcoses never considered his first marriage dissolved. Making matters even worse was that Manotoc, though apolitical himself, was the nephew of two leading oppositionists: Eugene Lopez, Jr., and Raul Manglapus, who had by then founded the Movement for a Free Philippines in the United States.

The Marcoses' response to their daughter's marriage bore no trace of the chess player's strategy that had won the President such admiration in the west. Imelda, inexplicably, became the spokeswoman during the tumultuous few weeks, and she flailed, contradicted herself, and gave several clues to her involvement in the kidnapping. As nearly six weeks passed without a word from the young hostage, Manilans felt mounting tension: would Manotoc live or be "salvaged" (Filipinos' polite word for "killed")? What would make the difference? The Manotoc family received a purported NPA ransom note seeking $2.5 million and the release of several political prisoners, neither of which, of course, they could possibly have produced. Tommy's stockbroker brother, Ricardo, called a press conference to denounce the note as fake, telling reporters that presidential security guards had visited his home to inquire about it a full hour before it was delivered. Days later, the U.S. Embassy received reports that the government was preparing charges against Ricardo for diverting investment funds.

The Philippine newspapers made no mention of the missing man's links to the Marcoses until Imelda herself revealed the marriage in a long, emotional interview with Agence France-Presse. She confessed that she had strongly objected after Manotoc asked for her daughter's hand during a meeting in the United States that December, saying it was "impossible" and "absurd," since he remained married to Pijuan. She added that her daughter had "the mind of a 40-year-old and the heart of a 10-year-old," and was engaged in a "sophisticated rebellion." Then she confided that the Marcoses were in a "no-win situation." If Manotoc was killed, they would be blamed, she said. If he reappeared, it would be assumed that they had kidnapped him. In another interview, she rashly promised to give up all her official positions if Manotoc was not returned alive. From a later perspective, her most chilling comment came when she declared that she sincerely hoped Manotoc was alive—just as much as she had hoped Aquino would remain alive after he left for his operation in Texas.

Between Imelda's overdone denials, she gave so many hints of complicity that even Philippine officials refused to discount the possibility when speaking privately with American diplomats. One supporter of the President went so far as to add, darkly, "This was definitely not an Ilocano operation." The embassy concluded that "while not likely to become a Philippine Watergate, in part because of effective government control over the media, the incident has strained Malacanang's credibility and has the potential to blacken the image of the first family, particularly Mrs. Marcos."

The notoriety was not undeserved, according to Zamora, who was closely involved in the crisis. Zamora had been friendly with both the Marcoses and their children—Imee was his son's godmother—and thus became a kind of go-between for them and Imee as family relations deteriorated. Both Marcoses had been shocked by the wedding, Zamora said, and Marcos had insisted he tell Manotoc that he would never inherit any money, "because that's all he wants." But Imelda was by far the more distraught. After hearing her daughter had married, she cried throughout an hour-long meeting with the lawyer, pleading, "It would be such a scandal—God would punish all of us." Soon afterward, when Manotoc disappeared, Imee knew immediately who was responsible. "She had a tantrum, said she'd kill herself if anything happened to him," said Zamora. "It prevented any more thoughts of doing him in."* A news story published in Manila in 1987 said Imee's confrontation with her mother included the smashing of numerous precious antiques on palace walls and floors.

It was forty-one days more before Manotoc was "rescued" by a detachment of soldiers in an elaborate charade. On February 9, 1982, flanked by Ver and Enrile, a shaken-looking Manotoc gave a press conference to describe how he had been roughed up and indoctrinated by the "communists." Enrile then told in dramatic detail how the troops, acting on a secret tip, had found him, trussed and blindfolded, in an isolated hut in the Sierra Madre of the northeastern Quezon province. One kidnapper had been killed in the assault, the minister claimed. Manotoc, speaking haltingly, made no mention of his marriage. He read a letter thanking the government and refused to talk about his plans.

General Pedro Balbanero, who had led the "rescue" operation, received a promotion several months later. But in 1987, he told Filipino reporter Nick Joaquin, "I had been used." No one had told him at the time that the operation was a fake, he said, although there had

---

*Zamora's memories of the kidnapping affair apparently became a bit shaky following my first interview with him about it, by telephone in August 1987, in which he said Imelda "instigated" the event. In a subsequent conversation with reporter Bonnie Weston, who was interviewing him on my behalf, he denied firsthand knowledge as to which of the Marcoses had been more responsible.

been signs. The "heavy gunfire" from "unseen enemies" that met his men as they advanced toward Manotoc's hut hit none of them, although they were clear targets. Nor did anyone see a bullet strike a rock or tree or even hear one whiz by. Moreover, the corpse of the "kidnapper" they discovered had been stiff and cold for hours.

For several months after Manotoc's press conference, the Marcoses tried their best to ignore the addition to their family. Imee continued to live in the palace, and was never seen nor photographed in public with her husband. When Imelda was asked about Manotoc in a June interview with her former biographer, she repeated, "The man is married. He has a wife. He has two children. He is bound by all that is decent and moral to support them, to give them not only material but also emotional sustenance. But if in the face of all this, this little boy continues to pursue Imee, one is forced to question his motives." Imee shot back, in another interview, "I cannot squabble in public with my family. I think that is really cheap, and vulgar, and common." Shortly thereafter, she drew speculation that the relationship was still alive by attending a public ceremony in a loose-fitting dress. Her pregnancy became obvious after a few more weeks, and she finally moved out of the palace and into a suburban condominium with Manotoc.

The U.S. Embassy had carefully monitored the kidnapping and sent back melancholy reports to Washington on the Marcoses' public relations blunders. The new American administration had been eager to see the Filipino rulers restore their reputations. The new ambassador, Michael Armacost, came to Manila feeling Carter officials "had gone overboard in keeping the Marcoses at arm's length," and he became so companionable in response that Filipinos called him "Arm-a-close." (The ambassador soon grew nervous, however, at how constantly the Marcoses photographed their meetings with him. The couple, he realized, put huge stock into symbols of personal connections: Imelda especially loved to haul out her photo album of Reagan's 1969 visit, telling over and over again how Governor Reagan had stayed at the palace and how she had told him, "You are family." Armacost felt the tug, too; neutrality was all but inconceivable.)

In June of 1981, six months after Marcos lifted martial law, the President had held new "elections" to install himself in another six-year term as president. The blatant cheating of 1978 was unnecessary this time. Though the nation's mounting debt, vast poverty, and unemployment would have made potent campaign issues, conservative and radical opposition groups had joined together to boycott the campaign after Marcos refused to change voting rules they found unfair. As a sign of unity, it was unprecedented, but it was also an admission of impotence. The mainstream opposition was fractious and leaderless; they reviled each other almost as often as they reviled the President, and short of reviling the President, they couldn't settle on issues capable of inspiring their people. They carped and schemed, in their ostentatious mansions, like toddlers oppressed by some older sandbox bully. Armacost's predecessor, Richard Murphy, saw them as "weak and flabby" and one former leader, Gerardo Roxas, fretted that they were already irrelevant. Even U.N. ambassador Young had been disappointed by his 1979 meetings with them, telling Murphy he found them "not ready for martyrdom."

The only man who was ready, as he proved two years later, was Aquino, but he remained in exile, living in a gracious brick Tudor mansion in Newton, Massachusetts (with a country estate in nearby Brookfield), while studying on a fellowship at Harvard University. The constitution would have prevented his running for president in any case, since at 48, he was two years younger than the minimum eligible age. But he was growing more and more impatient to get back in the fray. From Newton, he kept in constant touch by telephone with his cohort Psinakis, in San Francisco, as well as with frequent visitors from Manila. (Manila's government-controlled newspapers ridiculed them as "steak commandos.") From the first year of his exile, he was lobbying privately with administration officials speaking publicly against the regime, and longing to again confront Marcos directly.

*       *       *

Impatience was also building in Manila, and in a sign of their desperation, some disenfranchised "oligarchs" banded together in two terrorist movements, called Light-a-Fire and the April 6 Liberation Movement, that being the date of the largest 1978 election protests. Starting in August of 1980—barely two weeks after Aquino warned in a speech of the threat of "massive urban guerrilla warfare"—members bombed or set fire to several public buildings, selected for their links to the Marcoses or their cronies. Between August 22 and October 19, at least thirty Manila banks, office buildings, and hotels, as well as Imelda's Convention Center, were bombed, causing the death of one American and injuries to seventy others.

The Marcoses seemed taken aback at first. Imelda, in New York, summoned both Aquino and Psinakis to her "imperial suite" at the Waldorf-Astoria to plead against the use of violence. But in the same meetings, she boasted of the Marcoses' good standing with the new U.S. administration, and indeed, U.S. officials later aided in a crackdown. By June 1981, the bombings had long ceased to be a serious threat.*

It was at this point that Vice President George Bush visited Manila and gave the couple the strongest American endorsement any Philippine administration had received. It came after a celebration in Luneta Park for Marcos' unsurprising victory in staged presidential elections. U.S.-made Philippine armed forces jets buzzed overhead and a 1000-voice choir sang Handel's benediction, "And he shall reign for ever and ever," after which Bush, in a flower-draped barong tagalog, raised his glass and declared, "We stand with the Philippines. We stand with you, sir. We love your adherence to democratic principles and to the democratic processes and we will not leave you in isolation."

*        *        *

Philippine government radio and television stations played Bush's toast over and over again during the next few days, even as the Vice President was harshly criticized in editorials in leading U.S. newspapers. The Marcoses were determined to make the most of it: the preceding February, when they had sought similar affirmation from Pope John Paul II, they had been disappointed. First, the Pope had refused to stay at Imelda's Coconut Palace, a multimillion-dollar mansion built mostly from the shells of 100,000 coconuts and palm tree by-products. (To console herself, Imelda later flew in actress Brooke Shields to inaugurate the palace.) Then he criticized Marcos' human rights record, though he did so in careful generalities. "One can never justify any violation of the fundamental dignity of the human per-

---

*According to U.S. news reports, April 6 movement members had learned to build bombs in the desert near Tucson. A U.S. investigation began in 1981 after the arrest of one member in Manila, a Los Angeles food importer named Victor Lovely, Jr., who had been critically injured in September 1980 by the accidental explosion of a bomb he was preparing in his Manila YMCA room. Interrogated before he was turned over to U.S. authorities, Lovely implicated both Aquino and Psinakis in the bombings, but later recanted, saying he'd spoken under duress. In June of 1981, U.S. Secretary of State Alexander Haig reportedly gave Marcos a letter saying the State Department was pursuing prosecution of the "terrorists," and six months later, Psinakis' home in San Francisco was raided.

son or of the basic rights that safeguard this dignity," he said in a speech as Marcos sat stonily beside him. The comment was ignored by the controlled media, which instead played up the Pope's admonition to priests and nuns not to take an "exaggerated interest" in politics.

Before the February visit, eight of the Philippines' ninety-nine bishops had written to John Paul II to ask him to call the trip off, pleading their country couldn't afford the lavish reception he would inevitably receive, and that the Marcoses would twist the meaning of his visit into an endorsement of their rule. The Pope came anyway, and, thanks mostly to Imelda, proved the eight bishops right.

Foreseeing the Marcoses' designs, Manila's Archbishop Jaime Cardinal Sin, plump, bespectacled, and wily as the best of Manila's professional politicians, had wrested a letter from Malacanang conceding the Pope's visit would be sponsored by the Church, not the state. But once the Pope arrived, the Marcoses made the distinction moot, coopting his trip flamboyantly and entirely. There was not a day in his six-day visit that did not involve some ceremony at which the Marcoses and their children were prominently featured: they greeted him at the airport, received him at the palace, and turned a reception for him into an extravaganza exceeding Imelda's "barrio fiesta" for Lyndon Johnson.

Each guest at the palace affair was instructed to wear traditional Filipino attire, creating the air of a costume ball. White fabric was delivered to homes in advance to make ternos for the women, and barong tagalogs for the men. Bronze medals were struck for the occasion with likenesses of Marcos and the Pope, and passed out to be worn on yellow ribbons. Members of the presidential security command were decked out in feathered helmets. *New York Times* correspondent Henry Kamm, reporting on the affair, was struck by the buffet table "of noble woods, rich cloth, and lustrous crystal...the length of the long hall, heaped with carefully piled fruit, largely imported, resembling a seventeenth-century Flemish still life that had proliferated out of the painter's control."

Of the Marcoses, Imelda was far more determined in her pursuit of the Pope. She was always one step ahead: When he stopped in Manila's Tondo slums, she had already erected cheerful facades over the worst of the decaying shanties. When he visited the island of Cebu, she was waiting for him at the gangway of his plane, having arrived shortly before with her Italian friend D'Urso. The next morning, she met him again in the city of Davao, on Mindanao, and subsequently trailed him to the islands of Bacolod and Iloilo. On the fifth day of his visit, she took the pontiff on tour of the Indochinese refugee camp she had persuaded Marcos to set up in Bataan. On the last day, Marcos received the Pope in Baguio, after which the couple saw him off at the airport.

Both Marcoses had been especially eager then for demonstrations of the Pope's goodwill. John Paul's admonition to Philippine priests and nuns had not come in a vacuum. Increasing numbers of the clergy had openly joined the opposition. The more conservative Church hierarchy, in contrast, had kept close to the Marcoses for years, but in the 1980s there were occasional hints of the rustling of vestments as the elders shuffled ever so slightly to the side.

The most public Church-state confrontation was between Cardinal Sin and Imelda, after the Manila Film Festival of January 18, 1982. Following its notorious accident, the film center was completed fifteen minutes before opening ceremonies, at a cost of nearly $22 million. Deciding it had caused enough controversy, Marcos' recent appointee as prime minister, Cesar Virata—a respected "technocrat" whom Imelda called "Dr. No" for his periodic vetos of her schemes—declined to subsidize the $5 million festival. Unfazed, Imelda came up with an alternate plan: she got censorship laws relaxed to allow the showing of thirteen uncut soft pornography films in local theaters, attracting long lines and fat profits. The clergy called the shows a "river of filth," but she argued they would "contribute to the maturity of Filipino movie audiences." Pornography, she reasoned, "is all in the mind and the heart...if garbage affects us, then there must be something wrong with us."

Sin was beside himself. He told a reporter, "one of the fringe benefits of being a priest is that one does not have to argue with a woman." But in the next breath, he condemned Imelda's hopes for succession, asking "Where will this country go with this kind of leader?" Considering other issues on which Sin might have protested, Imelda's dirty movies were a silly reason for a turning point, but the cardinal up to that point had restrained himself in statements to the press. He remained on publicly cordial terms thereafter with the Marcoses, even embracing the President at a ceremony three years later. With Imelda, however, the battle lines had been drawn.

By choosing her audiences, Imelda found she could still receive the approval she craved. At home, her coterie of Blue Ladies, press aides, and technocrats still surrounded and revered her, treating her with the same awe she reserved for her husband. "I'd come to see her sometimes, and it would be like a Fellini film," said the wife of a close adviser. "There would be Imelda, giving some sermon or other, and everyone's head would be nodding in unison, with people telling her everything she wanted to hear: 'If they don't like you, it's because you're too beautiful,' etc., etc."

In the United States, it was also still easy to find praise in some circles. In November of 1981, Imelda visited Washington again for a day-long program attended by administration officials and conservative senators including Republicans Charles Percy of Illinois and Sam Hayakawa of Hawaii, and Democrat John Glenn of Ohio. Her forty-minute lecture covered familiar ground: she reminded them of the crucial importance of the bases and told them that the Philippines was misunderstood and unappreciated. But though she was "hurt and wounded," she vowed Marcos wouldn't be swayed by emotions, but would make decisions based on loyalty to the United States. U.S. memoranda detailing the meetings also noted that Imelda worried aloud, four times, about who might succeed her husband in office.

Senator Percy, sponsor of the day's lunch, called Imelda "a very remarkable person," who "gave a very good, strategic account of the position of the Philippines in the defense of the Pacific region," and "impressed me very much." He also declared America's relations with the Philippines had "never been stronger." Later that evening, Mrs. Bush gave a party in Imelda's honor.

Yet despite such havens of support, it was by then impossible for Imelda even outside the Philippines to avoid signs of her growing unpopularity. That very night, as she sat in the presidential box at the Kennedy Center, watching her protégée pianist Cecile Licad perform in a concert, four Filipinos stood up from the audience and shouted that there was an "unwelcome guest" in the audience. They then chanted, "Down with Marcos!" until they were hustled out and arrested. Imelda at first seemed startled, but then socialite Pat Hayes, sitting nearby in her box, rose to the occasion, asking the audience for a round of applause for the "distinguished First Lady of the Philippines." They obliged, and Imelda nodded serenely.

She faced more protests the next year on her return to the United

States. In April 1982, she graced a multimillion-dollar Bloomingdale's exhibit in Manhattan promoting Philippine exports. One floor, a "tribute to three heros" celebrated the lives of Douglas MacArthur, Carlos Romulo, and Ferdinand Marcos, calling Marcos the "most decorated member of the citizens' army." Another level held a display of ternos from Imelda's collection, with each mannequin resembling her and the display capped by a silvery gown studded with gilt-edged doves, worn for one of her speeches to the United Nations. Imelda called it a "fiesta of merchandise and free thought—these beautiful products can only be made by happy people." Outside, however, protesters hung her in effigy. And when the exhibit came to Washington, other demonstrators brandished a Miss Piggy doll to make their point.

If Imelda nonetheless seemed unfazed in the early 1980s, she had reason. At home, her influence was increasing. Though she still was barred from involvement in the most crucial government issues, the insurgency and the bases, she had been encroaching vicariously on them through her brother Kokoy. Earlier that year, for instance, Kokoy had sat across the negotiating table from Armacost, leading the scheduled talks on the U.S. bases in secret meetings at the ambassador's residence.

Moreover, Imelda seemed truly to believe she was popular, even though she was still making no effort at all to curb her ostentation. On occasion, a Philippine armed forces helicopter would fly her the few blocks from the palace to a restaurant in her bayside development for lunch. Security men in bush jackets would leap into action as she landed, clearing the area before her limousine would carry her the few remaining feet to the door. Then Assistant Secretary of State Richard Holbrooke recalled a 1980 trip he took with her around Christmas time, through Marcos' province of Ilocos Norte. As their large touring bus barreled along country roads, scattering pigs and chickens, its speakers blasting Frank Sinatra's "Have Yourself a Merry Little Christmas," peasants stood awestruck in the fields, watching them pass. "She pointed, and said, 'Look! Look how the people love me,'" Holbrooke recounted.

In September 1982, Imelda was particularly gratified by the success of the state visit. She had told Armacost beforehand of her fear that Congress would be hostile, but the ambassador assured her that she needn't be concerned about the welcome the Marcoses would receive from the administration. He also promised to precede them to Washington and spend some time on Capitol Hill "preparing the ground."

The White House hosted a dinner with some of the luminaries Imelda most admired: Oscar de la Renta, Margot Fontayn, Andy Warhol, and her special favorites, Van Cliburn and Mario D'Urso. To her gratification, officials also showed interest in what she called her "triangular diplomacy," a reference to her visits earlier that year to both Peking and Moscow. In the U.S.S.R., she had signed an agreement whereby some two dozen Soviet technicians would build a $120 million cement plant on the Philippines' Samerara Island, their first sizeable investment since relations were established in 1976. As usual, Imelda was treated like royalty in Moscow, and Presidium Vice Chairman Vasiliy Vasiliyevich Kuznetsov had complimented her as "the principal architect of the building of friendly ties between our two countries."

In Washington, at the suggestion of Bush, Imelda was debriefed on her impressions of the Soviet Union by CIA chief William Casey and Assistant Secretary of State John Holdridge, who by then had replaced Holbrooke. Earlier, in Manila, she had also offered to share her impressions with Ambassador Armacost, but as he later remembered, she had little of significance to offer. His most vivid impression from the meeting was that every chair and sofa in her reception room was filled with gold-framed Russian icons. Seeing him staring, Imelda gaily asked, "How do you like the loot?"

The meeting in Washington was somewhat more substantive. State Department records show Imelda told them she respected the Soviets' material achievements but regretted their lack of freedom and declining creativity. She added that she had been struck by Leonid Brezhnev's obvious physical decline and said she had sought unsuccessfully to get in touch with some younger leaders. The experience had made her all the more eager to discuss her own future, always foremost in her mind. At one point, talking to Holdridge, she lowered her voice and said, "We must be concerned with the post-Marcos situation." He responded that he anticipated no great problems, given the warm ties between the two countries, and the matter was dropped. Two months later, Imelda returned to the Soviet Union to attend Brezhnev's funeral and pledge continued friendship with his replacement, Yuri Andropov.

Holdridge had been ready for Imelda's hints. The issue of succession was also prominent in the minds of State Department officials, who, like Imelda, were worriedly watching Marcos' decline. In most other countries, the question wouldn't have been so fraught with danger. But power in the Philippines, in the 1970s, had gradually become centralized to an extent that would have surely impressed Brezhnev. Marcos watched his rubber-stamp parliament from monitors inside the palace. Through his cronies and servile underlings, he had a cut of nearly every sizable business and contract in the archipelago, and few major economic decisions, public or private, were made without his blessing. He took the same approach with the military, moving battalions via a telephone hookup in his study and overseeing its affairs so obsessively that he insisted on personally signing even routine authorization forms allowing soldiers to train in the United States. When Marcos was ill, Ver would never presume to make decisions on his own, and would postpone them, instead, until Marcos might be consulted. As delays became the norm, rank-and-file soldiers grew impatient and angry.

American officials, well aware of the trend, were by 1981 gently but often raising the issue of succession with Marcos, and their questions were also emerging in U.S. press reports. In a prescient comment in 1981, *New York Times* reporter Henry Kamm, at the end of a long magazine piece on the Marcoses, noted, "If, over the next six years, Mr. Marcos does not assure a peaceful succession by sharing and eventually surrendering power to persons who are not necessarily his cronies or members of his family, the military, whom Mr. Marcos created as a major political force, will be the most likely arbiter of the future of the Philippines, the kingmaker or the king."

In public, Imelda continued to deny in the strongest terms any wish to succeed her husband. "I would be a freak of a woman if I became president," she declared to a television audience in 1982, amid reports that Marcos was dying. But in private, American officials believed she was killing off their hopes for any rational process of succession, preventing anyone other than herself from emerging as a candidate.

And indeed, how could Imelda not have been obsessed with the "post-Marcos situation" in those years, watching her husband growing weaker and knowing—despite her delusions—how weak she would be in his absence. She was no Eva Peron; though genuinely loved in Leyte, her home province, she was by that time generally disliked elsewhere. The military didn't trust her, and the Church barely tolerated her. Nor had she reason then to think she'd win an American mandate. To her immense frustration, Marcos, too, seemed to be balking at decisively giving her the stature of his heir apparent. He was still too concerned with his own image in the United States, and perhaps also still unwilling to imagine a government without him to lead it.

Yet for Imelda, succession was paramount. It meant holding on to the identity she'd built; it meant survival. She hated inactivity more than anything, hated especially having time to brood or reflect. As she acquired more power, and seemed to find it ever more unsatisfying, her restlessness grew to the point where impulse and action were indistinguishable. She did everything in binges: ate, talked, danced, and planned her public programs all in great, thoughtless bursts of energy (her administrative weakness was always lack of follow-through). And of course, she bought in binges. Manilans, and, by the 1980s, Americans, too, never seemed to tire of hearing how and what she bought. She shopped wildly, almost desperately, and certainly indiscriminately. Her bodyguard, Morales, said that often, after shopping trips, she would stare blankly at the packages around her in her room, and mutter, "Could I really have bought all this?"

In just one of countless stories then circulating about her shopping escapades, Sotheby's was reported to have canceled a two-day art auction after she bought the whole collection with a $6 million check—and then tried to buy the apartment where it was kept. On another occasion, during a 1983 swing through New York, Rome, and Copenhagen, she spent more than $5 million, according to her private secretary's notebook, later found in the palace. The disbursements included: $3.5 million for what was noted as a "Michelangelo painting"; $43,000 for a silver service; $10,340 for sheets at an Italian linen store on Madison Avenue; $208,000 for a Cartier emerald and diamond bracelet; and more than $1.3 million for antique jewelry from other establishments, including the House of Faberge.

Quite often she bought for other people. In her basement she kept a storeroom—palace tour guides later called it the "mini-Rustan's" after Manila's huge department store chain—full of watches, colognes, scarves, and trinkets to give away. It was just one sign of how much she needed to feel needed, or powerful—another being her love of the campaign trail, when her schedule's demands always exceeded her ability to meet them. "When I lie down even for a minute, I tell myself I could be helping a hundred, perhaps a thousand people, in that time," she once said. Even then, she might have guessed the kinds of comments she would later make in exile in Hawaii: that it was like a tomb, worse than death, worse than crucifixion.

*       *       *

As part of his campaign for credibility, Marcos set up a fifteen-member committee in 1981, including, among others, Imelda, Virata, Enrile, and a Mindanao loyalist named Ali Dimapora. It was intended as a kind of group vice president, a succession mechanism and a council of advisors. But it never did much besides listen to the Marcoses, and was soon disbanded.

In the meantime, Marcos left the door just ajar for his wife's ambitions. During his September 1982 state visit, he told Washington journalists Imelda would not be the successor. But he added, in a typical, keep-it-vague tactic, "She may be needed to help the successor, because without her help or without my help the successor may not be able to succeed." Soon afterward, Imelda appeared on television in Manila, answering reporters' questions on a variety of topics for forty-five minutes. The *Far Eastern Economic Review* called her "quietly confident and competent, in the mold of a world leader."

Imelda was encouraged. By 1983 there was very little she felt she couldn't handle—even the biggest remaining obstacle to the fulfillment of her dream: her old nemesis, Benigno Aquino.

By May of that year, the former senator had let it be known that he planned to return to Manila. He felt guilty in his comfortable exile, though his wife, Corazon, would later call that time her happiest. For the past three years, he had been telling American officials and reporters that he meant to return. "If I am there, even in jail, at least I'll know the feel of things," he said in one interview. "I think a leader has to be with his people." As summer approached, it was clear he was finally determined to act soon. It was also clear to anyone who listened that he'd staked his pride on it. Aquino's pride was considerable. There was surely not much chance he could be swayed to remain in the United States. Imelda, true to form, thought she'd give it a try anyway.

She secretly summoned Aquino to her six-floor, East 66th Street townhouse, with its six kitchens, glass chandeliers, huge jacuzzi, and rooftop disco. It was a truly elegant residence, except for a few garish touches—particularly the life-sized portraits of Imelda, Marcos, the Jimmy Carters, and the Ronald Reagans, all painted against dramatic blue and white celestial backgrounds ("A Triumph of Purity" read the plaque under Imelda's). There were also the plastic golden cups, engraved with Imelda's initials, which she used to serve her guests, and her throw pillows, embroidered with such mottos as: "Nouveau Riche is Better Than No Riche At All" and "Good Girls Go to Heaven. Bad Girls Go Everywhere."

The May 1983 meeting was Aquino's third audience with the First Lady. The first had been in December 1980, when she'd invited him and Steve Psinakis to her Waldorf-Astoria suite, demanding they use their influence to stop the Manila bombings. Two years later she again called Aquino to the suite, but her purpose then was less clear. The former senator arrived to find her dining with the Swearingens, to whom he was proudly introduced before she led him to a more private room. Yet once they were alone, she simply smiled, and seemed to have nothing in particular to say. "Ninoy was furious," recalled his friend, scientist Guy Pauker. "He was convinced she'd trapped him in front of those people just to show him off."

That still didn't keep Aquino from accepting Imelda's third summons. This time it had a tone of urgency, and she indeed came right to the point. Grinning fiercely, she asked her longtime rival if he'd care to join the government. "We can do great things together," she promised. Yet Aquino politely declined. With hardly a pause, she switched tactics, urging him to drop his plans to return and stay where he was—in return for which she offered a loan of $10 million. It was easy money, she assured him—nothing to do with the government. She'd made a killing on the stock market recently, thanks to the expert advice of Felix Rohatyn, and had also recently agreed on a joint venture with Armand Hammer to build a hotel in China.* Still, Aquino remained unmoved.

Finally Imelda got tough. She told Aquino—"as instructed by President Marcos"—that there were threats against his life. "My advice to you is not to return home now," she said. "If you do, my husband will be forced to put you back into jail for your own safety. If something happens to you...we'll be blamed for it." She added, om-

---

*In 1987, both Rohatyn's secretary and Hammer's public relations office denied there was any truth in her claims.

inously, that the potential killers included "certain allies of the President who couldn't be controlled."

Aquino subsequently took precautions that showed he took Imelda's warnings seriously. But on leaving the meeting, he remarked to a friend, "She's really off her rocker. She's become single-minded."

He was at least equally determined, however, and nothing would stop his return. When the government refused to issue travel documents, he got a phony passport in the name of Marcial Bonifacio; "Marcial" for martial law and "Bonifacio" for the nineteenth-century Filipino nationalist whose name graced his former prison home. Surrounded by relatives and journalists, he flew from Taiwan on August 21, 1983, aboard a regularly scheduled China Airlines Boeing 767.

Early that month, the Philippine government had made the unprecedented announcement that Marcos would be going into seclusion for three weeks "to write books." But the pretense was obvious, especially after members of the presidential security command were asked to donate blood. Diplomats later confirmed that Marcos had a kidney transplant sometime around August 7.

Recuperation didn't come easy, and there were several weeks in which it seemed quite possible the President would die. It was that, above all, that inspired Aquino's timing. He had grown convinced that Marcos wouldn't last longer than a few weeks, after which Imelda would take over. Aquino felt he could reason with Marcos, but not with his wife. "If I delay any further, and the President goes," he wondered, "then with whom will I talk?"

He nonetheless knew the risks of his decision, and discussed them widely before he left. He told *Newsweek* he gave himself only a 10 percent chance of surviving the trip home. He wrote loving letters of provisional farewell to his children. He told a Japanese television crew accompanying him on the plane, "You have to be ready with your hand camera, because this action can happen very fast. In a matter of three, four minutes, it could be all over and I may not be able to talk to you again." And when he stepped off the plane in Manila that Sunday, surrounded by six soldiers in the blazing midafternoon heat, he was wearing, under his ivory safari suit, a thick bulletproof vest. It was "the kind Reagan wears," he had joked earlier. Still, it mattered little to Aquino's murderer, who simply stuck a revolver down his unprotected neck and fired.

Later testimony showed the fatal shot could only have come from one of the soldiers who hustled Aquino down a ladder from the plane to the tarmac. As they led him away, other soldiers thrust their bodies against the door, blocking the views of most of the passengers craning for a glimpse. Some of the reporters left their tape-recorders running, however, and they captured the revealing Tagalog jumble of speech from around the steps below. "Here he comes, let me, let me, let me, here it is...shoot!" the words came. As the slain Aquino fell from the arms of his escorts, other soldiers on the tarmac pumped sixteen bullets into the body of a man in denim trousers, who lay on the ground just a few feet away. Later that day, the government declared Aquino's killer to have been that dead man, anonymous but for his signet ring, engraved with the initial "R," and the word "Rolly" embroidered on his underwear. He was identified within the next week, however, as Rolando Galman, a hitherto obscure provincial farmer.

At the moment Aquino was murdered, Imelda was ten miles away from the airport, lingering over a Chinese lunch with the director of the national film censorship board. Called away to answer the telephone, she returned within a few minutes to say she had to leave. It had been Ver on the phone, telling her to get back to the palace as soon as possible.

If Imelda at that moment had any strong reaction to the news of her rival's murder, she kept it expertly disguised as she briskly left the restaurant. Yet a week earlier, caught off guard, she'd made a characteristic slip that was to cast suspicion on her role in the crime. An opposition politician who had told her of Aquino's plans to return said she'd been stunned by the news, falling silent for a moment, but then blurting out: "Let him come. But if he does, he's dead."

And three days after the murder, an American diplomat who met with Imelda at Malacanang described her behavior as "macabre." The meeting was the first time he'd seen her since the killing, he recalled, and he found her in a state of agitation, alternately professing her shock and angrily condemning Aquino's choice to come back. As the two were talking, they passed Imelda's palace shrine to the Santo Niño, the Christ child, and the First Lady's tone turned confidential. She pointed to the statue's neck, from which she'd hung the rosary Aquino gave her in 1980. She then declared that on hearing of his death, she had rushed to the shrine and exclaimed, "Santo Niño,

Santo Niño! I said to take care of him, but I didn't mean like this!"
She seemed to regard the story as funny, the diplomat noted.

When U.S. Ambassador Armacost heard of the murder, he immediately suspected the Marcoses, as did almost everyone else in
Manila. But the ambassador at first rejected the idea. The government just couldn't have done it, he thought, couldn't have been so
dumb as to stage something like that, in such a public place, with all
those windows on the plane and in the terminal. The next day, however, Marcos called him at home, and by the time he had hung up,
Armacost was deeply worried. The President had told him that he
couldn't see him then but wanted to discuss the murder. He then
launched into a long, convoluted explanation of why Galman was
responsible. Later that day, Armacost sent a long cable to Washington, describing the phone call in detail. He ended by noting that
it all sounded rather fishy.

It wasn't long before Marcos was publicly blaming the murder on
the communists. Meanwhile, Imelda was spreading the word in private that it was a CIA job. Armacost, along with his colleagues in
Washington, grew even more suspicious and finally frankly alarmed,
as it grew clear that the government's investigation was a joke. For
one thing, Galman's body had been allowed to lie on the tarmac for
several hours after he was shot, hindering an autopsy. But embassy
officers grew even more leery after talking with Major Prospero
Olivas, Ver's appointee to lead the investigation. They came away
thinking he had uncovered less in several days than a police cadet
might have found in ten minutes.

As months passed, the mystery for Filipinos and Americans became
not whether the government was involved—there was no doubt that it
was—but whether Marcos personally had ordered or even been informed in advance of the killing. There were wide reports by then of
the President's August 7 surgery. Rumor even had it that he was co-
matose on the day Aquino was killed, although Armacost, for one, never
subscribed to that theory. The ambassador had seen Marcos just three
days before Aquino's murder, and while he thought he looked terrible—
thin, weak, and puffy-faced—he believed him fully capable of responding to events, and was sure that Ver, at least, would have had access to
him. Since the soldiers at the airport were directly under Ver's command, the general was certainly implicated, and indeed was later
indicted with two dozen other military men by a government-appointed

investigation board. But Ver would never have taken such action on his own. Who gave him his orders?*

The question may well remain unanswered, one of the few secrets of the Marcos regime that wasn't confided to underlings or documents. But palace employees, including Imelda's former bodyguard, Captain Morales, have told varying stories about how Marcos, when he heard of the killing, threw his lunch tray at his wife, or at the wall, or on the ground. In the months after the murder, Filipinos close to the palace repeated the stories with conviction. Marcos couldn't have known, they'd say; that wasn't the wily, methodical ruler they knew. One of the most prominent officials holding this theory was Defense Minister Enrile, who told former assistant secretary of state Holbrooke that he knew that Imelda was responsible. "He cited a lot of technical reasons that I can't remember," Holbrooke said later. Enrile himself refused to discuss the matter in 1987.

Armacost eventually grew convinced Ver was responsible, but he remained suspicious also of Imelda and "Coconut King" Eduardo Cojuangco, each of whom, he thought, had obvious motives. Cojuangco, the cousin and bitter rival of Aquino's wife, Corazon, despised Aquino, apparently as much as Imelda did. A CIA officer who knew him well said Cojuangco had told him before 1983 that Marcos' biggest mistake was not executing Aquino when he had the chance.

Still, even Imelda later acknowledged that Aquino's killing brought ruin to the Marcoses. It immediately brought unprecedented protest demonstrations, which evolved into violent riots around the Mendiola Bridge near Malacanang Palace. The worst melee came that September, on the eleventh anniversary of the declaration of martial law. On that day, hundreds of thousands of Filipinos gathered to hear speeches from opposition leaders including former president Diosdado Macapagal and a political newcomer, Aquino's softspoken widow, Corazon. But some three hours later, the dwindling crowd met with lines of security forces. Some of the civilians began throwing bricks, while others tried to burn the army buses with Molotov

---

*The board that indicted Ver was known as the "Agrava Commission" since it was chaired by Justice Corazon Juliano-Agrava. Many Filipinos had expected it would end in a whitewash, since Agrava was an open admirer of the Marcoses and had gone so far as to lead fellow board-members in singing "Happy Birthday" to Imelda when the First Lady testified on July 2, 1984. But the decision was made by the majority in defiance of the chairman, after eight wrenching months of testimony and deliberations that year.

cocktails. The soldiers finally counterattacked, and by the end of the day eleven people had been killed and 150 seriously injured.

The violence brought dozens of foreign journalists flying into Manila from their bases in Tokyo, New York, and San Francisco. Gathering each day at the Mendiola Bridge, they became witnesses to the evolution of the "parliament of the streets," the ad hoc, diverse coalition of activists newly galvanized against the government. The parliament comprised a galaxy of what Filipinos called cause-oriented groups, most of which were known by their acronyms. They included ATOM, the August Twenty-One Movement; JAJA, Justice for Aquino, Justice for All; WOMB, an anti-Marcos women's association; and even ACRONYM, the Anti-Crony Movement. For the first time, even middle-class professionals were joining these rallies, their outrage at Aquino's murder finally moving them to action. They marched in their bright polo t-shirts and business suits, toting placards with gory pictures of Aquino's corpse and buying visors printed "Ninoy Forever." The newspapers also grew braver, egging each other into increasingly provocative anti-government innuendos.

For the Marcoses, however, the most devastating fallout of Aquino's death was economic. It came within a month of the murder, when alarmed foreign bankers started calling in hundreds of millions of dollars in Philippine loans and refusing to grant new ones. Wealthy Filipinos joined the foreigners in bailing out of their economy, changing their pesos for dollars and sending the cash out of the country, mostly to American banks. For a harrowing week, capital flight was measured at $3 million to $5 million a day.

Then came the startling news that President Reagan had canceled a planned stop in Manila on his trip through Asia that November. While his aides offered apolitical excuses, it was painfully clear that the administration, at last, had also begun to recoil.

Through it all, Imelda's image suffered the most damage, although it took her some time to realize it. Armacost and his colleagues believed the taint of her suspected involvement in the killing decisively ended her hopes to succeed her husband. Meanwhile, the ambassador who had begun his term believing closer relations were the key ended it convinced that the Marcoses—and particularly Imelda—had to go.

\*     \*     \*

For a week after the murder, neither Marcos nor his wife left the palace, prompting speculation that the President was dying. Marcos finally tried to refute the rumors by appearing on television, frail and wan, to say, "I am here. I am ready to wrestle with anybody." Then, on the night of August 29, 1983, Imelda made her own coming-out gesture, appearing in a simple black dress in the elegant lobbies of the Manila Hotel, the gathering place for the capital's foreign correspondents. The bellboys in their gleaming white suits and pillbox hats rushed to roll out the red carpet and present her with her routine bouquet. But she said no more than a muttered thanks before striding to the coffeeshop, smiling but declining answers to reporters' shouted questions. She shared a quiet meal with her entourage and left as quietly as she had come.

Yet after that ritualized end to her seclusion, Imelda suddenly seemed to be everywhere. She appeared almost daily on the television news and in photos on the front pages of Manila's newspapers, politicking with KBL leaders or signing government contracts in public ceremonies. At last on September 19 she met formally with a group of journalists, again at the Manila Hotel. She told them that she was so outraged at being linked to Aquino's killing that she'd decided to quit politics for good. She meant to switch to the private sector, she confided, in an ambitious if somewhat vague plan to revive the economy. "I hope to go to the rural areas and set up linkages, processing centers, financing, and technology relevant to people in the rural areas," she said. "I'm raring to go, to roll my sleeves up and get to work where the real ball game is."

It wasn't until November that Marcos also reappeared in public, claiming, in an interview with Roy Rowan, to have suffered a "horrible type of allergy...but I have recovered, thank God." His restraining influence on Imelda had been noticeably lacking in the three months of his absence. In the middle of October, for example, when Manila was jittery with news of riots and food shortages, the First Lady, still in her simple black dress—but with a bright black and golden silk scarf in a rakish knot at her throat—strode out to the presidential lawn, her camera crew in tow, and ordered hundreds of workers to tear up 26 acres of imported Bermuda grass and replace them with a vegetable garden. By one report, the commotion startled the President, who stuck his head out from his office window and demanded of his aides, "What the hell is she doing now?"

While such antics preoccupied the Marcoses' attention, society outside the palace grounds was unraveling. Throughout the islands, Aquino's killing had radicalized former moderates, and the ranks of the New People's Army (NPA) grew, by one U.S. estimate, as much as 24 percent, reaching a longtime high of more than 12,500 members. The armed forces, poorly paid and poorly led, were less and less of a worthy match for them. And in his isolation at Malacanang, Marcos did nothing to inspire them. The President in fact was out of action for most of 1984, working on the average less than two days a week, while weak and foggy-minded from dialysis treatments. He dropped out of sight altogether from October to December, when U.S. intelligence officials believe he was so close to death that he'd been given his last rites. He slowly recovered, but decisions continued to pile up on his desk, the government sputtering out of control. "In a system with just one guy calling the shots, you can imagine what it meant," said a high-ranking U.S. intelligence official. "The growth of the insurgency at that time came as a direct result.... Decisions just weren't getting made."

To be sure, the NPA's advances that year owed to a host of complicated factors, combining the social, political, and historical. Yet there was little denying the chaos that came due to Marcos' isolation. Morale plummeted among the cabinet ministers, who sometimes would not see the President for weeks at a time. "Only Imelda knew how sick he was," said Cristobal, the press aide. "He'd just telephone us, and not every day. She just stepped in. She'd always wanted to step in and this was her opportunity. We began sending less memos to Marcos because we were sure she was reading them. She shielded things from him, actually concealed the bad news concerning her people."

The high-level American diplomats trying to deal with Marcos in that period were just as frustrated. The Aquino killing had finally struck them with the urgent need for military reform, and the embassy had begun pressing the President to retire nearly thirty aging generals who had been kept on mostly due to their loyalty, while promotions were stalled for younger, more committed officers. Ver was one such aging general, and once indicted, he became a State Department cause célèbre. Under the gun, Marcos agreed to put Ver on leave, filling his job temporarily with General Fidel Ramos, an understated, cigar-chomping West Point graduate much admired by American military officers. But the move was a facade. Marcos forbade Ramos from making any policy or personnel changes without consulting him, while thwarting any attempts he made at leadership on his own. "Every time Ramos tried to do something, his underlings would run around to Ver or Marcos," said Gen. Theodore Allen, then head of the Joint U.S. Military Advisory Group in Manila.

As administration officials worked to get Ver retired, some became convinced it was Imelda who was standing in their way, working behind the scenes for the man who had once been her sworn enemy. This greatly increased her already vast share of their ill will. "I have no doubt that Marcos would have replaced Ver in 1984 without her fighting it," said a high-ranking intelligence official. Imelda persuaded her husband to stand firm by arguing that the Americans would smell blood if he gave up the general to them then. By siding with Ver, however, she antagonized not only the Americans, but also a new coalition of reformist soldiers then gathering under the guidance of Enrile and Ramos. Within two years, the Reform the Armed Forces Movement, or RAM, had sparked the anti-Marcos rebellion, propelled mostly by their fear of an Imelda-Ver takeover if Ferdinand Marcos died.

Imelda had good reason to be wary in 1984, but more and more her suspicions were driving her to hysteria. As 1985 began, her insomnia was worse than ever, and she would often summon fellow cabinet members to macabre, pre-dawn meetings at the palace. "We'd have to come...but then we'd all look for excuses to go to the comfort room," said her former ally, Labor Minister Blas Ople. Imelda by this time was convinced that Ople, Virata, and Enrile were scheming to take over as soon as her husband died, and with no apparent provocation she would suddenly begin to scream accusations of treachery at them. "The whole palace became paranoid along with her," said Ople. "The quality of your day could depend on what her children said at breakfast over the newspaper."

In fact, Ople did aspire to succeed Marcos, and in an interview in the spring of 1985 had revealed his willingness to run in the scheduled 1987 presidential elections. Making matters worse, he dismissed new talk of a draft-Imelda movement by calling the First Lady a "magnet of resentment" whose candidacy could hurt the country. As for Enrile, his hostilities with Imelda were by then well out in the open. Morales, Imelda's bodyguard, recalled seeing the minister approach Imelda at a public ceremony one afternoon late in 1984 to try to minimize rumors that she wanted him thrown out of government. As reporters hovered near, he began on a conciliatory note: "Ma'am, the press says we're supposed to be having a quarrel...." But Imelda drew back and snapped at him loudly, in a rare breach of her normal deference to public relations. "Well, it's because you're crazy!" she declared.

*          *          *

Even at that late stage, there were many in the palace who still hoped that they might boost the First Lady into power—and boost themselves by clinging to her skirts. But in 1985 Imelda ran into the worst spate of publicity she had yet endured. Much of it came from a string of embarrassments related to her chief aide and ally, Joly Benitez.

Fortified by two years of protests and international support, opposition legislators had grown bold enough to wage war on Imelda's superministry of Human Settlements. They had plenty of ammunition. In their nastiest attack, they dubbed Benitez, the deputy minister, "the Toilet King," in reference to his most glaring fiasco, the so-called Toilet Village of Cavite, a rural area just outside Manila. In 1985, the village was little more than hundreds of empty outhouses dotting a grassy hill, but at one time they had been part of a grand scheme to move thousands of squatters and relieve pressure on Manila, where a fifth of the eight million residents lacked any homes at all. A free toilet and a little plot of land were seen as fine incentives by the planners, but they'd forgotten a more important factor: jobs. There were almost none in or near Cavite, which meant that just as quickly as the government trucked squatters in, other squatters would sneak out. Before too long, the village of empty toilets became one more Marcos monument, this time memorializing the government's blindness to the simplest needs of the bulk of Filipinos, the poor.

Toilet Village was just one of many projects conceived by Imelda and Benitez which became wild disasters due to neglect or corruption or simple ill-conception. Imelda often had generous impulses, and quite a few Filipinos and Americans who worked with her believed she wanted to help poor people. For several years, in fact, Imelda's ministry had been in charge of allocating hundreds of millions of dollars in U.S. economic assistance. "Every time we got together, she showed clear concern," said AID director Fred Schieck. But her concentration was lacking, and she got snowed under by half-baked schemes—her prison-reform plan, for instance, to give each inmate a pig and window garden, or her fuel-reserve program to plant thousands of fast-growing ipil-ipil trees to burn as fuel.*

Whenever Imelda delegated, moreover, she picked people who were either sticky-palmed or as ill-suited as she was at management. While many of the ministry's projects, designed by Benitez, began with hopes of fundamental change for the poor, they quickly degenerated into handouts for the rich.

An example was the PAG-Ibig pension fund—a Tagalog acronym forming the word "Love"—to which all public workers were required to contribute. The fund was meant both to provide for retirement and to sponsor low-interest housing loans. Yet the interest was never so low as to be affordable by any but the upper-middle class, and few workers, meanwhile, had faith that any money would remain for their old age. Another ministry failure was the KKK, another Tagalog abbreviation that stood for "livelihood" and a system of generous government loans meant to foster industry in budding rural businesses. Begun in 1981, its budget grew to $457 million within a year. But very little of that money was distributed as announced. Though KKK recipients were supposed to be landless workers, urban slum dwellers, disabled people, and tribal minorities, many KKK dollars ended up going to military officials, while even more underwrote Imelda's multimillion-dollar promotional exhibit at Bloomingdales. Before too long, control of most of the small loans ended up in the hands of New Society Party (KBL) governors and mayors, who gave them to political favorites. Very few recipients ever paid anything back to the government.

By 1984, U.S. officials who dealt with the ministry were convinced that many of its officials were making fortunes from their jobs. In that year, four separate parliamentary investigations were pending involving the agency and Benitez. One investigation charged that Imelda's aide used ministry materials to build large homes for himself and his wife's parents. Another was based on a government audit that found the ministry unable to justify more than $10 million in expenditures, about $1 million of which were in the form of cash advances to Benitez.

---

*France and England financed seventeen of the would-be power plants, but the United States stayed aloof—wisely, as it turned out, since the land for the project was poor, and very few trees ever grew.

Most of all, Benitez and Imelda were blamed for wasting millions of dollars in the midst of the country's worst economic crisis. Ed Morato, Benitez's assistant, years later told how his boss inspired the ministry's crazed spates of construction, "just because the money was there. Joly would do things like offer a trip abroad to whoever completed the most 'livelihood' centers within a certain time—so at one point we had 119 two-story buildings go up in all sorts of places, mostly out of the way, where they'd never be used."

As pressures mounted in the parliament, the press, and even the palace for Benitez to quit, Imelda called in his wife, Joanne, a New York investment broker who had also become her friend. "You're the strong one," the First Lady began. "Like with me and the President." She then declared she had decided that Benitez would have to resign: there was nothing more she could do to protect him. "Joly's not a politician," she said. "Maybe it would be better if he quits and you two go abroad."

As Joanne Benitez told the story two years later in San Francisco, her husband stood silently chainsmoking at her side, letting his wife take charge much as she had done then with Imelda. "Marcos' men, Gapud and the rest, were grooming her in case Marcos died, and they didn't want Joly to be in there," Joanne said. "They were trying to make her get rid of him. But I started arguing immediately. I said, 'You can't do that to him. He doesn't just work for you. He loves you.' And she changed her mind right there."

Imelda's loyal impulse toward her mentor probably hastened the speed of her plummeting political stock, but by then it was too late for that to have made much difference. Members of the U.S. Congress had been alarmed by a 1984 General Accounting Office report revealing that the First Lady's ministry was in charge of distributing $200 million in U.S. aid. Marcos finally agreed to take jurisdiction of the money away from her, but even then she thwarted the move with her usual speed.

Marcos had signed a midnight order in August of 1984 to transfer control of the American aid from Imelda's ministry to the National Economic Development Authority, under the quiet and respectable Virata. In a typical stratagem, he made his move with utmost secrecy, and at a time when she was traveling outside of the country. Marcos' aides had persuaded him that the program wasn't getting enough management attention, and Schieck, the AID director, agreed. U.S.

officials had earlier insisted on monitoring each project supported with the funds, but no one in the ministry would take time to work with them. For lack of decisions, the money "just backed up and backed up and backed up," Schieck said. "In May of 1984, when I came in, the backlog was $80 to $90 million, all of it unused."

A Marcos aide checked with Schieck in advance of the President's order, asking if it posed any problem. "Hell, no!" came the response. But the change of management lasted only one week. Within a few days after Imelda returned from her trip, Marcos issued another order creating a new council to disburse the aid, and putting the First Lady back in charge.*

For all her sins, Imelda's most pernicious were those of omission. Together with many other Philippine leaders, she never once responded adequately to the most obvious needs of the poor. Despite her showy Nutricenter, for instance, she stubbornly refused to acknowledge malnutrition in the Philippines, and in fact tried to hide evidence of it, believing it a national embarrassment. "Her nutrition institution did research, but it wasn't ever allowed to publish," said Pratima Kale, the UNICEF representative in Manila in the 1980s.

In July 1985, however, Manila newspapers began publishing stories on the crisis of sugar farmers on the island of Negros. A severe drop in the world price of sugar combined with outrageous corruption and mismanagement had devastated the industry, and led to the point that children of plantation workers were starving. When international relief teams flew to the island, they learned the crisis hadn't happened overnight. "It began in 1979, and became an emergency in 1980," Kale said. "By the time we got there, we found close to 150,000 children who were malnourished."

The crisis was contained in the next year, partly thanks to the

---

*While many of the ministry's actions were legally or ethically questionable, Schieck said he witnessed only one case of abuse related to U.S. aid. It concerned the $80 million backlog, which was being held in a Philippine National Bank account, earning 20 percent interest, when he arrived. By bilateral agreement, the Marcoses couldn't touch the principal, but U.S. officials had learned of a presidential order letting him use the interest any way he saw fit. The dispute was never resolved, Schieck said, but during the 1986 election he heard provincial mayors claim that some new schools had been built with the aid money, even though the schools had never been approved. Then in December of 1985, Roberto Abling, a Human Settlements official with access to the fund, received a cash advance from it of more than $1 million. According to Schieck, Abling later claimed to have delivered the cash to the palace in a suitcase. "But there's no way to know what really happened to that money," he said.

Aquino government's cooperation. In a rare switch to a more localized, long-term approach, some 5000 home gardens were planted and research begun to find ways to rid the island of its dependence on the single crop. Still, Kale said she never completely blamed Imelda for her insensitivity. "Just like Hitler's Germany, the system has to provide a setting for individuals to act," she said. "There was always, and still is, an elitist approach to planning here, a focus on growth rather than equity."

In 1985, however, as in later years, these larger questions were pushed to the background by the Philippines' perennial rush of scandals and crises. In the forefront was Imelda herself, who, for the opposition, the Americans, and her own cabinet colleagues, was now the focus of hostility as never before. At rallies, protesters cheered when speakers demanded she resign all her posts. She was the constant butt of jokes, with increasingly pointed punchlines. One of the most celebrated gags had Marcos summoning Filipino chess champion Eugene Torre to his office to ask him the best strategy to save the country. Torre supposedly responded: "Easy. Sacrifice the Queen. If that doesn't work, resign."

# 13

# BECAUSE OF YOU

*All the perfumes of Arabia will not sweeten this little hand....*
—William Shakespeare, *Macbeth*, Act V, Scene 1

On a late November morning in 1985, the carved wooden doors of the Malacanang guest house flew open and Henry Byroade stomped out. He had only recently arrived in Manila, traveling as a private citizen on a tour with a few right-wing executives and television evangelist Jerry Falwell. The Marcoses, as usual, had taken him aside and insisted he stay at the palace. But he had realized the trip was a mistake from the first day, when he spotted Imelda at the airport. She had come with her film crew and was busily recording their arrival for a television broadcast that he knew would portray it as a signal of American support.

Nor was that the worst of it. It was less than a month after Marcos had made his shocking announcement that he'd hold early presidential elections. And Imelda had just finished saying that it had to be a landslide.

Byroade abruptly left the First Lady to go looking for his old friend. He tracked Marcos down in his study, and started right in. He knew what Imelda meant. "A landslide. That scares the hell out of me," he told the President. "The whole world is watching. It just won't be credible." The ex-ambassador to Pakistan and Egypt considered himself an expert on one-man governments, and he offered Marcos some of his wisdom. "A strongman comes in surrounded by backers," he

229

said. "The backers get stronger, and the boss still takes the blame. Then you find that when the chips are down, they're not cheating for you. They're cheating for them.

"Remember Bhutto," Byroade warned, watching Marcos' puffy face. Pakistan's ex-ruler Zulfikar Ali Bhutto had been overthrown by his army eight years earlier in the wake of outlandish electoral fraud. Within two more years, he was also convicted of killing a political rival and was executed by hanging. Marcos knew his story well, sharing Bhutto's driven sense of destiny, and the two words were enough. He beat his fist on his desk. "You put your finger on the problem," he blurted out. "Goddam it, I will control it."

The analogy seemed to have hit home, and yet Byroade left Manila depressed. Marcos couldn't control the system. More importantly, he couldn't control his wife.

Each night of his stay, Byroade had watched Imelda making the rounds of Manila's parties. She would huddle with groups of political leaders, a dozen at a time, chattering in her revved-up way and giving them all the same message that frightened Byroade so much. "I leave it up to you to take care of the President and deliver the votes," she would whisper in their ears. The system was securely in place, and as Byroade sensed, plenty of others besides the First Lady were ready to cheat to save their jobs. Imelda played on their greed like the pro she had long ago become. By day, she would telephone the wives of generals she had cultivated to remind them of their husbands' debts. "You know, Marcos has kept his hands off the military for all these years...," she would begin.

Imelda had fiercely opposed the plan to move up the elections. But in what had become standard procedure, Marcos had made his move while she was traveling in Japan, giving her no chance to convince him to hold back. When she heard of it, she simply said, "Oh, no!" But then she began to prepare for the campaign battle of her life.

It was a battle doomed from the start. By the fall of 1985, Marcos' illness was so evident that succession was on everyone's mind. Imelda remained, as one oppositionist phrased it, "the most visible noncandidate around," and many assumed she was Marcos' first choice to follow him. Yet all the years of publicity about her ambition and extravagance had finally taken its toll and Imelda's popularity had sunk to its nadir. It was already decided—not only by the opposition but the armed forces, the Church, Manila's business leaders, and the Americans—that she just couldn't be allowed to win.

The reasons were laid out explicitly in a confidential report released in September 1985 by a team of risk analysts from Frost & Sullivan, a New York firm that sells its wisdom to foreign investors. The four team members had impressive qualifications: two were Philippine experts with Ph.D.s in political science, a third was a U.S. government regional expert, and the last had served on a U.S. congressional foreign affairs staff. Their prognoses of an Imelda regime were dreadful. Military repression would grow more severe, and the armed forces could split, they wrote. The Communist insurgency would thrive from the chaos. Under Imelda, moreover, "an economic nationalist stance" could well emerge, the team warned, meaning the government might threaten bankers with debt boycotts until easier payback terms were offered.*

The report echoed the fears of U.S. government officials, most of whom felt sure Imelda would seize the presidency if given half a chance. "We were convinced she would make the play," said a high-level American intelligence official then in Manila. "But we were also aware that it would be very difficult for her to pull it off. Loyalties would not so easily be transferred. So we were not so much concerned that she would succeed as that the attempt would be so messy that the left would become the beneficiary, that it would create so much chaos in the government and in the military that it would be very hard for any kind of moderate center to keep power."

Nor was it any small matter that Imelda was personally loathed by many of Reagan's close advisers. "She was a pain in the ass," as Byroade put it. "She always wanted to be treated as a head of state, and that offended everyone. It got so that one way to curry favor in the White House was not to be in her good graces."

American pressure had already won the decision to call for early elections to be held in February 1986. And soon afterward more of the same achieved a second surprise concession—again made while Imelda was on the road and out of touch. After so many years of protesting his "allergy" to vice presidents, Marcos at last agreed to run with one.

For Imelda, this was a particularly cruel blow. She knew by then that she was too unpopular for a Marcos-Marcos ticket, but she had

---

*It is interesting to note that to various extents some of these predictions have come true under Aquino's rule.

thus far managed to block anyone else from running with her husband. She made a fast recovery, however, and found the ideal candidate for her purposes in former KBL senator Arturo Tolentino. Once a feisty Marcos critic, Tolentino more recently had acquired such an agreeable image that he was known as "The Jukebox"—willing to play whatever tune was requested. Fit and vigorous for his 75 years, he nonetheless made the Marcoses a private promise to resign after the election for reasons of his advancing age, according to a knowledgeable Marcos aide.

Imelda was fighting back hard, taking on even Cardinal Sin, whom she tried unsuccessfully to have transferred from Manila on her trips to the Vatican. That failing, she finally attempted to bribe the cardinal by dropping by his office two months before the elections with a cakebox full of one million freshly minted pesos, or $50,000. "This was the first time she offered money," said Sin, who accepted the box but maintained he turned it over to charity.

The rash attempt showed Imelda's very justified desperation. The early election call had weakened Marcos just as she had feared it would. Agreeing to it at all had been risky, but broadening the race to include vice presidential candidates was a terrible mistake, she felt, and one that Marcos, in better times, would surely have foreseen. Its effect was to increase the pressure for union on Corazon Aquino and Salvador Laurel, two fledgling opposition candidates who might otherwise never have formed their ultimately successful ticket.

"Cory" Aquino, the shy widow of the slain Ninoy, had been pushed into the race by her opposition colleagues. Her most powerful appeal was the shadow of her husband, by then a saintly image she kept constantly before the reverent crowds who waited hours to see her and hear her tell them, over and over again, how he had died. At 53, she had spent years training for martyrdom. The mother of five, she had bravely endured the seven years of her husband's imprisonment, pleading with his jailers for extra privileges and carrying his messages back out to reporters. She was always quiet, always putting herself second— even after Aquino's death, when she confessed she had prayed to him for political advice.

At the same time, Cory Aquino by her own rights was a confirmed member of the once powerful Filipino political elite. She had grown up in luxury, her family's immense fortune based on its 15,000-acre sugar hacienda in Tarlac province. Her background made her instinctively conservative and pro-American; she was educated mostly by foreign nuns, spending seven years of her schooling in New York, at the women's College of Mt. St. Vincent in the Bronx.

Though inexperienced politically and nearly bereft of charisma, Aquino alone had the moral mandate that could make the oppositionists, for once, put aside their own ambitions. There was much talk, then and later, of the "Filipino crab," which when placed in a bucket joins its fellows only when one starts to try to crawl out—at which point they all unite to drag their fellow back down. But the politicians immediately recognized Aquino's symbolic value, and in it, their own salvation. All saw it, that is, but Laurel.

"Doy" Laurel was an intensely ambitious politician and the son of the Supreme Court justice who had long ago ruled to spare Marcos' life. The younger Laurel had also supported Marcos until the late 1970s, after which he was generally spared from political persecution in acknowledgment of the old debt. By 1983, he had formed the twelve-party opposition umbrella, the United Nationalist Democratic Organization (UNIDO), of which he was president. Admired for his political skill, he was nonetheless suspected of ruthlessness and not widely loved. For those impatient for change after the long Marcos rule, Laurel, a very traditional Filipino politician, also seemed the least likely to bring true reforms.

Above all, Laurel's hunger for power worried many in the opposition. He was nothing if not determined: he told *Asia Week* magazine in a November interview that he had skipped rope 1000 times every morning for the past twenty-five years. ("The moment I reach 800 I start perspiring.") The exercise followed his morning ritual of Bible reading and prayers for divine guidance, he noted. Many feared that so driven a man would insist on running no matter what the majority decided and split the anti-Marcos vote. But the announcement of the Marcos-Tolentino ticket prompted several marathon meetings with Aquino, ending in Laurel's agreement on December 12 to campaign as her vice presidential nominee for the elections set for February 7, 1986.

The race became a morality play unequaled in Philippine history. Each campaign appearance was as laden with drama as the radio soap operas so beloved in the provinces. Marcos would limp to face crowds, his boldly striped, lucky "shirtjac" clashing with his pale, tired face. He struggled pitifully to stand, sometimes literally propped up by his aides.

A large van followed close behind, and at times, Marcos would abruptly retreat behind its doors. Still, official word went out that he limped from old "war wounds." His illness—in the past called bronchitis, blackwater fever, or allergies—now was "asthma." Soon, however, Marcos began to miss events, and it fell to Imelda once again to keep up appearances. She agreed with her usual zeal, and brought an even more outlandish contrast to the two campaigns.

There would be Cory Aquino, in her matronly spectacles and prim yellow dress, nasally urging the crowds to pray and making claims on their moral judgment with all the pizzazz of a postal clerk on a bad morning. She had no real plan for governing, she confessed, vowing, "The only thing I can offer the Filipino people is my sincerity."

Then there was Imelda, cracking salacious Tagalog jokes and throwing jasmine blossoms, pesos, or cheap watches to the crowds, the sunlight flashing from the diamonds at her ears or catching the shine on her blood-red fingernails. As she moved among the slum dwellers, they pushed and shoved to get close to her, but no one knew if they hustled for love or mere desire to be within tossing range.

The crowds who worshipped Aquino saw in her the two pillars of modern, middle-class Filipino faith: her closeness to the Church and her identification with America. Her holy aura came less from her Jesuit advisers and personal conviction than from all the Catholic symbolism of sacrifice, suffering, and redemption she evoked. Compared to her, Imelda looked increasingly tawdry and evil, and the First Lady's old supporters suddenly grew shameful of the baser responses she had always called forth in them. The Marcos rallies drew large crowds, but they were now mostly cynical crowds, paid on the spot with lunch boxes, t-shirts, 20-peso notes, or the chance to see a movie star bought off by the regime. The Aquino rallies brought the true believers. If the speeches were flat, the crowds were spontaneous and lively, full of spirit and new hope for the future.

Sensing this, Imelda redoubled her efforts. Aquino to her was a personal insult of the highest degree: She had come from the landed wealthy class that Imelda had always felt snubbed by, but even worse than that, she was a woman who was winning power seemingly without effort. The injustice of it all, after Imelda's long, hard climb, made her furious. She denounced Aquino as "the complete opposite of what a woman should be" and professed herself aghast that she would run against a man. The ideal woman, said the First Lady, is "gentle [and] does not challenge a man, but...keeps her criticisms to herself and teaches her husband only in the bedroom." She ridiculed Aquino for not wearing makeup and said yellow, her campaign color, reminded her of "jaundice, or a lemon." In a rally in Tacloban City, the heart of her Leyte political base, she called Aquino "worse than a Communist because she is allowing herself to be used by the Communists."

Still, it was obvious where the momentum lay. The controlled television stations were forbidden to film the vivid seas of yellow t-shirts and banners and people shouting "Co-ry, Co-ry!" that circled Aquino nearly every time she spoke, but Imelda didn't lack evidence. And it terrorized her: by mid-January, said a close friend, she was waking from nightmares before dawn and rushing from the palace with her guards in search of more hands to shake.

The rest of the palace joined her in her panic. No one had guessed how right Byroade was when he'd said the whole world would be watching. Days after Marcos' promise to move up elections, foreign reporters began to crowd into Manila, and they kept on coming until there were an estimated 1000 of them for election week, more than had ever come before. Network camera crews strode in their obligatory safari vests through the tony lobby of the Manila Hotel. NBC-TV's Tom Brokaw and Edward Kennedy, Jr., on special assignment for the *Boston Globe*, sat in on press conferences. The government office set up to assist and attempt to control the international press was besieged by Americans, Canadians, Italians, and Japanese. "It's one reporter for every vote!" shrieked one presidential aide.

Still, the general mood was one of welcome from each side. The Marcoses had long been unusually tolerant—even inviting—of foreign scrutiny, while oppositionists plainly regarded the visitors as helpmates in their struggle. The combination produced some strange results. When Marcos announced that he would call early elections, for instance, he did it on American television, in an interview with David Brinkley. And when both camps made victory speeches after the voting, they did so first before American network reporters. Aquino lined up her interviews with all three networks in a quiet room of her campaign headquarters, while a roomful of Filipino journalists were kept waiting for hours for her downstairs.

Finally, at a critical stage in the counting of votes after February 7, during one of the dozens of press conferences each side was holding, an Aquino spokesman named Rene Saguisag was handed what he declared was an urgent bulletin. A southern opposition mayor was seeking help. Pro-government officials in his province were refusing to count ballots for Aquino. "Please," Saguisag read, looking up and around the room for emphasis, "send foreign correspondents immediately." No one, by that time, raised an eyebrow. The foreign press had become a key actor in the Filipino drama.

Nor could the reporters be blamed for enjoying the windfall. The story was irresistible, full of conflict and color and injustice. Manila's appalling contrasts between rich and poor were rediscovered and made banal as reporters trooped from its putrid slums to the ostentatious enclaves of the rich. Meanwhile, unabashed Marcos loyalists jovially compared their voting system with Chicago's under Mayor Richard Daley or Louisiana's under Governor Huey P. Long. There was a constant supply of intrigues and scandals. And when all else failed, Imelda always made good copy.

The First Lady loved the attention but even she soon came to see how much of it was ridicule. As she had often done before, she flipped back and forth between courting the powerful foreigners and showing her hurt in anger. To the CIA station chief, she sent an early Valentine's Day bouquet, 4 feet tall and with huge red cardboard hearts placed among the imported blossoms. For Ambassador Stephen Bosworth, who had replaced Michael Armacost, she threw a large party to celebrate his wedding. The festivities, which she naturally televised, ended in a ceremony in which the ambassador and his wife, Christine, were seated on little thrones and presented with matching tiaras. ("I saw them crowned!" gasped Filipina journalist Paulynn Sicam, who watched the live afternoon broadcast.)*

Finally one evening that December, Imelda rushed to the U.S. Embassy building to try to persuade members of a hunger strike to quit their protest. "I was trying to free the U.S. Embassy of this irritation and apprehension," she told me days later. "I got no thanks, but it's all right," she added, giggling. "I did not do it for a pat on the back."

At other times she lashed out. That winter she made yet another

---

*Bosworth, in a brief telephone interview in 1987, said he did not distinctly recall the experience, but then added the "crowns" "may have been garlands of flowers."

high-profile trip to Moscow, where she presented the Soviet government with a statue of the Virgin Mary. Shortly after her return, she was overheard at a luncheon complaining about the Americans. "I was told during my trip to Russia that were it not for the Marcoses, with whom they can still communicate in a civilized way, the Soviets would have overrun the Philippines long ago," she began. "And believe you me, they are ready. They know their marbles." It began as a familiar rant, but it then took a strange turn. Imelda went on talking, with hardly a transition, but her subject had now become herself, and as she spoke it became clearer than ever just how much she had merged her own wounded self-image with her view of the Philippines. "America cannot accept a woman's superiority," she declared. "Especially tall and beautiful Filipino women who are smartly dressed . . . and they go even crazier if you are wearing high heels and looking very smart. Just because you are a woman, they think you are frivolous. Just because you can sing a little, you are not to be taken seriously.

"The trouble with America is if you're a friend, you're damned; if you're an enemy you're dead," Imelda concluded, oblivious, she claimed later, to the *Time* magazine reporter's tape recorder turned on nearby. "I'm waiting. I am already damned as it is. They really want me. I must be delicious. One of these days you will see me hanging from a tree. I'll be dead. . . . The moment [Marcos and I] are no longer here, the Russians will immediately take over. Stupid America!"

It was the First Lady's most naked moment to date, and afterward even Marcos had to concede how much of a liability she'd become. But his efforts to control her proved futile. "I was told several times by the President to tone down her media appearances," said Hermie Rivera, the palace press aide. "But how in the hell could I tell her that?"

Imelda still couldn't resist reporters and the feeling was mutual. "I found her fascinating," said Andy Hernandez, a Filipino photographer for the Associated Press and *Newsweek*. At 56, she still had much of the allure that made her, as her former aide Francisco Tatad once said, "the most look-at-able First Lady ever." Only recently had she gained weight and assumed a constant hunted expression. "She was so photogenic, and if you asked her to mingle with the crowd, to pose, she always would," said Hernandez.

Unlike her husband, Imelda was constantly trailed by a private camera crew, which by 1985 included a small movie crew and three still photographers for close-up, color, and black-and-white shots. They also acted as censors to the news photographers, warning them away from shots that would emphasize Imelda's double chin. Imelda herself once chastised Filipino photographers for taking a picture of her in which she cast what seemed to be a longing look toward the King of Spain.

Despite her occasional wariness of the foreign press, Imelda resolved to woo them for the crucial election. She had prepared for it apparently since 1984, when, in a luncheon meeting in New York, she asked her realtor, Joe Bernstein, about whether she might refinance her properties to pull out $70 million in 1987, then the scheduled election year.

She had reason to plan ahead. It had been a bad two years for both Marcoses, but especially for her. Parliamentary elections in May 1984—meant to show the regime could afford to loosen up—had ended in a New Society Party (KBL) disaster. The opposition had won more than 60 of 183 contested seats, whereas before it had held only 15. Most bitterly for Imelda, her slate was roundly defeated in Metro Manila, where she was still governor and had been expected to deliver. But opposition had grown to an enormous extent; most Filipinos were finding life much harder, and they blamed the Marcoses. The economy continued to suffer the impact of Aquino's killing: the GNP was down by 10 percent and nearly fifteen leading corporations had gone bankrupt by June of 1985. Even the most conservative executives who weren't paid off had joined the opposition. To all that must be added the fact that Marcos was sick for most of 1985. Imelda, increasingly, had to face the flak alone.

The Marcoses nonetheless had some advantages going into the 1986 elections. Among the most potent were the "warlords"—intensely loyal and powerful leaders scattered around the archipelago who routinely delivered votes with ruthless skill. Of the seventy-four Philippine provinces, thirty-four were considered "forbidden territory" to the opposition, mostly due to the warlords' influence. Among their ranks were Cebu's Ramon Durano, a former member of Congress who kept a 10-foot Statue of Liberty in his backyard and sent thugs to terrorize poll watchers; Ilocos Norte's Lieutenant Governor Roque Ablan, who promised Marcos his province wouldn't yield even one vote for the opposition; and Cagayan's Defense Minister Enrile, who controlled his province with equal force and determination. The warlords' greatest strength was their ability to co-opt the underpaid provincial constabulary. In many areas, the military men acted as errand boys and bodyguards to the wealthy Marcos loyalists, who in turn were heavily subsidized by the palace. Come election time, it wasn't rare to see the Philippines' finest in their military jeeps, decked out in Marcos t-shirts and with Marcos bumper-stickers plastered on their guns.

By 1985, the Marcoses' election war chest seemed limited only by imagination. While past elections had been funded by raids on the Central Bank, the 1986 campaign was underwritten with hundreds of millions of pesos from Manila's Security Bank and Trust Company, of which Marcos was half-owner.

Confronting all that force and money was the struggling Aquino campaign and 450,000 volunteers organized as the National Citizens Movement for Free Elections, or NAMFREL. The voting-list checkers, poll watchers, and ballot box guards of NAMFREL were the most selfless heroes of the revolution that was to come. Mostly they were middle-class Filipinos who had simply had enough and were ready to risk anything for change within the democratic system. It was a special shock to Imelda that some were former Blue Ladies, society matrons who rode sternly through Manila slums in their chauffeur-driven Mercedes to check voting lists.

NAMFREL was first created by Ed Lansdale with CIA funds in the 1950s for the campaign of Ramon Magsaysay. It was then resurrected in 1983 by Jose Concepcion, Jr., a rotund and wealthy flour merchant who would describe election abuses to foreign visitors over lunch at his office penthouse. (Under the Aquino government, Concepcion took a job as a trade minister, braving charges of a lack of the old social sensitivity, *delicadeza*, since it seemed counter to his former insistence on political neutrality.) In the 1984 election, NAMFREL volunteers had been shot at and beaten and robbed, yet they came back two years later with even greater zeal.

Their faith was boosted by increasing signals of American support. By the spring of 1985, high-level administration officials were making some remarkable statements against the Marcos regime. In March, for instance, Assistant Defense Secretary Richard Armitage told a congressional panel that Philippine communist guerrillas might win within three years without significant military reforms. "The Filipino people deserve better than the triumph of a communist insurgency or the continuation of economic, social, and political conditions which fuel insurgency," he declared. The same month, Assistant Secretary of State Paul Wolfowitz warned that U.S.-Philippine relations depended on the credibility of the ongoing trial of General Ver and the two dozen military men implicated as assassins of Benigno Aquino. (By December, however, the Philippine Supreme Court ruled to exclude key testimony against the defendants, and all were acquitted.) The policy shift was above all pragmatic: realization had sunk in that the Marcoses' misrule had allowed the communists to grow at an alarming rate. U.S. estimates of the New People's Army's strength had reached 15,000, sparking worries that they might soon threaten the security of the strategic U.S. bases.

The Reagan administration was moving slowly, but it was obviously now moving away from its former embrace. A team of congressional observers led by Republican Senator Richard Lugar of Indiana was sent to monitor the voting. More significantly, NAMFREL secretly received at least $300,000 in U.S. aid.

Other U.S. developments raised the pressure throughout the campaign. Representative Solarz's congressional committee held well-publicized hearings on the Marcoses' alleged corruption. And in Alexandria, Virginia, a federal grand jury began meeting on a separate case, trying to determine whether Marcos officials—specifically Ver—had diverted any U.S. military aid for their own use. In one of the cruelest blows, as far as Marcos was concerned, *The New York Times* published a story on January 23, based on previously unavailable U.S. reports leaked by Australian historian Alfred McCoy, alleging Marcos' war claims were "fraudulent" and "absurd."

\*       \*       \*

The Marcoses' last campaign began December 11 and ended two months later with rallies for the incumbent and challenger. Each was held in the bay-front Luneta Park, and each was a revealing portrait of the status of the respective campaigns. Aquino's was fervent and enormous, with estimates of 250,000 to half a million Filipinos in ecstatic attendance. Marcos', the next day, was glum and regimented, its low spirits dampened even further by a sudden tropical downpour. Less than 15,000 people showed up despite lures of free t-shirts and 20-peso bills.

At 7 a.m. on February 7, an estimated 24 million Filipinos began to cast their votes. "It could be liberation day, or it could be the start of civil war," said Vida Balboa, a suburban Manila housewife. She and others had good reason for their qualms. Marcos' henchmen were pulling out all the stops, and violence and confusion and bribery were recorded live throughout the archipelago for international television viewers. More than fifty Filipinos had already been killed in election-related incidents since the campaign began.

In several towns, voters were paid as much as 100 pesos, or $5—often the price of two days' work—to hand over their blank ballots to Marcos' supporters. (Cardinal Sin, meanwhile, was spreading the word that it wasn't a sin to take the money and vote for Aquino. "The money is a gift," he said. "It comes from the coffers of the country.") NAMFREL workers were shut out of many polling places. Whole precincts were redrawn at the last minute by the government-controlled election commission, known as COMELEC, leaving thousands waiting for hours for announcements as to where they should vote.

The vote-counting began in the midst of hourly charges of new fraud and abuse from what seemed to be one continuous press conference at the chaotic Aquino headquarters, the tall Cojuangco building in Manila's financial district of Makati. NAMFREL and COMELEC were each conducting separate counts. Foreign residents said they were stocking up on food, staying close to home, and in some cases, buying airplane tickets to provide for emergency exits.

Imelda tried to convey a sense of calm, sweeping into the Manila Hotel for several evenings in a row, with bellboys running to lay out her red carpet toward the velvet-draped Champagne Room, to the left off the lobby, or up a few stairs and through a lounge to the Caffe Roma, with its sloping glass roof and tall potted trees, where she liked the pasta and the muzak that played "Feelings." But later, in the early morning hours, she would often order the driver of her black, six-door Mercedes to drive her to the Villa San Miguel, the palatial residence of Cardinal Sin. There she would stay for as long as two hours at a time, Sin said later, pleading, "Why is this happening to us? We have done so much good for the country! And why don't they love me? I am so good." The cardinal merely nodded, except for one or two occasions when he couldn't resist admonishing her for "coming to the House of Sin at such an hour." Yet he said afterward that he began then to feel sorry for Imelda, despite all that she had done.

Both Marcoses in fact had begun to seem pathetic, while Manila waited with premonitions of inevitable change. It was then that Enrile made his move. For the past two years, the minister and two of his most trusted colonels, Eduardo "Red" Kapunan and Gregorio "Gringo" Honasan, had been plotting a rebellion—despite Enrile's later claims that he had acted on the spur of the moment and in self-defense, to save himself from being arrested by Ver. When the officers felt the time was right, in the chaotic week after election, one of their first recruits was Captain Ricardo Morales, Imelda's handsome young bodyguard. Imelda had taken a special liking to Morales, and had even paid for his schooling at the Asian Institute of Management. He, in turn, had never given any sign that he was anything but completely reliable. But after three years of watching palace life from the inside, Morales had grown disgusted. "I was ripe for the picking," he said. "The system was rotten."

Morales was approached by Honasan, a dashing, moustachioed young colonel who was one of Enrile's closest aides in the defense ministry. The plan, said Honasan, was for two dozen rebels to enter the palace on Sunday, February 23, set off explosives to assassinate General Ver, kidnap the Marcoses, and move them to Fort Bonifacio, where they would be forced to abdicate in favor of a civilian junta. "According to Gringo, the junta would include Cardinal Sin, [Cesar] Virata, and Jose Concepcion," Morales said in 1987. "I asked him point-blank if Enrile was involved. He said no. I realize now he must have lied."

Morales readily agreed to provide sketches of the palace interior and to lead a commando assault. But two days before D-day, Marcos' soldiers learned of the plan and arrested Morales and three other officers.

Enrile and his men changed their plans and instead of storming the palace, fled to Camp Aguinaldo, the armed forces headquarters, on Saturday. There they were joined by General Fidel Ramos. From his office, the minister called U.S. Ambassador Bosworth to advise him of his stakeout, while Enrile's wife, Cristina, urged reporters to head to the camp, saying her husband's life was in danger. Enrile also called Sin, pleading with the cardinal to help save his life, and believing that Enrile was in danger, Sin joined forces with the former architect of martial law.

At about 9 p.m. Sunday, the cardinal was heard over Radio Veritas, urging Manilans to come out to support the rebels. To his priests and nuns, he said, "Get out from your cells, proceed from the chapel with outstretched arms, singing. You are the Moses." He then called on residents around the military camps: "This is risky," he said. "But get out from your houses and proceed to Camp Aguinaldo." At least half a million obeyed and came to the camp gates, crowding the wide boulevard outside, known as Edsa, for Epifanio de los Santos. They treated the soldiers within like beloved guests, bringing them food, lending them rosaries, and wiping perspiration from their brows. When the rebels moved to consolidate at the nearby Camp Crame, the crowd surged alongside them like a vast corps of bodyguards.

The Marcoses seemed caught off-balance and reacted lethargically. The *Manila Post* later reported that Imelda ordered doctors to inject her husband with amphetamines so that he could address the nation. In any case, he didn't appear until 11 p.m. Sunday, when he weakly called on Enrile and Ramos to surrender.

For Cardinal Sin, political pragmatist that he'd become, the next three days were full of wonders. When the police released tear gas, he said, the wind blew it back toward their ranks. And soldiers charging the gates later told him they were stopped by the vision of "a lady with stars in her hair who said, 'Stop. I am the Queen.'" Yet the true miracle was something photographers could capture—and did—on Monday afternoon, when tanks and armored transports bearing some 3000 marines were halted en route to Camp Crame by a human barricade of tens of thousands of Filipinos.

Of the events that spelled the Marcoses' end, that moment was the most meaningful. It gave Aquino an instant international mandate and stirred sleeping pride within her people. From then on, things moved even more quickly: the White House statement later that day blaming vote fraud on the KBL; the mutiny, Monday, of an entire palace helicopter assault team; and the help, as it was reported later, of CIA agents who joined Enrile in his compound to disperse false propaganda that encouraged more defections.

At Malacanang Monday night, Marcos declared over government television that he had "no intention of going abroad. We will defend the republic until the last breath of our life and to the last drop of blood." But the family was at the haggard end of a terrifying day. One of the helicopter pilots who had defected had returned to the palace that morning to fire a barrage of six rockets. They landed near

Imelda's bedroom, demolishing her son-in-law Greg Araneta's car and sending the First Lady running to hide in the pantry.

At 3 a.m. Tuesday (3 p.m. Monday in Washington, D.C.), Marcos telephoned Republican Senator Paul Laxalt of Nevada, who had acted as Reagan's emissary on a trip earlier that year. He was threatening to "fight it out," but asked if it was true that even Reagan had turned against him. Two hours later, Laxalt called back to give advice which was soon published around the world. "Cut and cut cleanly," he said. "The time has come."

There was a long pause, after which Laxalt asked Marcos if he was still there. "Yes," came the answer. "I am so very, very disappointed."

Imelda called Nancy Reagan the same morning, and was reportedly assured that the Marcoses could come to the United States if they desired. Yet on Tuesday, the Marcoses weren't taking that idea seriously. They did by then intend to leave the palace but didn't plan for it to be permanent, and they weren't about to go until Marcos legally established himself as victor in the presidential elections.

Just before noon, Cory Aquino was inaugurated at the Club Filipino. Marcos was determined to have his own ceremony. Hastily planned, it was brief and spare, before a few hundred government employees, Blue Ladies, and others the Marcoses had made wealthy through the years. At its end, the President and First Lady stepped out on the balcony to pay respects to 3000 KBL loyalists assembled below, who shouted up to Marcos to "Capture the snakes!" Imelda wept and sang, "Dahil Sa Iyo," chanting her trademark Tagalog entreaties:

> *Because of you I attained happiness*
> *I offer you my love*
> *If it is true that you shall enslave me*
> *All of this is because of you.*

For a few hours afterward, the country lurched along with two presidents. (The two vote counts had been abandoned, and no reliable record was ever established of who had won the elections.) But even the most faithful Marcos loyalists could see their epoch was over. As she watched Imelda sing, "I thought of Marie Antoinette and the beating of the drums," said Carmencita Reyes, a former Blue Lady. "I thought, here is the end of a glorious regime."

\*          \*          \*

Imelda changed into trousers and spent much of the rest of the afternoon pacing back and forth in the grand reception hall, fretting with dozens of visitors who milled about under the tall portraits of past Philippine presidents. Marcos was out of sight—exhausted and ill, it was whispered. Joly Benitez, who had hurried back to Manila from Baguio that morning, stuck close to his protectoress. He had been in hiding since the revolt began, but had rushed back after hearing Marcos' televised call Monday night for all loyalists to return for the inauguration. "It all seemed so unreal," he said later. "Everyone was asking, how can it be happening? Why isn't the President moving? I asked the First Lady, 'What can be done?' and she said, 'Not much. We'll do what we can. Marcos will find some way to handle this.' Everyone was saying something had to be done, but by Tuesday it was too late. It should've been done before."

Yet Imelda was still trying to think of something. "Someone said we should have a command post, and Imelda said he should tell that to General Ver," Benitez recalled. But the palace was pitifully, surreally disorganized. Members of the presidential security command roamed about in fatigues instead of their customary formal clothes. No one seemed to know what to do next. Finally Imelda whispered to Benitez that the Marcoses were helpless "because of the U.S. Marines. The Americans were guarding the bay." It wasn't long afterward that she told him to get his things ready to leave.

Shortly after 6:30 p.m., Benitez came back to the palace with his luggage. Malacanang's halls were dirty and nearly deserted. He climbed the plush red-carpeted stairs, turned down the passageway to Imelda's room, and found her dazed and disheveled. She was standing motionless near her canopied bed with its carved wooden crown as her maid bustled about. Clothes were strewn on the handwoven bedspread; drawers were flung open and empty jewelry boxes lay all around.

"She was standing as if in a trance, asking the maid to find a pair of shoes," he said. He led her gently toward the elevator to take them both to the first floor and out the back door to the banks of the Pasig River. She was walking slowly and murmuring incoherently. As they moved through the passageway toward the reception hall, she snatched pictures of the family from the wall, and just before they entered the elevator, she came on a last photograph of Marcos, taken several years earlier and showing him looking healthy and relaxed in his golfing hat. Marcos wore a golfing hat that evening, too, as he walked outside to meet his family. Yet now he looked feverish and distraught, limping along on the arm of a valet. A few of the palace guard who weren't going with them watched him anxiously as he passed, and just as he reached the water, he turned back and shouted, "Don't worry, boys. I'll be back in three days!" It was close to 8 p.m., and they could all see the two large helicopters that had landed on the opposite bank.

The family was hoisted by their servants into a small Navy boat called the Captain's Jig. Bongbong was wearing fatigues, had grenades in his pockets, and was carrying what looked like an Uzi machine gun. Irene was carrying her violin case. It took five minutes to cross, and then they all hurried to the copters. The boat had to return two more times to get the eighty-odd friends, employees, and servants who went along, and it was dark by the time it made its last trip. Still, a lieutenant assigned to Marcos' security said he clearly saw his chief being carried under the arm of a U.S. Marine, "like a sack of rice." The sight made him weep, he said, adding, "I was ready to order my men to fire, but an officer told them to hold back." Another Marine hurried Imelda into the second helicopter, his hand tightly clasped around her upper arm. Sitting close to Benitez, she took out a rosary and began murmuring Hail Marys. As they took off, they saw for the first time the medieval tableau of the threat outside the gates: the thousands of angry Filipinos raising torches and shouting.

Marcos later said leaving Malacanang was the biggest mistake he ever made. When he flew off with his family, however, he believed he'd be taken not to America and exile but to Ilocos Norte, the most trustworthy stronghold of his support.

The arrangements had been made Tuesday night in a dozen phone calls back and forth between Brigadier General Theodore Allen, chief of the Joint U.S. Military Assistance Group, and Marcos and Araneta at Malacanang. Marcos had told Allen that he wanted to go to Ilocos Norte, stay there a day and a half, and tell the Americans then where he'd go after that.

"Our agreement when we went into the palace was we'd take him to Ilocos Norte," Allen told me in May 1987. But within a couple hours after the helicopters landed at Clark Air Base, things had changed dramatically. Ambassador Bosworth had talked to Cory

Aquino, by then the recognized Philippine president, and she had decided she couldn't tolerate Marcos staying in the country. Adding to the urgency, Allen had received a call from the commander of the Philippine Air Force detachment guarding the perimeter of Clark, who told him he questioned the loyalty of his troops, and couldn't guarantee they could keep mobs from the air base. "The word in the province was 'People Power' would be mobilized, that two million people would be marching to Clark," Allen said, adding, "I could just see it. A march on Clark."

The Marcoses were resting, but Allen roused Tommy Manotoc and Bongbong at about 2 a.m. Wednesday and told them he couldn't assure their safety if they stayed. The two young men went into the room where Marcos and Imelda were sleeping and came out after fifteen minutes, saying the couple had agreed to leave. Allen never really knew if they had told Marcos where he was going. But it disturbed him, he said later, how Marcos complained of his treatment afterward. "I think he's a proud man and probably would have stayed and died at Malacanang," said Allen. "But we saved his life, and there's not a grateful bone in his body."

Marcos had been awake for nearly three days running and was bleary-eyed and stumbling. He had to be carried from his room on a stretcher, and it fell to the American general to pick him up and lay him in the C141 transport plane bound for Guam. Imelda trailed behind, "out of touch, with a faraway expression in her eyes," as her maids helped her through the door.

Manila by this time had been celebrating for several hours. The night-shift workers at hotels and the airport greeted guests with giddy pride, calling, "Happy Liberation Day!" Calendar pages lined the streets of Makati, as if it were the New Year.

A few Marines were still walking around the palace grounds with yellow ribbons on their helmets, signifying their support for Aquino as they guarded the halls from looters and loyalists. Shortly after midnight, thousands of Manilans had stormed through the gates, and for a short time, many of them had run free through the palace halls, in a frenzy of possibilities. Outside, people stomped on the Marcos-Tolentino buttons littering the ground, enjoying the loud pops they made. Then suddenly, they all looked up at the balcony where the Marcoses had said their farewells. Two young boys had seized a large portrait of Imelda in an evening gown and were dangling it from the railing, making it dance in the long shadows from the paper bonfires below. Someone had painted horns above her head and a devil's tail behind her. The crowd in the courtyard reached up, yelling.

For a moment, it was as if Imelda were still just out of reach, above them all. Then the boys let the portrait fall, to be crushed under the stamping feet of the mob.

As for Imelda herself, she perked up a bit on the ten-hour flight to Guam, and began loudly complaining about the lack of windows and the draftiness of the big U.S. cargo plane. Then she began to sing. "Ferdie said he wished he had a hammer so he could hit me over the head and shut me up," she later told an American reporter. It may have been mere *palabas*—it was almost too perfect a touch—but the song she was later reported to have sung, over and over again on that long flight to exile, was one of her favorite American show tunes, "New York, New York."

# 14

# MORE ABOUT
# NEW YORK

*All I ever dreamed of when I was a tiny girl was a little house with a
little picket fence by the sea.*
                    —Imelda Marcos, in an interview with the author,
                    December 1985

The Marcoses arrived in Hawaii on Wednesday afternoon. With them,
in thirty-two boxes, crates, attache cases, and leather Louis Vuitton
and Gucci bags, they carried almost $9 million in jewelry, cash, and
bonds. Among the jewelry, according to U.S. Customs records, were
a $58,286 tiara of pearls and diamonds; a $44,410 diamond-studded
hair comb; a matching set of a bracelet, earrings, and broach in sap-
phires, rubies, and diamonds priced together at $1,487,415; and an
emerald and diamond pendant worth $74,825. In one suitcase alone,
a red russet leather bag marked "777," 93 items of jewelry confronted
the stunned Honolulu customs agents. They included a sea of pearls,
blue-, pink-, and silver-toned, loose and strung in chokers; single
globes set in gold earrings and twisted freshwater strands with ruby
and diamond clasps. Other bags held handguns, videotapes, more
watches (Cartier, Rolex, and Geneve) and millions of dollars worth
of freshly minted American and Philippine currency.

Former labor minister Blas Ople said Imelda had told him six
months before the fall, "I may not be able to be president, but I can
be kingmaker and fund you to eternity." It was not until that week,
he said, that he realized she wasn't exaggerating.

The U.S. Customs Service took control of the cargo and maintained custody of it pending a federal court's resolution of claims by

the new Philippine government. Getting back the Marcoses' "hidden wealth" was already a top priority of Aquino's administration: on Wednesday, her first day in office, she had set up the Commission on Good Government to recover as many of the overseas investments as possible. Within a year, the commission had seized 295 companies; $87 million in Philippine currency; $44 million in Philippine real estate; a Princeton, New Jersey, mansion worth $1 million; Philippine stock valued at $50 million; forty-two airplanes and helicopters; fifteen ocean-going ships; and thirty-three mansions built around the country. Yet the new administration's most dramatic coup took place one week after its creation.

On Wednesday night—Thursday morning in Manila—a young Filipina attorney named Severina Rivera got a call at her Washington, D.C., home from Jovito Salonga, the Good Government Commission's new director. Salonga had heard the Bernstein brothers were at last going to buy three of Imelda's New York properties: Herald Center, 40 Wall Street, and the Crown Building. Rivera, a fiercely anti-Marcos activist, who just that day had taken her bar exam, found herself suddenly being authorized by Salonga to supervise the entire legal effort to get control of the buildings in a hurry. "Find some more lawyers—but we have no money to pay them," Salonga told her.

"Sure," she replied. She then hung up, whispered, "Omigod," and got to work. The next four days passed in a blur. On Thursday morning, she called the Center for Constitutional Rights in New York, a nonprofit law center with rare expertise in international cases. The center's lawyers started work that day but were not formally retained until Friday with a telex from Salonga in Manila. Also on that day, the Philippine government's new lawyers read an article in *The New York Times* about the impending sale, in which Joe Bernstein was quoted as saying it was already too late, since "The deal is done. We are the new owners."

All through the weekend, five attorneys and two political activists gathered documents and news articles to support their suit for a judicial order to prevent the sale of the buildings. They finished drafting the complaint on Sunday evening, by which time they had found a superior court judge, Elliot Wilk, who was willing to hear them at his home.

At 11 p.m. Sunday Rivera was still collating documents in Wilk's living room as the attorneys were making their case. The presentation was brief, and after requesting one or two clarifications, Wilk agreed to issue the order. At 8 a.m. the next morning, the Bernsteins' paperwork arrived at the Superior Court clerk's desk, but Wilk's order prevented the clerk from recording it. It wasn't long thereafter that attorneys at the Center for Constitutional Rights were debating whether to hold their summer fundraiser at Lindenmere.

# EPILOGUE: SENTIMENTAL JOURNEY

*We have fed the heart on fantasies*
*The heart's grown brutal from the fare...*
—W. B. Yeats, "Meditations in a Time of Civil War," 1922

Imelda's fall confirmed her as an icon of popular ridicule. Children in the streets of Manila sold rolls of toilet paper with her face stamped on each square. In America she inspired a category on the *Wheel of Fortune* television gameshow, won *Esquire* magazine's Dubious Achievement Award, and was named, along with Lyndon LaRouche and Sean Penn, as being among the world-class "Bozos" for 1987 by the original television clown. Newspapers published teary quotes from her lavish rented Honolulu mansion—about how she now wore $9.99 pants from J.C. Penney's; how George Hamilton wasn't calling anymore; how she dressed all in red, white and blue, and sang "Sentimental Journey" for her guests. Her life had become a vaudeville routine, with barely a memory remaining of all its former promise.

The Philippines, meanwhile, sank into a worsening crisis made up of its familiar plagues of corruption and dissension. In its first year, President Corazon Aquino's government stumbled through five attempted coups and endured embarrassing charges of nepotism. Officials seemed helpless to change old habits of privilege; the guerrilla New People's Army continued to challenge government troops and lines of applicants for visas in front of the U.S. Embassy grew longer than ever before. Filipinos, fed so long on fantasies, seemed more and more cynical, and the reality of their lives surely more brutal.

In hindsight, many aspects of Imelda's life had served as a striking metaphor for the nation's decline. She began by embodying the best of the traits often ascribed to Filipinos: their industry, humor, and intelligence—and ended by reflecting the worst: their frivolity, clannishness, and greed. What she mirrored most faithfully of all, however, was the bitter confusion, caused by centuries of colonization, that remains the Philippines' most awful burden. She was raised by an aloof father whom she idealized—just as she later, however resentfully, looked up to Americans. And her early years were marred by the stigma of being poorer and less worldly than her relatives. By the mid-1970s, when Imelda was telling reporters she came from a "third-rate province in a third world country," it was clear that she'd sacrifice anything for status in the earnest belief that it was all for the national good.

Imelda began her stint as First Lady by building a fantasy to captivate her country. She ended it as a prisoner of a ridiculous dreamworld. Yet it was most striking how long many other Filipinos and Americans shared in the romance, though few would admit that today. A very large assortment of journalists and politicians helped build the glamorous Marcos myth, while ignoring or justifying corruption evident as early as 1970. And even much later, even after Imelda's noisy fall, many members of the tiny, westernized Filipino "elite" clung to her visions.

In April of 1986, just a couple of months after the "People Power" revolution, I took a tour of the Coconut Palace, the elaborate mansion Imelda had built for the Pope five years earlier. My stylish young government guide led me briskly through rooms draped with hand-embroidered curtains and crammed with antique ivory and jade, dutifully elaborating on the number of children who might have been fed for a week for the cost of one satin pillow. But as I trailed her clicking stiletto heels, I sensed a counterpoint to her complaints in the very voluptuousness of her appreciation of the cost and quality of each outrageous item. Should the government have foreseen a threat in such awe?

The palace had ironically and stubbornly remained a shrine to Imelda. Though guards had removed her portrait, set in Mikimoto pearls, her grandeur, energy, and excess filled the place; I easily imagined her bustling, grinning, through the halls. My guide concluded the tour in a small sanctuary attached to the palace, with a final round of protests over a tortoise-shell and ruby shoehorn displayed in its own glass case. But then she paused, and I wasn't surprised when she asked me, sotto voce, what I'd thought of the Marcoses. I muttered something neutral about difficult jobs, and, encouraged, she confessed, "Well, I'm a loyalist, myself. They were so elegant—and so intelligent."

I have tried not to overestimate Imelda's power, or the guilt she bears. She was partly molded and, for many years, controlled by her husband, handicapped by her upbringing and disposition, and forced into many of her initial lies by the rules of her contradictory society—a matriarchal society overtly ruled by men—and a society in which President Aquino remains a historical accident. Nonetheless, Imelda shared with her husband at the very least a profound sin of omission. Along with Marcos, she was handed historic opportunities, especially in 1965 and again in 1972. The "conjugal dictatorship" had resources, popularity, foreign support, and nearly absolute license to make serious changes. More than that, the Marcoses' speeches continually showed they knew what was needed for their country. They might easily have enriched themselves several times over and still moved the Philippines ahead with overdue reforms in land ownership, housing, and the creation of meaningful jobs. Imelda, especially, had the vehicles to achieve these goals with her official welfare posts, while she might also have been a strong force for change through her undeniable influence on her husband. Yet throughout twenty years, Imelda ignored her historic chance—an act of selfishness far uglier than any shopping binge. She made comic opera out of her opportunity for greatness, and in the end, earned her fate.

# Acknowledgments

This is an unauthorized biography. Imelda Marcos talked to me only once, in a three-hour interview for the *San Jose Mercury News* in December of 1985. She never agreed to be interviewed for this book, despite considerable efforts to persuade her—among them three registered letters (never claimed), more than ten phone calls, attempts to reach her through the Marcoses' southern California public relations man, Jay Hoffman, and an entire morning in January 1987, which I spent waiting in her garage in Honolulu. (I'd flown to Hawaii after being guaranteed interviews with both Marcoses by the couple's press aides, Gemmo Trinidad and Leone Tan, who then abruptly canceled the meeting for reasons that were never explained.) In addition to Imelda, I would also have liked to have talked to George Hamilton and Van Cliburn, but neither made any reply to my letters, while George Hamilton's Los Angeles agent specifically turned me down on his client's behalf.

*     *     *

On the subject of disappointments, I was also unpleasantly surprised by the U.S. Freedom of Information Act, which as a daily journalist I had always looked forward to using if I ever got time to write a book. Only when I got that chance did I discover that the act—at least as far as the U.S. State Department is concerned—is virtually useless, not just for those concerned with current news, but also to anyone without more than a year to wait. In 1987, there was a minimum nine-month waiting period before one could get documents from the State Department, the recipient of most of my requests. I began filing requests in November 1986 and received only one full-fledged response before January 1988, and then only because that specific request had already been processed for someone else. I think there's something wrong with those kinds of delays, and with the fact that one not only must wait but, in many cases, must also hire lawyers to pry meaningful information from the U.S. government.

*     *     *

These two setbacks aside, I was overwhelmed by the help I received from friends and from the more than 100 others I interviewed for this book. I owe the most to Jack Epstein, Bernice and Ellis Ellison, and John Ruark, for reasons they all know well.

I'm also indebted to Ray Bonner for his extraordinary generosity with his time, advice, and loan of government records and articles. Without Ray and the National Security Archive in Washington, I would have had virtually no access to any State Department records for this book.

Much valuable help in Manila, San Francisco, and Washington came from three skilled journalists, Bonnie Weston, Loren Stein, and Craig Nelson. Reporter Abby Tan also helped out at the last minute with important Manila interviews. And without my friend Karel Littman, I never would have been sure I had read nearly every major U.S. news article in existence about the Marcoses. I'm also grateful to my *San Jose Mercury News* colleagues Pete Carey and Lew Simons, my agents, Elise and Arnold Goodman, and my editor at McGraw-Hill, Tom Miller.

*San Jose Mercury News* photographer Karen Borchers contributed her pictures and encouragement and also shared a memorable morning in the Marcoses' garage. *Mercury News* metro editor Jon Krim and author David Bain read parts of my early drafts and gave expert advice. Bernard Wideman, publisher of the *Bethel Citizen* and a Philippine hand of note, generously took the time to comb through his files for a stranger on the phone. Carnegie Endowment Philippine expert Richard Kessler offered very helpful early suggestions. Charlie

Steiner gave his fine pictures and counsel. My sister, Dr. Jean Robinson, and brother, Dr. James Ellison, and friend, Emily Goldfarb, were also insightful and gentle advisers. David Zeltner helped at a critical stage with inspiration and his xerox machine. Journalists Roy Rowan and David and Leonor Briscoe all contributed valuable background and insights. Finally, my editors at the *San Jose Mercury News*, particularly Bob Ryan and Victoria Loe, were more patient than perhaps they thought they should have been, for which I'll always be grateful.

Some institutions I relied on were the Philippine Resource Center in Berkeley, the Data Center in Oakland, Amnesty International in New York, the National Security Archive in Washington, D.C., and the Bread Loaf Writer's Conference in Middlebury, Vermont. Special thanks also to Evelyn Gimenez, Digna Santiago, and the rest of the staff at Malacanang Palace.

Among others who stood out for generosity with their time, enthusiasm, and useful recollections are: Father James Donelan, Severina Rivera, Henry Byroade, William Sullivan, and William McCormick Blair. I would also like to thank General Theodore Allen, Steve Le Vine, Doreen Fernandez, Paulynn Sicam, Frazier Meade, Colonel Saturnino Domingo, Guy Pauker, Cristina Ford, Dennis O'Leary, Ronny Zamora, Eugenio and Fernando Lopez, Blas Ople, Fred Schieck, John Silva, Mahlen Perkins, Celia Laurel, John Nance, Ben David, Andy Hernandez, Teddy Lovina, Joly and Joanne Benitez, Sister Belarmine, Richard Holbrooke, Pratima Kale, Vicente Chuidian, Captain Ricardo Morales, Lewis Gleeck, Diosdado Macapagal, Tom Breen, Sol Vanzi, and several others, including many I'm not free to name. I hope all feel that the time they gave so kindly was well spent.

# Notes and Sources

## Prologue: The Legacy of Lapu-Lapu

The story of the origin of the yo-yo comes from the Duncan Toy Company in Baraboo, Wisconsin. Lapu-Lapu's history was culled from Parr's *So Noble a Captain*, Zweig's *Conqueror of the Seas*, and Guerrero-Nakpil's essays. Most of the rest of the historical background came from the U.S. Army's *Philippines: A Country Study*; Bain's *Sitting in Darkness*; Agoncillo's *A Short History of the Philippines*, and Schirmer's *Republic or Empire*.

## 1. Leavetaking

Most of this chapter was based on my own reporting, primarily from trips to Malacanang Palace on the night the Marcoses left and on two later occasions. Interviews with witnesses of the inauguration and palace employees filled in details. William Buckley's description of Imelda appeared in his interview with her released November 24, 1977, for the *Washington Star* Syndicate. Ian Buruma wrote with insight of *palabas* in Philippine politics in the *New York Review of Books* on June 11, 1987.

I gave no precise estimate of how much the Marcoses have stolen because estimates thus far have varied widely, and the probable existence of foreign bank accounts yet undiscovered makes it likely that no one will ever know the couple's real net worth or their debt to the Philippines. Claims filed by the Philippine government before the U.S. District Court in the southern district of New York say the amount they looted "may even equal or exceed the national debt of the Government of the Philippines, which is approximately $30 billion."

## 2. Origins

For help in this chapter, I am indebted to Imelda's two sisters, Conchita Romualdez Yap and Dulce Romualdez, who became Sister Belarmine of the Convent of the Holy Spirit in Quezon City. Sister Belarmine, especially, was generous with her time and candor and in providing notes on the Romualdez family history. Loreta Romualdez Ramos was also helpful, speaking at length to two reporters assisting in my research. Help from Teddy Lovina, Lily Montejo, and Letty Locsin was invaluable. I visited Leyte twice, and reporter Bonnie Weston went once more, on which occasions other neighbors and friends of Imelda's were gracious with their time and memories. Some close friends quoted in this chapter and throughout the book provided insights in exchange for a guarantee of anonymity.

The main written sources I relied on were Quijano's *Reportage on the Marcoses;* the three biographies of Imelda by Polotan, Navarro Pedrosa, and Crisostomo; Breur's *Retaking the Philippines;* Manchester's *American Caesar;* and Steinberg's *The Philippines: A Singular and Plural Place.* For descriptions of Manila at various times, Keith's *Barefoot in the Palace* and Horn's *Orphans of the Pacific* were helpful, as were interviews with other visitors of the time.

Imelda's grades were still on file at St. Paul's. Her parents' marriage record was found at the San Marcelino Church. Some information on Vicente Romualdez came from *Don Vicente Orestes Romualdez: The Man,* a 1984 pamphlet written with obvious assistance from Imelda by Marcelino Foronda.

Marcos' "virginitis" quote appeared in Mijares' *Conjugal Dictatorship* and in *Newsweek* magazine in 1986. Constantino was quoted in

Agoncillo's *A Short History of the Philippines*. Imelda's comments about being poor were made to Roy Rowan, who graciously allowed me to read over his transcripts. Her comments about "anchoring" her life to someone came from a 1983 interview with reporter Ina Ginsburg.

## 3. Waiting for Destiny

Interviewees for this chapter included Celia Laurel, Benito Legarda, Willie Jurado (a Manila observer who later became a Marcos press aide), Mrs. Luz Lacson, Conchita Yap, Sister Belarmine, and Loreto Romualdez Ramos, especially as interviewed by Leonor Briscoe.

Among the main written sources were Bain's *Sitting in Darkness*, Keith's *Barefoot in the Palace*, Horn's *Orphans of the Pacific*, Agoncillo's *Short History*, Lynch's *Four Readings*, Joaquin's *Reportage* and *The Aquinos of Tarlac*, Shalom's *The United States and the Philippines*, and Freedom of Information Act (FOIA) records from the Department of State concerning Benigno Aquino's conversation with U.S. officials about having dated Imelda. Lew Gleeck provided a copy he had on file of a long letter to *Life* magazine in August 1966 by Rosario Trinidad, Remedios' niece, which concerned both Remedios' background and Imelda's years at her cousins' home in Manila.

Among newspaper articles I relied on were "I Discovered Imelda," by Angel C. Anden of the Philippines' *This Week*, and "In Memory of Arsenio H. Lacson," *Manila Standard*, April 15, 1987.

## 4. Romance of the Year

The Marcos courtship, as I've suggested, may never be rendered entirely accurately, and my own efforts to do so have left me somewhat frustrated. The story of the meeting in parliament, the watermelon seeds, the two roses, and the hot pursuit to Baguio has appeared in many books with slightly varying details, and many relatives and friends who have no real claim to inside knowledge have insisted their descriptions are the correct ones. At the same time, as I've noted, the newspaper accounts most likely were not to be trusted. Since Guevara was one of the few constant witnesses, I've let his version dominate the others, but have done so with some helpless skepticism. Other details were culled from the three Imelda biographies, Spence's *Marcos of the Philippines*, Joaquin's *Reportage*, which included Imelda's recollections, and the day-to-day newspaper accounts, chiefly *Kislap*'s "The Beauty and the Solon," of May 12, 1954, and part II, "Operations 'Queen' Imelda," May 26, 1954. Where possible, I have also excerpted Imelda's memories of the romance from later interviews she conducted throughout her life. (It was a rare interview that did not at least mention the fabled eleven-day courtship.) Descriptions of the wedding came mostly from the *Manila Times* and *Manila Bulletin* of that week.

Good background on Marcos came from Spence's book, from "Philippine 'No. 1'" in *The New York Times*, November 13, 1965, and from *The New York Times*' January 22, 1986, report on his false war claims. Keith's *Barefoot in the Palace* and Horn's *Orphans of the Pacific* provided color on Manila and Baguio in the 1950s. My own trips to Baguio in 1986 and 1987 filled in details.

The notes on Lansdale came from Bonner's *Waltzing with a Dictator* and Fitzgerald's *Fire in the Lake*. The Recto condom story came from Joseph Burkholder Smith's *Portrait of a Cold Warrior*. (Burkholder Smith's book also had an interesting passage about Lacson, who as he remembered had a practice of visiting the Filipinas Hotel every afternoon at 4 p.m. for what he called his "Chinese tea." What that meant, he said, was that each day "the people who ran such things in Manila provided a lovely young Chinese girl for the mayor's pleasure. Sometimes more than one." Lacson eventually died of a heart attack during one such tea party in the 1960s.)

Aside from Guevara, major interviewees for this chapter included Sister Belarmine, Conchita Yap, Loreta Romualdez Ramos, Roque and Manuela Ablan, Joseph Burkholder Smith, Celia Laurel (for the insight into her father-in-law), and Diosdado Macapagal.

Finally, I make the first reference in this chapter to Marcos' diaries. These are a collection of what appear to have been private notes written in longhand on Malacanang Palace stationery, and discovered a full two years after the Marcoses fled. I gained access to some of the papers soon after they were found, in the spring of 1988, but I believe they must be approached with caution. There is good reason to believe that the President—a prolific author whose favorite subject was himself—was often writing for history rather than self-scrutiny. Thus one reads Marcos denying, in January 1970, that he meant to stay in power much longer, or waxing indignant in the same year over the claims of a woman who was well-established to have been his mistress. Nonetheless, the writings occasionally reveal private facets of the lives of Marcos and his wife. Notable among these is the immensity of Marcos' sense of himself as savior of his country and his belief that he had telepathic powers. Even his emotional notes for posterity claiming fidelity to his wife and subservience to his country revealed something—at least, in these cases, the depth of his capacity for denial. As for Imelda, she kept no diaries I could find, nor for that matter did I interview anyone who said they had ever received a letter from her.

## 5. Educating Imelda

For background on Filipinas, I've relied mostly on Carmen Guerrero-Nakpil's insightful essays, historian Agoncillo's discussions, and on smatterings from many other interviews. It is interesting to note the strides Philippine women have made since the 1950s: *The New York Times* of March 17, 1978, reported that women by that later date made up nearly half the nation's doctors, 60 percent of its college students, and 71 percent of its graduate students.

As for Imelda's nervous breakdown, she has discussed it herself repeatedly in interviews with journalists through the years, apparently beginning with Nick Joaquin, who described it in his eloquent essay in the *Philippine Free Press*, "Image of Imelda." Not surprisingly, it was difficult to find more details of Imelda's treatment in New York. In 1987 I interviewed a Filipina psychiatrist in New York who had told others that her supervising physician in the 1960s had treated Imelda and confided to her that he had diagnosed her as manic-depressive, a condition that may be treated but rarely cured. The woman, whose name I agreed not to reveal, confirmed what she had told others, but declined to provide more details. Since her statement remained hearsay, I resisted including it in the main text, but I've brought it up here because it became a familiar rumor in Manila.

For details on the campaign and convention, I relied on dozens of sources, among them interviews in 1987 with participants, including Blas Ople, Celia Laurel, Fernando Lopez, Diosdado Macapagal, Doreen Fernandez, Lewis Gleeck (who also provided an article he wrote about his recollections of the 1950s for the *Bulletin of the Amer-*

*ican Historical Collection* of January 1987), Presentacion Psinakis, and Jose Guevara.

Philippine newspaper accounts helped tremendously, especially those of the *Philippine Free Press* and *Manila Chronicle* of 1964 and 1965. As additional background, I used Polotan (especially for the convention) and Spence. In particular, I found *Life* magazine's Philippine election reporting superb. Imelda's quote about bribing the bellhops came from Ray Bonner's interview with former assistant secretary of state William Bundy, published in Bonner's *Waltzing with a Dictator*.

U.S. Embassy First Secretary William Owen's memo of November 19, 1965, was declassified through the Freedom of Information Act and proved extremely useful as general background on Macapagal, the campaign, the convention, and Imelda. Also helpful were post-election analyses, similarly declassified, by Ambassador Blair in 1966 and a copy of Blair's secret testimony in 1967 before the House Committee on Foreign Affairs.

A note on the Spence book: I found it interesting that, while it was written with full cooperation from the Marcoses and was meant to help their campaign, the book nonetheless seemed aimed at an American audience, and in fact became controversial in the Philippines for that reason. Spence again and again praised Marcos by distancing him from his fellow Filipinos, stressing his "light-brown color," contending he "intellectually is closer to the West than to the East," and adding that in a culture "addicted to graft and political corruption," Marcos "has a reputation as an honest man. Among people who are essentially lazy, Marcos is a dynamo."

## 6. Camelot

As is clear in the text, interviews with ambassadors Blair, Byroade, and Williams, all in 1987, supplied background and details for this and the following chapters. The Marcos government's view of Imelda's accomplishments was provided in *A Biography of Deeds*, by Imelda's press secretary Ileana Maramag.

Together with an interview with Willie Jurado, *Time* magazine of July 15, 1966, and *Life* of July 25, 1966, illuminated the story of the Beatles. Imelda's recollections of the state visit were mostly culled from a long interview she gave to the Philippines' *Woman & Home* magazine of October 16, 1966. Bishop's *A Day in the Life of President Johnson* also added helpful details.

## 7. A Share of the Brickbats

Imelda's speeches on the Cultural Center came from *The Ideas of Imelda Marcos*, volumes I and II. Martinez' *Grand Collision* gave helpful descriptions of Imelda's clash with Aquino over the Cultural Center, while Joaquin's *The Aquinos of Tarlac* had excellent background on Benigno Aquino.

*Life*'s "Solemn Event in a Fiesta City," gave the best account I found on the Manila summit, while Alex Campbell's "Sugar, Rice and a Great Deal of Vice" (*New Republic*, March 12, 1966), Klitgaard's "Martial Law in the Philippines," and *The New York Times Magazine*'s cover story on the Marcoses on February 26, 1967, offered particularly good background on the Marcoses and Manila in the 1960s. Of great help in describing Marcos' construction of his power base and events leading to the 1970 student riots was Lela Garner Noble's January 1985 study, *The Marcos Era*.

"A Fishwives' [sic] Fairy Tale" in the *Philippines Free Press* of August 22, 1970, provided background on the two Imelda biographies.

## 8. Disenchantment

I interviewed Hermie Rivera in April of 1986. He then emphasized that he did not believe (nor do I) that the Beams scandal inspired martial law, yet he said he was convinced that it pushed Marcos to do it sooner than he might have done.

I was unable to talk to Beams, after many efforts. I did, however, speak to the Tennessee psychiatrist quoted in the *Republic Weekly*, who said he recognized his statement as cited in the deposition. *The Washington Post*'s "New Spotlight on Marcos' Lovey Dovie," of March 13, 1986, provided useful details, as did, "Duet with Marcos Unveiled," in the *Nashville Tennessean*, March 14, 1973.

Ver's background came mostly from the *San Jose Mercury*'s "Accused General Owes Everything to Patron Marcos," October 24, 1984.

Details on the Lopez rift came in part from The *Manila Bulletin*'s "Who's to Blame in the Marcos-Lopez Crisis," March 5, 1969, and from my interview with Fernando Lopez in April 1987.

Luis Beltran's column in Manila's *Evening News*, October 6, 1970, gave details on Imelda's trips, as did State Department cables declassified under the FOIA.

Among articles I used for background on Imelda's travels in 1971 were a long piece by Kerima Polotan in the *Asia-Philippines Leader*, December 17, 1971, and Sally Quinn's reportage on the Iran party in October 1971. The *Nation* of November 1, 1971, also provided useful background on the event.

John Swearingen's quote came from *The New York Times Magazine* of June 6, 1977.

## 9. The Magic Lamp

State Department records declassified under the Freedom of Information Act provided the underpinnings of my descriptions of Imelda's trips to Washington and other overseas destinations, although some details were provided by friends who went along. The FOIA records also provided details of the Manila visit of Andrew Young. Of great help in understanding the Marcoses' foreign policy was Richard Kessler's Ph.D. thesis, *Development Diplomacy: The Making of Philippine Foreign Policy Under Ferdinand E. Marcos*.

Author John Nance, the former AP Manila bureau chief, attended Imelda's party on the eve of martial law and graciously provided a description. For other details of the look of the beginning of that era, I'm grateful to Sol Vanzi, Jun Medina, Bernard Wideman, and others. Frazier Meade, whom I interviewed in Washington in March 1987, provided helpful general background from his experiences in Manila from 1966 to 1971 and again from 1973 to 1976, as did ambassadors Blair and Newsom and former assistant secretary of state Richard Holbrooke, also interviewed the same month. My interviews with Steve Psinakis, Eugenio Lopez, Jr., and Fernando Lopez in 1985 and 1987 illuminated the Lopez-Marcos rift.

The poll on politicians' standing with the public came from Shalom's *The United States and the Philippines*. Imelda's quote about Elvis was published in *US* magazine, August 24, 1987. Imelda spoke about the assassination attempt against her with journalist Beth Day (who later married Filipino statesman Carlos Romulo) in an interview for *Ladies Home Journal* in 1973. The account of Imelda's Nobel Prize nomination was from the *Hong Kong Standard,* September 6, 1987. Both Marcoses' comments about how Marcos used his wife on diplomatic missions came from their interviews with Roy Rowan in 1979, transcripts of which were provided to me. I also used Rowan's transcript of Imelda's "star and slave" quote, it being the most expansive I found.

William Sullivan offered his intriguing recollections in a February 1987 interview at his home in retirement in Cuernavaca and in later telephone conversations. Imelda's attitude toward him was described by aides and in Mijares' *The Conjugal Dictatorship.*

The CIA profile on Marcos I cited was described in a footnote to Richard Condon's *The Manchurian Candidate.* The profile on Imelda was provided to me.

The story of the Imelda parable play in Manila came from the notes of Bernard Wideman, and my account of the PAL takeover was largely based on his write-ups for *Insight* magazine and the *Washington Post* in July 1978. For Imelda's encounter with Congress that same year, I relied on a tape recording of the session provided to me. I interviewed Richard Chesnoff in two long phone calls to Paris in March 1987.

Imelda's "George Hamilton" schedule was published in Pedrosa's biography. Joseph Bernstein's description of the actor as business representative came in a deposition in 1987 for the Good Government Commission.

I interviewed Bonnie Swearingen by phone in April of 1987, and Mario D'Urso in person in Manhattan in March of the same year. My description of D'Urso was supplemented with background from Ken Auletta's *Greed and Glory on Wall Street.* Charito Planas was interviewed on my behalf in April 1987.

## 10. Dynasty

My own trips to "Marcos-land" and "Imelda-land" in 1986 provided descriptions of Sarrat, Batac, Bongbong's home, and the Santo Niño shrine. For details on Irene's wedding, I supplemented Philippine and U.S. news accounts with details from interviews with two witnesses, the AP's David Briscoe and a photographer whom the Marcoses hired to record the event.

The best articles on cronies included *Time*'s "Tales from Disiniland," January 23, 1978; the *Asian Wall Street Journal*'s "In the Philippines, It's Whom You Know that Can Really Count," January 12, 1978; *Insight*'s "Winning Ways of the Marcos Cabal," September 1978, and a *Christian Science Monitor* profile of Imelda published on September 18, 1980.

Many details for my description of Bongbong came from an interview with Farinas, "Candidly Speaking of Bongbong," in Manila's *Sunday Inquirer Magazine*, April 20, 1986. Some details for the section on Imee came from Manila journalist Paulynn Sicam's interviews, notes, and recollections, including her three-part series for *Mr. & Ms.* magazine, "Imee Marcos, the Girl, the Woman." Abby Tan in Manila interviewed friends of the children for additional background, while my own interviews with a Marcos security guard and a Blue Lady rounded out the picture.

Philippine newspapers provided the background on Edgar Jopson, from the substantial number of eulogies that ran after he was killed. Of particular help was "Death of a Rebel," *Bulletin Today*, September 29, 1982.

## 11. The Crossroads of the World

The bulk of this chapter is based on my own reporting, from unpublished notes from the *San Jose Mercury News* series on capital flight, and later interviews for this book. The story of how Imelda liked to ask who owned the Crown Building came from Ronny Zamora. I also relied on the *Mercury News* series itself, published in June of 1985, and, particularly, on the following articles: "Marcos Takes Manhattan," *Village Voice,* October 15, 1985; "Much Marcos Wealth, Still Carefully Hidden, Eludes Investigators," *Wall Street Journal*, February 11, 1987; "Agents Admit Role in Marcos Land Deals," *San Jose Mercury News*, April 20, 1986; "Secret Agents," *Manhattan, Inc.*, May 1986; "Lawyer Links Imelda Marcos to New York Real Estate," *San Jose Mercury News*, January 24, 1986.

Joseph Bernstein never returned my phone calls, but my interviews with the following people all proved helpful: Victor Politis (New

York Land Company's former executive vice president), December 1986; Ronald Zamora, August 1986, August 1987; and an unnamed Marcos "division head" whom I interviewed several times from 1985 to 1987.

Carino's affidavit was provided to me. In addition, I used the complaint and related documents of New York Land Company's suit against the Republic of the Philippines; of Pablo Figueroa's suit against Ancor Holdings, N.V., Imelda Romualdez Marcos et al.; and of the Philippine Government's suit, in the U.S. Court of Appeals (Second Circuit), against the Marcoses.

Also of use and of interest in itself was the January 28, 1987, affidavit of Rolando C. Gapud, which was provided to me in Manila. In his statement, signed in Hong Kong, and in earlier talks in Manila with Philippine government investigators, Gapud confirmed his role in the New York investments and myriad other Marcos financial schemes. He left Manila "through the back-door" (i.e., the covert southern route to Malaysia) in June 1986, fearing, he said, for his life. Though widely known as the Marcoses' financial adviser, Gapud said in his statement that he was more accurately a "Financial Executor," since he chiefly carried out their orders. He is believed to have had the most thorough knowledge of the workings of Marcos' multibillion dollar financial empire, an ultrasecret, intricate network of several scattered "divisions" most of whose managers were strictly barred from knowledge of the doings of their colleagues. (According to other sources, nominees spoke on scrambler phones, used dozens of numbered accounts, wrote huge checks to "cash," and rarely committed details of their transactions to writing.) Gapud alone knew which of the secret accounts held the Marcoses' five "trust" accounts. In his sworn statement and earlier talks with investigators, he described the network below him, naming fifteen principal "cronies" as fronts and listing the companies held in their name that in fact were almost all partly or wholly owned by the Marcoses. "As far as I can remember," Gapud concluded, "there was only one instance of what I can describe as a legitimate earning of Mr. Marcos, namely, the retirement benefits of Mr. Marcos coming from the Government Service Insurance System (GSIS), but this was a very small, insignificant amount—around one hundred thousand pesos...or the equivalent today of about $5000—which was given to him through the Security Bank when he reached the age of 65."

Marcos' 1961 tax return showed a gross income of a little over

$55,000, a net income of less than $40,000, and total assets of $40,000 as of December 31, 1961. No income was reported from Imelda.

## 12. Imelda Years

Major interviews for this chapter included General Theodore Allen (in 1987), former head of the Joint U.S. Military Advisory Group in Manila, and palace aides and intelligence officials speaking about the degree and details of Marcos' centralization of government, as well as the progression of his illness. In addition, a high-level United States official privy to Armacost's impressions in Manila spoke about them on condition of anonymity.

My description of lupus was based on facts provided by *The Columbia University College of Physicians and Surgeons Complete Home Medical Guide*. Details on the Manotoc kidnapping and on Imelda's trips to Washington came mostly from U.S. State Department cable traffic declassified under the Freedom of Information Act.

Some of the details on Aquino's fatal trip to Manila and Imelda's reaction to it came from "A Welcome Home Murder," *Newsweek*, September 5, 1983; "Why Is this Man Going Home?" *Ang Katipunan*, July/August 1983; "Politics Luring Marcos Opponent Back to Uncertain Fate in Philippines," *San Francisco Examiner*, July 27, 1983; "Anatomy of a Dying Regime," *Philadelphia Inquirer Sunday Magazine*, January 8, 1984, and Lewis Simons' book, *Worth Dying For*. Henry Kamm's "Creating a Dynasty in the Philippines," in *The New York Times Sunday Magazine*, May 21, 1981, also provided useful background, particularly on the Pope's trip.

My descriptions of Imelda's ministerial fiascos mostly came from my own reporting for the *San Jose Mercury News* in 1985. It was supplemented by Paulynn Sicam's interview with Ed Morato in April 1987, my own interviews with Benitez in the summer of 1987, and the excellent reporting in the *Far Eastern Economic Review*.

## 13. Because of You

As in the last chapter, much of the information was based on my own previously published and unpublished reporting, and on later supplementary interviews. Among major interviews specifically for this chapter were Henry Byroade, General Theodore Allen, Captain Ricardo Morales, Cardinal Sin (from whom I also used quotes in a speech he gave to Filipino clergy on May 6, 1986, in San Francisco), Blas Ople, Joly Benitez, Carmencita Reyes, Fred Schieck, Cristina Enrile, Netty Wild, and a number of former Marcos bodyguards and aides who spoke only on condition of anonymity.

Some of the articles on which I relied include: "Mao, Marx, and Marcos," *Far Eastern Economic Review*, November 14, 1985; "Running Like an Underdog," *Time*, November 25, 1985; "Campaign: Marcos, Aquino Pull Out All Stops," *Los Angeles Times*, January 12, 1986; "Bandaged Marcos Limps into Battle," *San Francisco Examiner*, January 19, 1986; "Marcos Assails Media for 'Rumormongering,'" *Washington Post*, February 2, 1986; "Confusion Mars Philippine Voting," *San Jose Mercury News*, February 7, 1986; "Marcos' Campaign Ends in Fizzle," *San Jose Mercury News*, February 6, 1986; "A Rotten Election," *Newsweek*, February 17, 1986; "Diary of a Revolution," *San Jose Mercury News*, March 2, 1986. Bonner's *Waltzing with a Dictator* provided background on the National Citizens Movement for Free Elections (NAMFREL).

Especially useful for some details of Enrile's plot and the Marcoses' last days was the two-part series called, "Coup!" in *Veritas*, October 1986.


## 14. More about New York

A list of the contents of the Marcoses' luggage was provided by a U.S. Customs Service list provided by the Philippine government and titled: Articles Accompanying Marcos Party Upon Arrival Honolulu Hawaii, March 10, 1986. Bernstein's quote was in "Marcos' Mansions Suggest Luxury," *The New York Times*, February 28, 1986.


## Epilogue: Sentimental Journey

Useful accounts of Imelda's exile have appeared in: "Forgotten by Friends & Hounded by Lawsuits; Tales of Woe from an Exiled First Lady," *New York Post*, April 28, 1986; "Marcos Disguise for Return Told," *San Francisco Chronicle* (reported by Reuters), April 8, 1987; and "Imelda: A Fate Worse than Crucifixion," *Malaya*, April 30, 1987.

# Bibliography

As background for this book, I read most of the major articles concerning the Marcoses published from 1965 to 1986 in *The New York Times*, *Washington Post*, *San Jose Mercury News*, *Time*, *Newsweek*, and the *Far Eastern Economic Review*. A complete list of the books I used as background follows.

Agoncillo, Teodoro. *A Short History of the Philippines*. New York: New American Library, 1975.

Auletta, Ken. *Greed and Glory on Wall Street: The Fall of the House of Lehman*. New York: Random House, 1986.

Bain, David Haward. *Sitting in Darkness: Americans in the Philippines*. Boston: Houghton Mifflin Co., 1984.

Barry, Stephen P. *Royal Service*. New York: Macmillan, 1983.

Bishop, Jim. *A Day in the Life of President Johnson*. New York: Random House, 1967.

Bonner, Raymond. *Waltzing with a Dictator: The Marcoses and the Making of American Policy*. New York: Times Books, 1987.

Bresnan, John. *Crisis in the Philippines: The Marcos Era and Beyond*. Princeton: Princeton University Press, 1986.

Breuer, William. *Retaking the Philippines*. New York: St. Martin's Press, 1986.

Condon, Richard. *The Manchurian Candidate*. New York: McGraw-Hill, Inc., 1959.

Crisostomo, Isabelo T. *Heart of the Revolution*. Quezon City: J. Kriz Publishing, 1980.

Day, Beth. *The Philippines: Shattered Showcase of Democracy in Asia*. New York: M. Evans and Co., Inc., 1974.

Fanon, Franz. *The Wretched of the Earth*. New York: Grove Press, 1963.

Fitzgerald, Frances. *Fire in the Lake*. New York: Vintage Books, 1973.

Gregory, Harry. *Khadafy: A Penetrating Look at the Mad Dog of the Middle East*. London: Paperjacks, 1986.

Horn, Florence. *Orphans of the Pacific*. New York: Reynal and Hitchcock, 1941.

Joaquin, Nick. *The Aquinos of Tarlac*. Manila: Cacho Hermanos, Inc., 1983.

Johnson, Lady Bird. *A White House Diary*. New York: Holt, Rinehart & Winston, 1970.

Kessler, Richard, Jr. "Development Diplomacy: The Making of Philippine Foreign Policy Under Ferdinand E. Marcos." Ph.D. thesis, Medford, Mass.: Fletcher School of Law and Diplomacy, Tufts University, 1985.

Lynch, Frank, et al. *Four Readings on Philippine Values*. Manila: Ateneo de Manila, 1973.

Manchester, William. *American Caesar*. Boston: Little, Brown & Co., Inc., 1978.

Marcos, Imelda. *The Ideas of Imelda Marcos*. vols. I and II. Manila: National Media Production Center, 1978.

Martinez, Manuel. *The Grand Collision*. Hong Kong: APG Resources, 1984.

Means, Marianne: *Woman in the White House*. New York: Random House, 1963.

Mijares, Primitivo. *The Conjugal Dictatorship*. San Francisco: Union Square Publications, 1976.

Miller, Stuart Creighton. *Benevolent Assimilation: The American Conquest of the Philippines 1899–1903*. New Haven: Yale University Press, 1982.

Nakpil, Carmen Guerrero. *Woman Enough and Other Essays*. Quezon City: Vessel Books, 1963.

Parr, Charles McKew. *So Noble a Captain: The Life and Times of Ferdinand Magellan*. New York: Thomas Y. Crowell, 1953.

Pedrosa, Carmen Navarro. *Imelda Marcos*. New York: St. Martin's Press, 1987.

Polotan, Kerima. *Imelda Romualdez Marcos*. Cleveland: The World Publishing Co., 1969.

Poole, Fred and Max Vanzi. *Revolution in the Philippines: The United States in a Hall of Cracked Mirrors*. New York: McGraw-Hill, Inc., 1984.

Psinakis, Steve. *"Two Terrorists" Meet*. Dobbs Ferry, N.Y.: Morgan & Morgan, 1981.

Quijano de Manila (pseudonym for Nick Joaquin). *Reportage on the Marcoses, 1964–1970*. Manila: National Media Production Center, 1979.

Rotea, Hermie. *Marcos' Lovey Dovie*. Cockeysville, Md.: Liberty Publishing, 1983.

Schirmer, Daniel B. *Republic or Empire: American Resistance to the Philippine War*. Cambridge: Schenkmann, 1972.

Shalom, Stephen Rosskamm. *The United States and the Philippines, A Study of Neo-colonialism*. Quezon City: New Day Publishers, 1986.

Shaplen, Robert. *Time Out of Hand*. New York: Harper & Row, 1970.

Simons, Lewis. *Worth Dying For*. New York: William Morrow and Co., Inc. 1987.

Smith, Joseph Burkholder. *Portrait of a Cold Warrior*. New York: G.P. Putnam's Sons, 1976.

Spence, Hartzell. *Marcos of the Philippines*. Cleveland: The World Publishing Co., 1969.

Steinberg, David Joel. *The Philippines: A Singular and a Plural Place*. Boulder, Colo.: Westview Press, 1982.

Sullivan, William M. *Obbligato, 1939–1979: Notes on a Foreign Service Career*. New York: W. W. Norton & Co., 1984.

Terrill, Ross. *The White-Boned Demon*. New York: William Morrow & Co., 1984.

U.S. Department of the Army. *Philippines: A Country Study*. Washington, D.C.: Area Handbook Series, 1984.

Wolff, Leon. *Little Brown Brother: America's Forgotten Bid for Empire which Cost 250,000 Lives*. London: Longmans, Green & Co. Ltd, 1961.

Zweig, Stefan. *Conqueror of the Seas: The Story of Magellan*, New York: Viking, Literary Guild, 1938.

## Pamphlets and Articles

Foronda, Marcelino. "Don Vicente Orestes Romualdez: The Man," *Leyte-Samar Studies* (1984).

Gleeck, Lewis E., "The Editor's First Manila Years," *Bulletin of the American Historical Collection* (Manila, 1986).

Klitgaard, Robert E., "Martial Law in the Philippines," Santa Monica, Calif. Rand Corporation Report (November 1972).

# Index